Colin Gunn & Joaquin Fernandez Present

INDOCTRI

PUBLIC SCHOOLS AND THE DECLINE OF CHRISTIANITY

D0685427

CONTRIBUTORS INCLUDE:

R.C. Sproul, Jr.
Ken Ham
Doug Phillips
Voddie Baucham, Jr.
Howard Phillips
E. Ray Moore
Kevin Swanson
Israel Wayne
John Taylor Gatto
Samuel Blumenfeld
and many more

First printing: August 2012
Second printing: July 2013

ISBN: 978-0-89051-685-0
eISBN: 978-1-61458-262-5
Library of Congress Number: 2012942446

Content Disclaimer: *IndoctriNation* contains writings from 30 contributors. The views expressed by these authors are solely their own and are not necessarily shared in their entirety by IndoctriNation's directors, producers, writers, the editor of this book, or the other authors featured herein.

Cover design by Nawelle Noor; page layout by Ryan Glick

Taken from Christianity and the Constitution: The Faith of Our Founding Fathers by John Eidsmoe (Grand Rapids, MI: Baker Academic, a division of Baker Publishing Group, 1987). Used by permission.

All scripture quotes, unless otherwise noted, are taken from the New King James Version®. Copyright © 1982 by Thomas Nelson, Inc. Used by permission. All rights reserved.

Scripture quotations marked KJV are taken from the Authorized (King James) Version.

Scripture quotations marked ESV are taken from The Holy Bible, English Standard Version® (ESV®), copyright © 2001 by Crossway, a publishing ministry of Good News Publishers. Used by permission. All rights reserved.

Scripture quotations marked NASB are taken from the New American Standard Bible®, Copyright © 1960, 1962, 1963, 1968, 1971, 1972, 1973, 1975, 1977, 1995 by The Lockman Foundation. Used by permission.

Please consider requesting that a copy of this volume be purchased by your local library system.

Printed in the United States of America

Please visit our website for other great titles:
www.masterbooks.net

For information regarding author interviews,
please contact the publicity department at (870) 438-5288

Master Books®
A Division of New Leaf Publishing Group
www.masterbooks.net

Special thanks first and foremost to Jesus Christ, our loving and merciful Savior, who is the source of all wisdom, knowledge, and understanding, and without whom we would all be lost to the utter vanity of our own foolish thoughts.

We would like to acknowledge the following families and organization for graciously opening their personal libraries to us for research materials: The Phillip Bradrick, Barry Daming, Doug Fletcher, Sean Gill, Rick Muse, and Chris Young families, as well as Scott and David Brown at the NCFIC. We love you all dearly and are so grateful for the help you extended to us in support of this project.

Thank you to all the contributing authors and publishers for allowing us to use your work. This project would not have been possible without your support.

We dedicate this book to our dear wives, the co-educators of our children, Monica Fernandez, Emily Gunn, and Sarah LaVerdiere: thank you for your love, patience, and wise counsel; you are truly precious gifts from the Lord and your worth is indeed far above rubies

Contents

The Big Yellow School Bus

Colin Gunn

"In my mind, there is no better emblem of this madness than the big yellow school bus. That is why it played the part of the antagonist in our film."

COLIN GUNN

Colin Gunn is an award-winning writer/director/producer and accomplished animator. His early documentary films include *Shaky Town* and *The Monstrous Regiment of Women*. His most recent films are *IndoctriNation* and *Captivated*. He was also executive producer of *Act Like Men*. As an actor, Mr. Gunn played Wally the Mailman in the award-winning feature film *The Widow's Might*, which premiered in U.S. theaters in April, 2009. Originally from Hamilton, Scotland, Mr. Gunn lives in Waco, Texas, with his wife and eight children.

The Bible says, "By the mouth of two or three witnesses every word may be established" (Matt. 18:16). That's simply what documentaries do. They bring forth evidence and establish truth by presenting an audience with a collection of witnesses. The power of documentaries often lies in bringing the experiences of others to an audience that might not be readily persuaded by a book or sermon.

It's always the eyewitnesses to an event that can present the most powerful testimony — there's something about looking into someone's eyes and hearing their story. In the film *IndoctriNation*, and in this companion book, you'll see how persuasive those testimonies can be, and how moving and meaningful it is to hear firsthand stories of Christian educators working in the government schools.

I could try to explain to you the conflict of being a Christian teacher in a public school, but Christian teacher Sarah LaVerdiere can make that argument with power and authenticity. She was the teacher that everyone wanted for their child. She loved the kids, and the kids loved her, yet her damning indictment of the schools is made with irrefutable honesty.

Likewise, Mike Metarko capably stands up against the "salt and light" argument, offering little hope to the parents who argue that their child will be that succesful missionary to the schools. If an elementary school principal had little success, what hope has little Johnny?

Both Sarah and Mike lived their story. What they say is authentic, and the audience knows it. After all, they sacrificed their careers to deliver their message to you!

Again, I could express to you my opinion that parents are accountable for the spiritual and physical risk their children face in the public schools. That's my opinion, and you could take it or leave it. But when you hear the testimony of Brian Rohrbough, there's no debate. Brian lost his son in the Columbine shooting, and he leaves every parent with the unforgettable words, "I put him there." These are some of the bravest words I have ever heard.

There are many other eyewitnesses in this book who will detail to you the decline of American public education from the inside. From R.C. Murray, who exposes the dumbing down of the curriculum, to Karl Priest, who participated in a textbook war and documents the futile thirty-year struggle to reform the schools in West Virginia. Then we have Robert Ziegler, who powerfully testifies to his ultimate offense in the public schools — naming the name of Christ!

Like any good trial, we also need our expert witnesses. I often have to remind people while fielding questions about the film that I'm not the expert. Our job as documentarians is to find those experts and interview them. And what an honor it is for us! Many of these men, such as Samuel Blumenfeld, Howard Phillips, and E. Ray Moore, are the founding fathers of the present-day homeschooling movement and are longtime defenders of the liberties that home-schoolers like me now enjoy.

Then let us bring you John Taylor Gatto, the author of *The Underground History of American Education*. As Teacher of the Year in New York City and New York State, he now stands as both an expert and eyewitness chronicling the disaster that is the public school sytem.

Mr. Gatto's memorable quote in our film sums it all up for me. He says, "Is there an idea more radical in the history of the human race than turning your children over to total strangers whom you know nothing about, and having those strangers work on your child's mind, out of your sight, for a period of twelve years? . . . It's a mad idea!"

Indeed it is. Public schooling is unatural, it's weird, it's outdated. It's based on a model that is neither American (it was imported from Prussia), nor Christian (it was founded by Unitarians, progressives, and utopians).

In my mind, there is no better emblem of this madness than the big yellow school bus. That is why it played the part of the antagonist in our film. As an outsider, these clunky, noisy, polluting monsters stand out as uniquely American symbols of federal uniformity and statism. The bus is loaded with every anti-Christian ideology from utopians like Robert Owen and Karl Marx, to the evolutionist Charles Darwin, to the psychologist Edward Thorndike and the humanist John Dewey. Using the bus is not a neutral act, but a decision that opens a child to multiple ideologies that oppose the Christian faith.

In presenting this book as an accompaniment to our film, one of our objectives is to equip the homeschooling public with the ammunition necessary to effectively defend our educational choices and attack our adversaries' choices. In the pro-life movement, sidewalk counseling has been successful where political action has been less than effective. Now is the time for us to be as bold in the same manner, using these resources to graciously challenge our brothers and sisters who are still deceived by the public school system. No one finds it easy to broach this subject with friends or family. So maybe you can let this book or film be the grenade you throw in the room and leave! We'll take the flak for you.

Please remember, this is the time to be bold. For those with children in the government schools this might be a matter of life or death.

Filmmaking with Fear & Trembling

Joaquin Fernandez

"In a very real sense, filmmakers are teachers, and when our films include a rebuke for the bride of Christ, we should consider well how we admonish the brethren."

JOAQUIN FERNANDEZ

Joaquin Fernandez is an award-winning writer, producer, and director of documentaries, television commercials and educational and marketing videos. He has shot extensively in the United States and has filmed on location in the Caribbean, France, Italy, Portugal, Israel, Russia, Japan, and the Philippines. IndoctriNation is his first feature-length film, on which he was also director of photography and editor. Mr. Fernandez is president of The Lighthouse, a video production and graphic design firm in Wake Forest, North Carolina, where he lives with his wife and four children.

In his book *Millstones and Stumbling Blocks*, Bradley Heath writes:

> [R]emoving scales from the eyes requires touching the eyeballs, always an uncomfortable proposition. Although the goal is better vision, the process may feel like a poke in the eye; the natural reaction is to close one's eyes and turn away.[1]

IndoctriNation was a challenging project for this very reason. It addresses an extremely sensitive issue for both families and churches — how we ought to train up and educate our children in a way that is pleasing to the Lord — and we knew that in order for this "poke in the eye" to be well received, we had to not only deliver the right message, but also do it with the right heart.

As Christian homeschooling parents, we wanted our film to

share our objections to the public schools' methodology and subject matter, and also to convey our clear desire that Christian parents remove their children from these schools for the sake of Christ's Kingdom. We wanted to share our deepest convictions about what God's Word has to say in the area of educating our children.

We began by writing a basic outline of some of the things we wanted to say and how we wanted to say them. We compiled a list of the people we wanted to interview on our *IndoctriNation* Tour where we would take a big yellow school bus, which we didn't even have yet, all around the country. We raised support from friends and ministries, got the word out at events and online, and began shooting footage at conferences. But then we began compiling all the material, *and our knees started shaking.*

You see, the Lord Jesus loves His Bride. He gave His life for her. Her enemies are His enemies. And one day He will say "Bring here those enemies of mine, who did not want me to reign over them, and slay them before me" (Luke 19:27). This should strike fear in the hearts of all unbelievers, but it should also give great pause to those who have anything negative to say to or about the Church of the Lord Jesus Christ. It's no wonder the Apostle James said "My brethren, let not many of you become teachers, knowing that we shall receive a stricter judgment" (James 3:1).

In a very real sense, filmmakers are teachers, and when our films include a rebuke for the Bride of Christ, we should consider well how we admonish the brethren. But it is equally true that we all are responsible for what we do with what the Lord has revealed to us. As it is written in the Book of Proverbs:

> Deliver those who are drawn toward death, and hold back those stumbling to the slaughter. If you say, "Surely we did not know this," does not He who weighs the hearts consider it? He who keeps your soul, does He not know it? And will He not render to each man according to his deeds? (Prov. 24:11–12).

Most of us who are involved in the *IndoctriNation* project are deeply committed to home education. We have been blessed with a vision for multi-generational faithfulness, humbly seeking to apply God's Word to every area of life including the training of our children. But with this understanding comes responsibility. Will we not have to give an account to Him who weighs the hearts, as to whether we did our part in trying to deliver an entire generation stumbling into public school classrooms all across our land?

Our film has been received by homeschoolers and public schoolers in a way that has far exceeded our expectations. We have received letter upon letter from both parents and teachers who are getting out of the system and turning to God's Word alone as their guide. In this way God has blessed this film, and we are so thankful to Him for the way He has allowed it to impact the lives of so many.

My prayer is that the Lord would now use you, your friends, and your church leaders — equipped with this book and our film — to blow the trumpet, as it were, and call God's people to seriously consider their ways regarding the training of their children. There is just too much at stake for us to remain silent.

> I set watchmen over you, saying, "Listen to the sound of the trumpet!" But they said, "We will not listen." Therefore hear, you nations, and know, O congregation, what is among them. Hear, O earth! Behold, I will certainly bring calamity on this people — the fruit of their thoughts, because they have not heeded My words nor My law, but rejected it (Jer. 6:17–19).

Will you sound the alarm with us?

Notes
1. Bradley Heath, *Millstones and Stumbling Blocks: Understanding Education in Post-Christian America* (Tuscon, AZ: Fenestra Books, 2006), p. 12.

Reality 101

Chuck LaVerdiere

"The one-room schoolhouses of the past did not mutate into the monster that is today's public school system; they were beaten up and bullied out of existence . . ."

CHUCK LAVERDIERE

Chuck LaVerdiere is a wretched sinner saved to joyful service in Christ by God's magnificent, undeserved grace. He holds a B.S. in Structural Engineering from the University of California in San Diego, and now lives in the Raleigh, North Carolina area where he runs his small engineering firm, Stonewall Structural Engineering. He has a passion for street evangelism, shepherding his family, and applying the Word of God to all of life. He has been married to Sarah for three years, and they have a one-year-old daughter, Perpetua Faith.

When I first set out to research material for the *IndoctriNation* book, I already arrogantly considered myself well-educated on the state of America's public schools. After all, I experienced them firsthand growing up. My wife even taught in public schools during the first few years of our marriage. I can remember those days when she'd come home each evening with a new horror story to share over an otherwise peaceful dinner. I don't miss those stories one bit.

Like many of America's youngsters today, I started attending a public school at around age four — *kindergarten*. Unlike many of my classmates, I was blessed to have a stay-at-home mom, and she was steadily involved with my schooling throughout those early years. When my parents saw the poor academic standards of the public schools, they transferred my younger brother and me out of the system. Over the next seven years, we attended parochial, Christian, and even military schools, then wound up back at our local public high school for the last few years.

Sadly, the behavioral differences I witnessed between my public and private school classmates were minimal. Instead of smoking pot and sniffing glue, they were dropping ecstacy and snorting cocaine. The vices were simply more expensive where the kids had bigger allowances. I wasn't caught up in every sin on the menu, but I certainly had my share.

None of the schools I attended taught *the fear of the Lord*, and as a result, my education actually led me away from true knowledge (Prov. 1:7).

My personal standard of "normal" for the first 20 or so years of my life was the moral acceptance of abortion and homosexuality, the normalcy of violence, racism, drug and alcohol abuse, rebellion, foolishness . . . the list goes on. These things weren't all necessarily heralded from the classroom but were definitely taught on the playground.

Like slowly removing a Band-Aid, grade by grade my heart was painfully pulled away from my parents', and there were a lot of rough years ahead for my family — to my regret, some of those wounds are still sore today.

In my early twenties, I traded in much of my wild liberalism for a secularized conservatism, and I desperately sought out someone to blame for the deteriorating state of our nation — looking anywhere but within myself. Like any good talk-radio-listening conservative, that blame conveniently landed on the hippies. The 1960s generation that cozied up to Karl Marx has so thoroughly overhauled every other established institution in American society, and modern school curricula clearly reflect their ideology. How could the hippies not be responsible for the demise of American education?

Needless to say, when I began working on the *IndoctriNation* book, I had many preconceived notions about how bad the schools really are, how they got this way, and what should be done about them. But I found that many of my assumptions were only partial truths. While it's true that the hippie generation is now basically running the United States of America into the ground with their terrible policies, I have discovered that they *themselves* were an intentional byproduct of America's public schools. Their mindset, or worldview, is the result of the work of several previous generations that were all indoctrinated by government schooling. The seeds of the humanistic values of the 1960s were planted in America more than a century before that revolutionary decade even occurred. Many of those same seeds were also sown in me and, most likely, in you as well.

The history of public schools is briefly examined in the book you now possess. I am confident that most individuals who consider themselves to be well-informed on the sociocultural issues of our day can read this book and realize that their knowledge on this topic has barely scratched the surface. And the deeper you dig, the dirtier it gets.

Suffice it to say that the one-room schoolhouses of the past did not mutate into the monster that is today's public school system; those schoolhouses of old were beaten up and bullied out of existence by a bigger, badder, government and big business–backed machine that has completely turned any sense of true education on its head and made off with the taxpayer's lunch money. While there are some who would call this educational takeover a grand conspiracy, we should remember that we live in a representative republic. Previous generations of "We the People" gladly handed over their children, first to the one-room schoolhouse then to the government, all for convenience.

We are now reaping the results of nearly two centuries spent sowing corruption — and it is a massive harvest of rotten fruit. The multitude of disturbing trends in our schools today is troublesome to say the least, as recognized by nearly every cross-section of society regardless of creed, ethnicity, gender, or political affiliation.

But the problems we see on the surface are symptoms of a greater disease. As Christians, let's call the schools' problems what they are: bad fruit. Knowing that *a bad tree cannot bear good fruit*, we should consider that when we support the latest school reform we are just polishing up foul, moldy apples to which there will be no end. If we truly desire to fix education, we must find the root of this bad tree, hew it down, and cast it into the fire — figuratively speaking, of course.

Dear parent: This book is meant to persuade you to remove your children from public schools. Think of it as Reality 101 — a crash course in a subject that wasn't offered in any school you or I ever attended. The vital prerequisites for this course are (1) a love for God, (2) a love for your children, and (3) an open mind.

Many may be offended by what is written in this book. It's not easy when things we think we know with certainty are challenged, but that's why the first prerequisite is an absolute necessity for this course. If you truly have it, it will do its part well by focusing you on what really matters when your personal sensibilities suffer injury.

One thing I've learned is that I can't blame the hippies for the deteriorating state of our country when I know from Scripture that it is only when we Christians, who are called by God's name, humble ourselves, pray, seek His face, and turn from our wicked ways that God will hear from heaven, forgive our sins, and heal our land (2 Chron. 7:14).

So please set your preconceptions aside and approach this material with the noble mind of a Berean (Acts 17:11). Challenge what you read herein. Verify the sources. Test these things against the solid rock of the Word of God. And if you find your practices out of alignment with Scripture, repent and cast yourself upon the mercies of Jesus. "Humble yourselves in the sight of the Lord, and He will lift you up" (James 4:10). Then be moved to action with the zeal of Josiah (2 Kings 22–23) to swiftly tear down your altars of ungodly educational traditions and seek to model your life according to His revealed Word.

May there arise a generation of fathers and mothers who recognize the beauty of God's intended system of education: personal parent-to-child daily discipleship. May that generation, along with their progeny, reap the good fruit of lives lived in faithful obedience to the commands of God.

Soli Deo Gloria!

"Do not lay up for yourselves treasures on earth, where moth and rust destroy and where thieves break in and steal; but lay up for yourselves treasures in heaven, where neither moth nor rust destroys and where thieves do not break in and steal."

— *Matthew 6:19–20*

Heavenly or Earthly Treasures

Brian Rohrbough

"It was my responsibility to make sure that my son was educated properly. But I failed that. I put him in a pagan school where they teach there is no God."

BRIAN ROHRBOUGH

Brian Rohrbough is the father of Rachael, Isaac, Dan, and Joshua. He is married to Lisa and together they homeschool their children. Mr. Rohrbough is a small business owner and serves as a director at LifeCommercials.com. He and his family attend Calvary South Denver Church. Mr. Rohrbough became a public figure after the Columbine massacre in which his son Dan was murdered. Since then, he has been an active speaker in support of the pro-life and homeschool movements. He has been interviewed on local and national media including *Oprah, Good Morning America, The Today Show, Sixty Minutes, The O'Reilly Factor, Dateline, CNN*, and others. Mr. Rohrbough formerly served as president of Colorado Right to Life and was nominated as Dr. Alan Keyes' vice presidential candidate in 2008. The following introduction was written by Mr. Rohrbough for the *IndoctriNation* book.

A Ferrari Filled with Dirt

Recently, a friend of mine called and asked if I would have time to do some work for one of his customers who was in town for a few days. When I called to discuss the job, the customer told me, during a very short conversation, about his Ferrari convertible that he wanted me to work on. He went on to say that he was very wealthy but he didn't want to be taken advantage of and that he was 67 years old and had cancer.

Later I met him at my friend's shop. He was foul mouthed, talking about the trashy women that he was involved with and how he was traveling around in his car and living it up. He went on to say that he had told his kids that when he dies he wants to be buried in his Ferrari with the top down and the car filled with dirt.

His comments reminded me of the conversations that I was involved in when I attended junior high school. It struck me that I had been taught the same value system. His worldview, his desires, his outlook, and his core values were all the same as those that I once held many years ago. I'm saddened to think that, like all of us, he needs a Savior; but he was taught, just as every child in our nation's public schools is taught, that there is no Savior. The schools that this man attended "trained him up in the way he should go," and now that he is old and dying, he will not depart from it (Prov. 22:6).

Looking back, I realize that my church upbringing didn't stand a chance against all of the immersive "education" that I'd received. There are some who will point out that while this may have been my experience, it didn't happen to them, and it did not happen in their school. They say, "I attended public school, and I turned out okay. My children will be just fine."

Perhaps even I would have said that until one Tuesday morning in April 1999. I was standing on the sidewalk looking past the playground at all of the commotion when an overpowering sense of loss came over me: "Oh, Lord, please don't let this be true. Please, Lord, let this just be my emotions."

Throughout that day I waited as every public official stated that they had no information. That evening a representative of the sheriff's office told us, "Go home, and we will send an officer to your home tonight as soon as we have any information."

The next morning we opened the newspaper and there was a picture of my son lying dead on the sidewalk at Columbine High School. No police officer, no sheriff, no district attorney ever came to my home. There were no phone calls. Our official notification came from that picture. The sheriff and DA did, however, notify the perpetrators' parents on Tuesday, and they would later admit that they did in fact have the names of all 13 homicide victims on Tuesday, even as they told us that they didn't know. I had been standing less than 300 yards away from my son Dan, but he was out of my field of view. They left him lying there for 27 hours.

Dan was dead, and I turned to the Lord and asked the most important question a parent can ever ask — the same question you, as a Christian, are probably asking as you read this. "Jesus, is Dan with You? Lord, where did I send my son?"

I spent seven long years demanding answers from the sheriff, the district attorney, the school, and the murderers' parents. I (along with others) forced the release of more than 52,000 documents, opened secret files and recordings, exposed secret meetings, and even forced a grand jury. We held press conferences at the front door of the district attorney's office and at the sheriff's office exposing the outright lies they had told. And after seven years I finally knew most of the details of how and why my son was murdered.

Exposing how and why Columbine happened was necessary and valuable. But there was an additional area that had to be investigated. The results of that investigation would be found in a simple device hanging on my wall. You probably have one yourself. Whenever I look into this device, I am reminded of the awesome responsibility that every parent has, a responsibility from which we can't escape. This device, a mirror, reflects me.

My son died not because of some choice that he made, but ultimately because of a choice that I made. People sometimes ask me why I talk about my guilt in my son's death. They seem to think that if I talk about these things, it must mean that I haven't received forgiveness from the Lord. But I have indeed received both the forgiveness and grace that only the Lord can provide. I speak about these things not because it is pleasant but because it is true. I want others to learn from my failings in the hopes that they will not experience the loss of their own children.

The truth is that every sin can be forgiven, but the consequences of sin often remain. Our sin usually hurts other people, especially our own children. Receiving forgiveness is not the same thing as having never sinned. Sin has a price, and it always requires a high cost from somebody; and where our children are concerned this may be a cost paid throughout eternity. There was no biblical justification for me to send my son to a Godless public school. He died because I ignored God's Word, even though I knew better.

The good news is that Jesus is able to and will forgive every sin of every truly repentant person who believes in Him as Lord and Savior.

***

Are you the one who asks your kids to respect their teachers, pay attention, and do what they're told? Do you ask them to do their best and to study hard? Do you tell them that school is very important for their future and that, while there, they must learn all the information and do well on every test?

Is the school you send your kids to a Christian school (preferably in your home or, if that isn't possible, a Christian school that you monitor to be sure that it stays true to Bible-centered teaching)? Is the fear and admonition of the Lord being taught as a foundational belief?

Or have you chosen public education?

Make no mistake. Sending your kids to public school is full of risk. I took that risk. My son was murdered. There are many ways for our children to be destroyed by the public schools. My son died at Columbine High School, but that is a relatively small risk compared to all of the dangers that are part of the required curriculum in government schools.

These schools will undermine your child's Christian upbringing by teaching as fact things like evolution where the strong rule, without moral consequences, and there is no right or wrong. They teach there is no God, we came from the slime, and do what you will.

The public schools teach sex education with the intent of promiscuity. This is one area where they really succeed. But with this success comes the death of the innocent. As pregnancy occurs, the school is there to "help," quite often by arranging and facilitating the murder of these babies through abortion. I can't help but wonder how many of our Christian families have had their grandchildren killed as a result of sending their kids to public school. The schools teach, "Kill the baby, cure the problem."

Of course you know about the diversity training, the false science, and the revisionist history being taught. But do you also accept the social environment and political agenda of your child's school? And do you deny the widespread availability of drugs and alcohol to which your child has access?

If you place your children in public school, within a few years, you will find a division growing between you and them. Will you tell yourself that this separation is normal and that it is just part of your children growing up? Do you really believe hatred between parents and children is normal?

In reality, this too is part of the public school agenda. Parents are replaced as their children's mentors by the teachers and school counselors who teach that they are the ones who truly understand your children. After all, from a very young age children are taught in school that their parents just don't understand them or today's world.

I have only scratched the surface with this list of dangerous ways by which your children are being purposefully misled and spiritually destroyed while attending government schools. My challenge to parents is for you to ask this most important question: "Lord, am I training my children to love and want to learn about You, or am I sentencing them to reject You?"

As Christians, we are in the world, but we are not to be of the world. For the sakes of your family and our nation, I urge you to make the necessary changes now to remove your children from the public school system. It is your responsibility to raise, protect, and properly educate the children God has graciously placed under your care. Please heed the Lord's call to train them up in the way they should go, that they might desire an eternity of righteousness instead of a Ferrari filled with dirt.

"Let us go up against Judah and trouble it, and let us make a gap in its wall for ourselves, and set a king over them. . . ."

— Isaiah 7:6

CHAPTER ONE

America's Trojan Horse: Public Education

Michael J. Metarko

"I went into the public schools as a Christian, basically looking at Matthew 5 and wanting to be 'salt and light' in a system that I knew was darkness."

MICHAEL METARKO

Michael J. Metarko holds a degree in commerce and engineering from Drexel University, a certificate in elementary education from Moravian College, and a master's degree in educational leadership from Wilkes University. He worked for nine years in the financial and technical sales arena before becoming a fourth grade teacher and middle school supervisor for curriculum and instruction. Heeding God's conviction, Mr. Metarko resigned his position in 2010 after working for 14 years in public education, the last five of which were as an elementary school principal. He is currently writing a book about his time inside the system. Mr. Metarko and his wife, Beth, have two children, whom they homeschool. The following is taken from an article written by Mr. Metarko that was published in the Chalcedon Foundation's *Faith for All of Life* magazine.

REMEMBERING THE TROJAN HORSE

The crafty Odysseus won the Trojan War for Greece by deception with the Trojan horse. An entire city was desolated by sleight of hand, worship of a false goddess, and false security. The Trojans sincerely thought the war was over, but sincerity is insufficient without the truth. They found out too late that they were wrong. They unknowingly led the enemy right into their city's heart, blindly trusted the enemy's word, failed to do their own research and inspection, and became complacent, focused on their own pleasures. Because of these foolish actions, they lost their children, families, city, and lives. *America is Troy; our public education system is the Trojan horse.*

INDOCTRINATION

Seventeen years ago, God called me to His Son. As I sought His will for my life, I believe that He led me out of engineering and technical sales into a career in education. For the last 15 years, I have held the following positions in public education: fourth-grade teacher, middle school assistant principal, and most recently, elementary principal. I have also served as adjunct faculty at a respected college, and taught for Johns Hopkins University's Center for Talented Youths. My goal has always been to be a godly example of excellence, a male role model, and "salt and light" in a system I knew had long ago expelled God.

Over the years I have had many opportunities to be that "salt and light" and have plugged up more than a few pinholes in the dike. Administratively, I have fought for the Good News Club to use facilities for which other organizations are never questioned. I have staved off the Anti-Defamation League's "No Place for Hate" campaign promoting the "acceptance" of questionable beliefs and lifestyles. I have argued to keep the names Easter and Christmas on the school calendar beside Rosh Hashanah and Ramadan. Educationally, I have focused teachers, students, and parents on state and federal mandates to the extent that my school is consistently one of the top in our state.

But over the past few years, I have been inspecting the foundations of the public education system. Research, reading, and observation have proven to me that the foundations of the system are broken. It is crumbling away under my feet, our children's feet, the family's feet, the feet of our cities and our nation, under the feet of future generations.

Why do I say this? Let me respond Socratically. How many well-intending parents wanting the best for their children, Christian or non-Christian, can answer the following:

- Where and why was public education established?
- Who were public education's "founding fathers"; what were their beliefs and goals?
- What is the foundation of knowledge?
- Is there ultimate truth? What are the ramifications if the answer is "yes" or "no"?

- Are schools void of religion? If you say "yes," are you sure? If you say "no," what is their religion and why does it matter?

- What science and history are being taught? Are they true science, accurate history?

- What is education's ultimate role? Who determines it?

- Are we truly educating our children in our public schools, or are we indoctrinating them?

I daresay most public school employees would be hard-pressed to answer; I admit that I would have been three years ago. Why? Partly ignorance and lack of education, but mainly because the education we have received is captive to the system itself. Our education system is

FROM THE FILM: "The [public school system's] foundation is not built upon God, not built upon His Word, not built upon His truths; it is built upon man, man's desires, man's wants."

such a part of us and of society that we no longer even think to question it. We accept it, work within its boundaries, polish it to look better, and rename it to sound better. Just as the people of Troy welcomed that horse, we have naïvely welcomed public education into our cities and homes without discernment, willingly accepting the words of "leaders" of the system just as the Trojans unwisely took the Greek captive at his word without questioning if it were a trap, a setup.

In opening up that Trojan horse, I was stunned and appalled. I not only realized what the horse was but saw the deceivers' plans. In a phrase, *what I found was indoctrination in an anti-Christian worldview called humanism.*

My eyes having been opened wide, I realize that we are in a war for the truth, the souls of our children, and the future of our country. The hardest thing for me to accept is that I have been the Trojan soldier listening to the Greek captive and accepting his description of the horse as a gift to society! My sweat, my energies, were tearing down the wall of my city and wheeling this horse inside. By not questioning and inspecting public education deeply enough, I put my family and America's children right into the archenemy's hands.

We must act! We must understand that education is not a neutral enterprise because there is no neutral territory, no neutral thought. Rushdoony states, "Such a view presupposes neutrality in the *knower and the known. . . .* For us as Christians, this view is false."[1] "God forbid that we should rebel against the LORD, and turn this day from following the LORD" (Josh. 22:29). We cannot be passive and watch our children, families, cities, and nation turn into slaves by the enemy's sleight of hand and by our complacency.

LOOK INSIDE THE HORSE: THE CURRENT STATE OF EDUCATION

I have seen firsthand the issues we face. I know the results of taking our focus off educating children as individuals created in the image of God with unique talents and gifts. I have witnessed how special interests promote their own agendas and obstruct efforts to improve our schools. Most Americans only see the attractive outside of our Trojan horse: the "gift" of education provided by a government wanting the "best for all." But if we take off our rose-colored glasses and approach this with discernment, we will notice its many blemishes and faulty workmanship; we will notice the hatch leading inside the beast. If we peer into it to see what's there, we will see many uncomfortable sights. If we will only shine the light

FROM THE FILM: "In the morning we pledge to the flag and have a moment of silence. And in that moment of silence I pray. Really that's the only area anymore that God is in the schools."

of truth into the cracks and crevasses deep inside the system, we will see what it is truly made of.

I do not doubt that teachers, parents, administrators, and school board members are often sincere in their desire to educate children.

But anyone reading the news will quickly note that there is a growing culture of corruption and the sacrifice of ethics for self-interest and personal gain in public education.

Accountability, national standards, class size, and teacher qualifications are all red herrings, draining taxpayer coffers with no statistically significant gains in achievement.[2]

Our government has enacted legislation such as the Safe and Drug-Free Schools and Communities Act and the Gun-Free Schools Act of 1996 under No Child Left Behind. Employees engage in intruder training, bomb threat training, and Drug Abuse Resistance Education (D.A.R.E), but all to no avail. All one has to do to see this is to read or listen to the news. According to the National Center for Educational Statistics' Indicators of School Crimes and Safety 2009 report, "For the first time, rates of violent crime victimization at school were higher than rates of violent crime victimization away from school. In 2007, there were 26 violent crimes per 1,000 students at school, compared to 20 violent crimes per 1,000 students away from school."[3] This same report indicated that "in 2007–08, 75 percent of public schools recorded one or more violent incidents of crime" and "17 percent recorded one or more serious violent incidents."

Well-intentioned people scratch their heads and ask why. There is plenty of blame to go around. We can blame the teachers' unions, the largest lobbying organizations in political history, for demanding to be treated as professionals while maintaining a union-bully mentality. But we must also blame fathers who have abandoned the principles of Deuteronomy 6:7 and Ephesians 6:4; we have shirked our responsibilities. As a by-product, we can also blame children who become *"disobedient to parents."*

To get the true picture of the future of the statist education system, do an Internet search on our current leaders: Secretary of Education Arne Duncan and Safe School Czar Kevin Jennings. Jennings is founder and prior executive director of GLSEN, the Gay, Lesbian, and Straight Education Network placed into position by President Obama with no congressional confirmation, possessing great power and authority over schools. What is being promoted? Brace yourself *and make sure no little eyes are watching*! Search "the little black book queer in the 21st century," "Homosexual movement + Kevin Jennings," or "Fistgate tapes."

Many have probably pondered at least some of this already. But, as we probe further into the egalitarian equine of public education, we must do away with the mindset that is so much a part of our culture, if we are really going to understand it. When I started researching what my education history classes failed to teach, I realized how far we have strayed from true biblical education. I took for granted the concept of age-segregated teaching — as do most churches — because I neither looked into its socialist roots nor considered its complete focus on class management and psychological remedies that breed mediocrity and social promotion. But G. Stanley Hall, the "father of adolescence," friend to Jung and Freud, planned this monstrosity from the start. Hall used evolutionism and Haeckel's recapitulation theory to form the concepts of age-segregated learning and racial eugenics.[4] Is that not why we fought Hitler?

It is not hard to imagine the next step the social engineers of public education took: remove God from schools, not all gods, of course, just that "intolerant" Old Testament God demanding, "Thou shalt have no other gods before me" (Exod. 20:3), and that "intolerant" New Testament God claiming, "I am the way, the truth, and the life. No one comes to the Father except through Me" (John 14:6; NKJV). True Christianity is what the Anti-Defamation League defines as bigotry because of its exclusivity. They do not accept my belief but tell me I must accept everyone else's.

Do not be fooled; our public schools do teach religion. Oh, I know about the separation of church and state comment by Thomas Jefferson that most Americans believe is part of our founding documents. That separation only applies to Christianity. Public schools are deeply entrenched in the religion of secular humanism. As Sam Blumenfeld points out:

> [O]n March 4, 1987, U.S. District Judge W. Brevard Hand, in *Smith v. Board of School Commissioners of Mobile County, Ala.*, ruled that secular humanism is a religion. The 172-page ruling defines religion and concludes, after reviewing the relevant aspects of humanism, that "For purposes of the First Amendment, secular humanism is a religious belief system, entitled to the protections of, and subject to the prohibitions of, the religious clauses."[5]

This man-centered religion is indoctrinating our American children in many ways. To name a few:

- Evolutionism at the expense of true science

- Revisionist history (creatively called social studies)

- Socialism with their mantra, "We're the experts. We'll handle all your educational needs."

- Psychology focused on segregation, self-esteem, and what "feels" right

- Androgyny: the feminization of our boys and the masculinization of our girls

- Acceptance, not just tolerance (unless you disagree with their point of view)

- Misguided environmentalism: mother earth versus God the Father

- Rebellion against the family (Google "We Generation")

The Effects of the Unknown Horse: Where Education Stands in Our Nation

Where does all this leave us as a nation in which 90 percent of professing Christians send their children to state schools? We have become exactly what the system is designed for us to become: apathetic, uninformed, uninvolved, and uneducated (or educated for very little). We have become uncreative nonthinkers lacking reasoning and rhetoric. On one hand, we have become a society of self-focused, self-indulgent couch potatoes growing only enough sprouts to text our sweet-potato friends on Facebook. On the other, we are gerbils on a wheel that run our children to every imaginable program and sport.

Let me also name a few of the effects of indoctrination in secular humanism through public education: abortion, divorce, single-parent families, euthanasia, gay marriage, condoning homosexual behavior, pornography, racism, and no public nativity scenes or Ten Commandments. These societal effects directly transfer into schools in the forms of removing God from the Pledge, banning the teaching of creation, expelling prayer, increasing violence, and casting Christ out of Christmas. America's children are becoming slaves to a government telling them "we control and dole out all rights." John Dewey, the illustrious "Father of Experiential Education," states the need for such indoctrination as follows:

> The superficial explanation is that a government resting upon popular suffrage cannot be successful unless those who elect and who obey their governors are educated. Since a democratic society repudiates the principle of external authority, it must find a substitute in voluntary disposition and interest; these can be created only by education.[6]

Who Made This Horse? History the Halls of Higher Education Do Not Teach

When earning my teacher certification, I innocently assumed I was getting the full picture of public education in my educational history classes. As a young Christian I questioned everything I read, but I did not think to question if what I read was everything. We read about Dewey but never went back to the true roots of his educational philosophy. We never studied Rousseau, a major philosopher of the Enlightenment and a key figure in the development of humanist educational theory. Nor did we research G. Stanley Hall, Lev Vygotsky, or Jean Piaget in any depth or look into the lives of these educational icons. My studies never looked at their ties to social engineering, Marxism, communism, or Platonism. But it is all there.

Vladimir Lenin once said:

> If we can effectively kill the national pride and patriotism of just one generation, we will have won that country. Therefore, there must be continued propaganda abroad to undermine the loyalty of citizens in general, and teenagers in particular. By making drugs of various kinds readily available, by creating the necessary attitude of chaos, idleness, and worthlessness, and by preparing him psychologically and politically, we can succeed.[7]

I have had days working in the public schools when I vividly remember thinking, *Dear God, we are in trouble!*

How did public education begin in America? Many point back to 1647 and the Massachusetts General School Law of 1647, known as "The Old Deluder Satan Law" because it opens with "It being one chief project of that old deluder, Satan, to keep men from the knowledge of the Scriptures. . . ." This law is said to be foundational to the socialist mindset of the government school system, but this proves untrue at a deeper look; its central focus was to combat the neglectful, infidel parents who were not raising their children in the Lord.

The real beginning was later in Massachusetts when the Unitarians and their clandestine counterparts, the secularists, approached the Puritans to initiate a more formal public sys-

FROM THE FILM: "When I really look at [Matthew 5:13], I realize that there is no Christian that can be in the public school system that can truly be salty, because if you are worth your salt and your light, you will not be in the system for long."

tem to educate poor, illiterate Catholics immigrating to New England. But the watered-down Christian education of the Unitarian-Puritan alliance quickly turned secular when the Puritans and Unitarians disagreed among themselves and withdrew from the table. The secular socialists were right there to take the reins.

Evolution has unquestionably played a role in public education. As Aldous Huxley, the evolutionist leftist grandson of "Darwin's Bulldog," T.H. Huxley, states:

> I had motive for not wanting the world to have a meaning; consequently assumed that it had none, and was able without any difficulty to find satisfying reasons for this assumption. The philosopher who finds no meaning in the world . . . is also concerned to prove that there is no valid reason why he personally should not do as he wants to do, or why his friends should not seize political power and govern in the way that they find most advantageous to themselves. . . . For myself, the philosophy of meaninglessness was essentially an instrument of liberation, sexual and political.[8]

During the post–Civil War era, Andrew Jackson's social-engineering paradigms used against American Indians, Mormons, etc., combined with the visions of Horace Mann, first Secretary of

Education for Massachusetts, into a destructive political force. Ever since then, special-interest groups have ferociously fought to control the mechanisms of state inculcation, with each group attempting to use the hammer of compulsory attendance to impose their worldview. No one has done this better than secular humanists, "Who changed the truth of God into a lie, and worshipped and served the creature more than the Creator, who is blessed for ever. Amen" (Rom. 1:25).

As the Humanist Manifesto I and II point out, the goals of secular humanism, now endearingly referred to as postmodern liberalism, are simple: firstly, remove the foundations of Judeo-Christian morality and beliefs, and secondly, fill this gap with a new enlightened, man-centered religion. But this takeover cannot be too overt; it must be under the guise of religious freedom, tolerance, equity, and scientific fact.[9]

The Origin of Education: The Biblical View

Was there education before Dewey, Mann, Hall, Rousseau, and Plato? Many think Plato, Socrates, and classical education were the start. But any Bible-reading Christian must disagree, for "The fear of the Lord is the beginning of knowledge: but fools despise wisdom and instruction" (Prov. 1:7).

Genesis 1 through 11 give the foundation upon which to build our knowledge of religion, history, geology, biology, anthropology, astronomy, physics, chemistry, and more. Ken Ham points out, "If the history leading up to Jesus Christ, all of the earthly things, is not true, then the spiritual and moral things are not true also." Ham continues, "Christianity is based in real history, not just interesting stories, and Jesus Christ's birth, death, and Resurrection happened in history." It is that history that leads to Jesus Christ. We must look at all things through the lens of the Bible.[10]

God and Genesis do matter; the family, children, and home also matter. Deuteronomy 6:5–9 clearly tells fathers:

> And thou shalt love the Lord thy God with all thine heart, and with all thy soul, and with all thy might. And these words, which I command thee this day, shall be in thine heart: And thou shalt teach them diligently unto thy children, and shalt talk of them when thou sittest in thine

house, and when thou walkest by the way, and when thou liest down, and when thou risest up. And thou shalt bind them for a sign upon thine hand, and they shall be as frontlets between thine eyes. And thou shalt write them upon the posts of thy house, and on thy gates.

God purposed that each chapter of Proverbs 1 through 7 include the following:

- My son, hear the instruction of thy father, and forsake not the law of thy mother (1:8).
- My son, if thou wilt receive my words, and hide my commandments with thee (2:1).
- My son, forget not my law; but let thine heart keep my commandments (3:1).
- Hear, ye children, the instruction of a father, and attend to know understanding (4:1).
- My son, attend unto my wisdom, and bow thine ear to my understanding (5:1).
- My son, if thou be surety for thy friend, if thou hast stricken thy hand with a stranger (6:1).
- My son, keep my words, and lay up my commandments with thee (7:1).

The New Testament is just as clear:

- The disciple is not above his master: but every one that is perfect shall be as his master (Luke 6:40).
- Casting down imaginations, and every high thing that exalteth itself against the knowledge of God, and bringing into captivity every thought to the obedience of Christ (2 Cor. 10:5).
- Study to shew thyself approved unto God, a workman that needeth not to be ashamed, rightly dividing the word of truth. But shun profane and vain babblings: for they will increase unto more ungodliness (2 Tim. 2:15–16).

In all these Scriptures we see that ultimate truth matters, worldview matters, and education matters.

WAKE UP TROY, DESTROY THAT HORSE, REPAIR THAT BREACH: A CALL TO THOSE WITH CHILDREN INSIDE THE WALLS

With 90 percent of Christians still sending their children into this statist educational system, I need to be brutally direct. According to current research, if you send your child to public school, you WILL most likely lose your child to the secular humanistic worldview. In two reports to the Southern Baptist Convention, T.C. Pinckney found that 70–88 percent of evangelical teens will leave the faith within two years of graduating from high school.[11] The fatal combination of secular education and the lack of true biblical discipleship is reflected in separate studies by the Barna Group and Britt Beemer of America's Research Group. They found that one-third of twentysomethings who were churched as teens have disengaged spiritually. Over "60 percent of the children that grow up in our churches will leave them as they reach the threshold of young adulthood."[12] We are losing more children much younger than previously thought: 83 percent of those surveyed started doubting the Bible in middle school and high school.[13]

FROM THE FILM: "We came to Proverbs 1:7, 'The fear of the LORD is the beginning of knowledge, but fools despise wisdom and instruction,' and I was stopped dead in my tracks."

> But when the righteous turneth away from his righteousness, and committeth iniquity, and doeth according to all the abominations that the wicked man doeth, shall he live? All his righteousness that he hath done shall not be mentioned: in his trespass that he hath trespassed, and in his sin that he hath sinned, in them shall he die (Ezek. 18:24).

We cannot sit idly by and let secular public education destroy our children. We must "cease . . . to hear the instruction that causeth to err from the words of knowledge" (Prov. 19:27).

The biblical model of education is what is needed — an education centered in the Word of God, and the family where the father is in charge and engaged. This is becoming the clarion call from the likes of E. Ray Moore Jr.,[14] Voddie Baucham,[15] Bruce Shortt,[16] Doug Phillips,[17] and Scott Brown.[18] Rushdoony heralded it for years.[19] Even the Southern Baptist Convention has joined the call.[20]

I challenge you to be a "repairer of the breach" (Isa. 58:12). Return to the Bible, "For the nation and kingdom that will not serve thee shall perish; yea, those nations shall be utterly wasted" (Isa. 60:12). Return to Genesis, for "Thou, Lord, in the beginning hast laid the foundation of the earth; and the heavens are the works of thine hands" (Heb. 1:10). Return to Matthew Henry's "church in the house,"[21] and "Set your hearts unto all the words which I testify among you this day, which ye shall command your children to observe to do, all the words of this law. For it is not a vain thing for you; because it is your life" (Deut. 32:46–47). Return to manliness and end female chauvinism. "Watch ye, stand fast in the faith, quit you like men, be strong" (1 Cor. 16:13), for "I would have you know, that the head of every man is Christ; and the head of the woman is the man; and the head of Christ is God" (1 Cor. 11:3). Return to learning about and learning from accurate history, "For the transgression of a land many are the princes therof; but by a man of understanding and knowledge the state thereof shall be prolonged" (Prov. 28:2). Return to the home: men standing up and leading their families, and women standing beside them in support; "And, ye fathers, provoke not your children to wrath: but bring them up in the nurture and admonition of the Lord" (Eph. 6:4). And return to true education, repudiating the indoctrination of public education, for "The wicked worketh a deceitful work: but to him that soweth righteousness shall be a sure reward" (Prov. 11:18).

Van Til writes:

> You cannot expect to train intelligent, well-informed soldiers of the cross of Christ unless the Christ is held up before them as the Lord of culture as well as the Lord of religion. It is of the nature of the conflict between Christ and Satan to be all-comprehensive.[22]

We must act now!

Endnotes

Taken from "America's Trojan Horse: Public Education" by Mike Metarko, *Faith for All of Life* magazine (July/August 2010), used by permission from the Chalcedon Foundation, www.chalcedon.edu.

All scripture quotes in this chapter, unless otherwise noted, are taken from the Authorized (King James) Version (KJV).

1. R.J. Rushdoony, *The Philosophy of the Christian Curriculum* (Vallecito, CA: Ross House Books, 2001), p. 165.
2. According to the National Assessment of Educational Progress' Nation's Report Card, www.nationsreportcard.gov.
3. This information may be found at the National Center for Education Statistics, www.nces.ed.gov/programs/crimeindicators/crimeindicators2009/index.asp.
4. See "A Brief Biographical Sketch of G. Stanley Hall," www.ithaca.edu/beins/gsh/gsh_bio.htm.
5. Samuel Blumenfeld, "Is Humanism a Religion?" *The New American* (February 23, 2010), www.thenewamerican.com/index.php/opinion/sam-blumenfeld/3001-is-humanism-a-religion.
6. John Dewey, *Democracy and Education* (Stilwell, KS: Digireads.com Publishing, 2005), p. 53.
7. This quote from Vladimir Lenin, Bolshevik ruler of Russia 1917–1924, can be found at: www.itwillpass.com/quotes_stupid_quotes.shtml.
8. Aldous Huxley, *Ends and Means, an Enquiry Into the Nature of Ideals and Into the Methods Employed for Their Realization* (London, England: Chatto & Windus, 1941), p. 270ff.
9. See "Humanist Manifesto I & II," American Humanist Association, www.americanhumanist.org/who_we_are/about_humanism/Humanist_Manifesto_I and www.americanhumanist.org/Who_We_Are/About_Humanism/Humanist_Manifesto_II.
10. Ken Ham, podcast entitled "Genesis: Reclaiming Culture," Answers in Genesis Ministries; similar information can be found at www.answersingenesis.org/PublicStore/product/Genesis-The-Key-to-Reclaiming-the-Culture,4741,190.aspx.
11. T.C. Pinckney, *Report to the Southern Baptist Convention Executive Committee*, Nashville, TN, September 18, 2001. See also the *2002 Report of the Southern Baptists Council on Family Life*.
12. Ken Ham, Britt Beemer, and Todd Hillard, *Already Gone* (Green Forest, AR: Master Books, 2009), p. 25, 141.
13. Ibid., p. 172.
14. E. Ray Moore and Exodus Mandate can be contacted at www.exodusmandate.org.
15. Voddie Baucham can be found at www.voddiebaucham.org/vbm/home.html.
16. Bruce Shortt can be found at web.me.com/voddieb/vbm/Blog/Entries/2010/3/9_The_Continuing_Collapse__March_2010.html. See also Bruce's groundbreaking book *The Harsh Truth About Public Schools* available at www.ChalcedonStore.com.
17. Doug Phillips and Vision Forum can be contacted at www.visionforumministries.org.
18. Scott Brown and the National Center for Family Integrated Churches can be contacted at www.ncfic.org.
19. See R.J. Rushdoony, *The Philosophy of Christian Curriculum, The Messianic Character of American Education* and *Intellectual Schizophrenia*.
20. Robert Parham, "Southern Baptist Convention Top Exec Boosts Anti-Public School Agenda," Ethicsdaily.com, June 10, 2009, www.ethicsdaily.com/news.php?viewStory=14356.

21. Matthew Henry, *A Church in the House, Restoring Daily Worship to the Christian Household* (San Antonio, TX: The Vision Forum, Inc., 2007).
22. Cornelius Van Til, *Essays on Christian Education* (Nutley, NJ: Presbyterian and Reformed Publishing Co., 1974), p. 26.

"Train up a child in the way he should go, and when he is old he will not depart from it."

— *Proverbs 22:6*

CHAPTER TWO

Drugging Them Up

Dr. Bruce Shortt

"[The prescribing of behavior modifying substances] is probably the largest uncontrolled drug experiment in the history of the world."

DR. BRUCE SHORTT

Bruce N. Shortt attended public schools through 12th grade; his mother was a public school nurse; and both of his grandmothers were public school teachers. He is a graduate of Harvard Law School, has a PhD from Stanford University, was a Fulbright Scholar, and serves on the boards of directors of the Houston Ebony Music Society and the Exodus Mandate. He is a member of North Oaks Baptist Church and currently practices law in Houston, Texas, where he resides with his wife and homeschools their sons. Mr. Shortt and T.C. Pinckney were cosponsors of the Christian Education Resolution that was submitted for consideration at the 2004 Annual Meeting of the Southern Baptist Convention. The following excerpts are taken from Dr. Shortt's book *The Harsh Truth about Public Schools*.

RITALIN: RUNNING FOR THE SHELTER OF TEACHER'S LITTLE HELPER

In 1966, the Rolling Stones recorded "Mother's Little Helper," a song about adults hypocritically using drugs to escape the unpleasantness of their lives.[1] In case you're wondering, the "mother's little helper" was, of course, a little yellow pill that helped "mother" through her "busy day." It seems that in the last 10 to 20 years, government school educators have discovered that psychotropic drugs can help them get through the unpleasantness of their "busy days." In this case, however, the drugs are being given to children, and especially to little boys.

Ritalin, Adderall, Prozac, Zoloft, Paxil, and other psychotropic drugs,[2] but mostly Ritalin and Adderall, are being used to drug schoolchildren at rates that are difficult to comprehend.[3] According to a 2000 ABC News story, Ritalin is prescribed to an estimated 4 million schoolchildren each year.[4] Roughly 75 percent of those children are boys.[5] The Drug Enforcement Administration has estimated that 8 million children and adults were on Ritalin in 2000.[6] Prescriptions for Ritalin increased by 700 percent from 1990 to 2001.[7]

In testimony before a panel of the United States House of Representatives in May 2003, medical experts testified that psychotropic drugs such as Ritalin and Adderall are being over-prescribed to children for the purpose of calming them down.[8] In fact, according to the testimony of the director of Behavioral Pediatrics at Children's Hospital of Philadelphia, Dr. William B. Carey, psychotropic drugs such as Ritalin are being prescribed to up to 17 percent of school-aged children.[9] What is Ritalin, and what is it being used for?

THE POOR MAN'S COCAINE

"Ritalin" is a tradename for a psychotropic compound called "methylphenidate" that was approved by the Food and Drug Administration in 1955 and that was often prescribed in the 1960s for behavioral control.[10] By 1999, the Drug Enforcement Administration was reporting that more than 19 percent of the world's Ritalin is bought and consumed in the United States.[11] Methylphenidate is pharmacologically classified with amphetamines.[12] In fact, the textbook *Treatments of Psychiatric Disorders* notes that cocaine, amphetamines, and methylphenidate are neuropharmacologically alike and that their clinical effects cannot be distinguished in laboratory tests.[13] Moreover, both the World Health Organization and the Food and Drug Administration place methylphenidate in the same high addiction category (Schedule II) in which they place amphetamines, morphine, opium, and barbiturates.[14]

So it should come as no surprise that Ritalin is being abused as a street drug, sometimes being referred to as "Vitamin R" or "Poor Man's Cocaine." Perhaps it may be more surprising that a 1999 survey of 6,000 Massachusetts teenagers attending government high schools found that *13 percent reported using Ritalin recreationally*.[15] The main source of the drug is, of course, the schools themselves. In a *New York Times* article, Janet Douglass, a director of the School

Health Institute at the University of Massachusetts at Lowell, commented on the prevalence of psychotropic drugs after visiting a nearby *elementary* school:

> I think they give out more psychotropic medication than a psych hospital did when I did psych. . . . Not just Ritalin, but heavy-duty psychiatric medications.[16]

According to a study conducted in Wisconsin and Minnesota, 34 percent of government school students ages 11 to 18 taking medication for ADHD reported being approached to sell or trade their drugs.[17] In addition, according to the DEA, Ritalin is one of the ten most stolen pharmaceuticals.[18]

The problem of the recreational use of Ritalin has become so pronounced that federal officials had to begin investigating government schools over the theft, illegal sale, and abuse of Ritalin and similar drugs.[19] Moreover, this problem involves principals, school nurses, and other school employees, not merely students.[20] Indeed, in 2000 the chairman of the House Committee on Education and the Workforce, William Goodling, characterized Ritalin as perhaps "the greatest drug problem we have in this country."[21] Researchers at the University of California have found that Ritalin is also a "gateway" drug to other drugs, especially cocaine.[22] According to the lead researcher for the study, "[Ritalin] makes the brain more susceptible to the addictive power of cocaine and doubles the risk of abuse."[23] Government schools are awash in this stuff. So why is it there?

ADHD and Drugging Schoolchildren

The most diagnosed "mental illness" among American children is Attention Deficit/Hyperactivity Disorder (ADHD),[24] and it is the ADHD diagnosis that has led to the mass drugging of America's schoolchildren. ADHD's status as a mental illness was established in 1987 by a vote of a committee of psychiatrists belonging to the American Psychiatric Association (APA).[25] According to the APA's *Diagnostic and Statistical Manual of Mental Disorders (DSM–IV)*, there are two types of ADHD, one characterized by inattention and the other by hyperactivity-impulsivity.

Each of these types of ADHD has nine symptoms, and a child is diagnosed with ADHD if (1) he exhibits six or more of the symptoms from either category and they persist for more than six months to a degree that is maladaptive and inconsistent with developmental level; (2) there is clinically significant impairment in social, academic, or occupational functioning; (3) the impairment is evident in at least two settings (e.g., home and school); and (4) there must be the onset of symptoms causing impairment by age seven.[26]

ADHD: A DIAGNOSIS IN SEARCH OF A DISEASE

What are these symptoms? Here are the nine symptoms for the "inattention" form of ADHD:[2]

- Often fails to give close attention to details or makes careless mistakes with schoolwork, work, or other activities
- Often has difficulty sustaining attention in tasks or play activities
- Often does not seem to listen when spoken to directly
- Often does not follow through on instructions and fails to finish schoolwork, chores, or duties in the workplace (not due to oppositional behavior or failure to understand instructions)
- Often has difficulty organizing tasks and activities
- Often avoids, dislikes, or is reluctant to engage in tasks that require sustained mental effort (e.g., schoolwork or homework)
- Often loses things necessary for tasks or activities
- Is often easily distracted by extraneous stimuli
- Is often forgetful in daily activities

The symptoms of the hyperactivity-impulsivity form of ADHD are:[28]

- Often fidgets with hands or feet or squirms in seat
- Often leaves seat in classroom or in other situations in which remaining seated is expected
- Often runs about or climbs excessively in situations in which it is inappropriate (in adolescents or adults, may be limited to feelings of restlessness)
- Often has difficulty playing or engaging in leisure activities quietly

- Is often "on the go" or often acts as if "driven by a motor"
- Often talks excessively
- Often blurts out answers before questions have been completed
- Often has difficulty awaiting turn
- Often interrupts or intrudes on others (e.g., butts into conversations or games)

Plainly, many, if not most, children "often" display six or more of these "symptoms," and they certainly do so both before and after reaching age seven. Moreover, even a cursory examination discloses the utterly subjective nature of the *DSM–IV* diagnostic standards (notice, for example, how the diagnostic criteria rely on the term "often"). For those who believe, however, that ADHD is a specific mental illness or brain disease, these symptoms tend to be seen as identifying a mental disorder with a genetic and biochemical cause.[29] This is generally the view of the ADHD industry.

In 1996, an article in *Scientific American* repeated the Ritalin advocates' view; namely, that by pointing to the rapid rise of ADHD diagnoses as evidence of overdiagnosis, the critics had things backward.[30] According to the experts quoted, the rise in diagnoses just reflected the fact that ADHD had previously been underdiagnosed.[31] The article admitted that diagnosing ADHD is subjective, and cited several studies that had been done which, while they *did not establish any physiological basis for ADHD,* were characterized as beginning to bring the biology of ADHD into focus.[32]

In essence, those who advocate the use of Ritalin to mitigate the behavior diagnosed as ADHD have generally argued that (1) ADHD has a physiological basis in some abnormal brain structure or brain chemistry, (2) ADHD seriously impairs 5–10 percent of schoolchildren, (3) Ritalin is a relatively mild, safe drug, and (4) those who reject the claim that ADHD is a mental illness properly treated by psychotropic drugs are mired in outmoded, unscientific views of disorders and, instead, are wrongly blaming ADHD on parents and schools.[33]

In 2002 and 2003, a spate of stories supportive of the ADHD diagnosis appeared in the popular press with headlines such as "Ritalin Is Safe — and It Works" (*Detroit Daily News*) and "Attention-Deficit Gene Is Located" (*Wall Street Journal*).[34] These stories, and others like them, report that there is now substantial evidence to indicate that ADHD is a neurological problem. Case closed. Or is it?

QUESTIONING THE ADHD ORTHODOXY

This view of ADHD and Ritalin has been sharply questioned.[35] In 1999, Dr. Richard Bromfield, a member of the faculty at Harvard Medical School, expressed his concern over the use of Ritalin:

> Ritalin is being dispensed with a speed and nonchalance compatible with our drive-through culture, yet entirely at odds with good medicine and common sense. The drug does help some people pay attention and function better. . . . But too many children, and more and more adults, are being given Ritalin inappropriately. The five-fold jump in Ritalin production in the past five years clearly suggests that . . . Ritalin is being *vastly over prescribed*[36] [emphasis added].

One of the oddities of the ADHD epidemic is that it has been essentially an American and Canadian phenomenon.[37] For example, into the mid-1990s, ADHD was rarely diagnosed in European countries such as Denmark, Norway, and Sweden.[38] As of 2000, it was reported that fewer than 6,000 children in France were being prescribed stimulants.[39] In 1997, the British Psychological Society published a major report in which British physicians and psychologists were warned not to apply the ADHD label to the wide variety of behaviors to which it is applied in the United States and Canada.[40] Indeed, the report questioned whether ADHD was a mental illness at all: "The idea that children who don't attend or sit still in school have a mental disorder is not entertained by most British clinicians."[41] In particular, the report expressed concern that the widespread practice of prescribing Ritalin and similar drugs for children diagnosed with ADHD in the United States not be replicated in Britain.[42] Further, the International Classification of Diseases published by the World Health Organization, which is the diagnostic manual used by most European health professionals, does not include as a mental illness any broad, ill-defined disorder comparable to ADHD as it is defined in *DSM–IV*.

THE ADHD DIAGNOSIS: DISSENT EMERGES

In the late 1990s even those who had been prescribing Ritalin began to question vigorously what was being done in the name of ADHD.

One example is Dr. Lawrence Diller, whose 1998 book, *Running On Ritalin*, points out that schools are pressuring parents to put their children on Ritalin, and that the result is widespread use of the drug when it isn't necessary. Interestingly, this came from a doctor who prescribes Ritalin and believes that there are circumstances when its use is appropriate. As a result of the publicly expressed doubts of health practitioners such as Dr. Diller, however, a more fundamental critique of the ADHD/Ritalin phenomenon began to receive more attention.

Recall that ADHD is alleged by its partisans within the American Psychiatric Association to be a specific "mental illness," not just a way of describing how children can misbehave. Resorting to Ritalin (and similar drugs) has been justified, in turn, on the grounds that a child with ADHD has a genetic and/or biochemical problem that the drugs are needed to overcome.[43] In light of this, one might reasonably ask whether there is clear evidence that the broadly defined forms of common childhood misbehavior set forth in the *DSM–IV* as symptoms of ADHD are the result of brain malfunction. This is the question that began to get more serious public attention after the publication of Dr. Diller's book.

One of the leading voices against ADHD as a diagnosis is Dr. Fred Baughman, a pediatric neurologist. Like a number of other critics, Dr. Baughman points to the lack of scientific data to show any link between brain malfunction and the "symptoms" of ADHD:

> This is a contrived epidemic, where all 5 million to 6 million children on these drugs are normal. The country's been led to believe that all painful emotions are a mental illness and the leadership of the APA knows very well that they are representing it [ADHD] as a disease when there is no scientific data to confirm any mental illness.[44]

Dr. Peter Breggin, psychiatrist and author of several books, including *Talking Back to Prozac*, has similarly argued that not only does ADHD not exist, "there is a great deal of scientific evidence that stimulants cause brain damage with long-term use."[45] So, is there substantial evidence to support the claim that ADHD is a mental illness, or is it, as many have suggested, an example of normal childhood behavior being voted into an "illness" by a professional organization?[46]

Putting "Therapy" Before Science?

Because of the controversy surrounding ADHD and skyrocketing levels of administration of psychotropic drugs to schoolchildren, the National Institutes of Health convened a Consensus Development Conference on the Diagnosis and Treatment of Attention Deficit Hyperactivity Disorder in 1998. Thirty-one scientific presentations concerning ADHD and its treatment were made to the panel, which concluded:

> We *don't* have an independent valid test for ADHD; there are no data to indicate that ADHD is due to a brain malfunction; existing studies come to conflicting conclusions as to whether the use of psychostimulants increases or decreases the risk of abuse, and finally after years of clinical research and experience with ADHD, our knowledge about the cause or causes of ADHD remains speculative[47] [emphasis added].

Apparently stung by their failure to get the NIH Conference to declare that ADHD is a real brain malfunction, ADHD partisans eventually drafted their own "International Consensus" letter in which they graciously compared those who question the validity of the ADHD diagnosis to "flat-earthers."[48] This letter has proved a useful public relations tool with those who are not familiar with the conclusions of the NIH conference. All in all, the debate among psychiatrists on the validity of the ADHD diagnosis often seems to resemble politics more than science.

ADHD: A Disease That Disappears During Summer Vacation?

The lack of any identifiable brain, biochemical, or genetic abnormality and its absurdly broad and subjective diagnostic criteria are not the only strange things about ADHD as a disease. Dr. Peter Breggin points out that the *DSM–IV* states that a child may manifest "symptoms" of ADHD when in settings "that lack intrinsic appeal or novelty" and tend to disappear when "the person is under very strict control, is in a novel setting, is engaged in especially interesting activities, is in a one-to-one situation."[49] Breggin also notes that most supporters of ADHD as a diagnosis admit that it tends *to disappear during summer vacation!*[50] Could it be that the fidgeting, lack of attention, and many of the other "symptoms" of ADHD do not reflect a mental illness but that children, and especially boys, are bored with, frustrated by, and alienated from the schools in whose custody they are placed? Could it also reflect a lack of parental attention and effective discipline at home and at school? Of course, this is just speculative, but, then, it seems so is the validity of the ADHD diagnosis.

RITALIN: A DRUG THAT CAN GIVE ANYONE A "BUZZ"

Some have attempted to claim that the existence of ADHD is confirmed by the fact that children diagnosed with ADHD tend to become more focused and obedient after taking Ritalin. The truth is, however, that giving Ritalin to normal children also has the same effect.[51] In fact, almost everyone's attention is improved by stimulants such as Ritalin, amphetamines, caffeine, and nicotine.[52] Consequently, seeing an improvement in someone's attention span after taking Ritalin doesn't establish that he has some disorder known as "ADHD." If it did, then we would have to conclude that virtually everyone in the world has ADHD.

A recent study gives further reason to question just what is being diagnosed when a child is labeled as having ADHD.[53] According to the study, which was led

FROM THE FILM: "Nobody really knows what the long-term effects of these medications are on young developing bodies and minds."

by researchers from the Boston University School of Medicine, children with sleep disorders manifest symptoms of ADHD at a higher rate than other children. In fact, snoring or other sleep-disordered breathing problems were found to be associated with a two-fold increase in the symptoms of ADHD. These sleep disorders affect an estimated 2–3 percent of children. But if sleep-disordered breathing problems are associated with an increase in the symptoms of ADHD, could it be that other factors causing children to get insufficient sleep are also associated with an increase in the symptoms of ADHD? Could we be drugging many children for ADHD, when the real problem is a lack of sleep because of over-scheduling, too many late hours in front of television or playing computer games, and a failure by parents to enforce reasonable bedtimes?

Don't Worry, It's Perfectly Safe

But if the very existence of ADHD is questionable, what about the benign public perception of Ritalin as a mild stimulant and the safest psychotropic drug available?[54] This appears to be not quite true either. Sweden banned Ritalin in 1968 because of abuse.[55] The International Narcotics Control Board has reported that Ritalin's pharmacological effects are essentially the same as those of amphetamines and methamphetamines (i.e., "speed").[56]

In 1995, the Drug Enforcement Administration reported that Ritalin is similar to cocaine: "It is clear that Ritalin substitutes for cocaine and d-amphetamine in a number of behavioral paradigms."[57] In 1996, the Drug Enforcement Administration held a conference on the use of stimulants in treating ADHD. In a report about the meeting, Gene Haislip, deputy assistant administrator of the Drug Enforcement Agency's Office of Diversion Control, pointedly warned parents about a *lack of candor* in how Ritalin has been promoted, especially as a drug for schoolchildren:

> Regrettably, much of the literature and promotion of the drug in recent years has ignored or understated the potency and abuse potential of methylphenidate and Ritalin. . . . This appears to have misled many physicians into prescribing the drug as a quick fix for problems of school and behavior.[58]

In fact, even the official version of the risks of taking Ritalin indicates that the dangers are far from trivial.

Well, Now That You Ask, There Are a Few Side Effects

Here are some of the side effects for Ritalin listed by the *Physicians' Desk Reference*: inability to fall asleep and stay asleep, nervousness, loss of appetite, abdominal pain, weight loss, abnormally fast heartbeat, chest pain, dizziness, headache, hives, jerking, pulse changes, skin rash, Tourette's syndrome, and severe and multiple twitching and writhing movements. Users are also warned that "suppression of growth has been reported with the long-term use of stimulants," long-term abuse can lead to tolerance and mental dependence with varying degrees of abnormal behavior, and *"long-term effects of Ritalin in children have not been well established."*

Critics of Ritalin are less circumspect about the risks so blandly described by the *Physicians' Desk Reference*. Dr. Peter Breggin, for example, notes the following:[59]

- Ritalin can cause inattention, hyperactivity, and aggression — in other words, the symptoms of ADHD!

- Ritalin can suppress a child's growth (height and weight), but there are no studies of how this growth suppression might affect the child's brain development. Moreover, there are studies that indicate that long-term use of Ritalin can result in shrinkage of parts of the brain.

- Ritalin can cause permanent, disfiguring tics and muscle spasms.

- Ritalin can often make children anxious, sometimes causing them to act in ways that seem "crazy."

- Ritalin can cause withdrawal symptoms when one or more doses are missed.

A 2001 study by researchers at the University of Buffalo reports that Ritalin may cause long-term changes in the brain similar to those produced by amphetamines and cocaine.[60] More specifically, Ritalin was found to activate certain genes linked to addiction known as "c-fos genes." Moreover, these genes were activated "in a pattern similar to that seen among those who use cocaine and amphetamines,"[61] which may provide the biological basis for the University of California study's findings that Ritalin is a "gateway" drug.

THE LONG-TERM EFFECT ON YOUNG CHILDREN? WHO KNOWS?

Dr. Jerry Rushton of the University of Michigan emphasizes how little is really known about how Ritalin and other psychotropic drugs affect young children:

I think the safety of these medications — in the young child especially — is not known, and when you take them in combination it's a whole new level of safety concern. . . . It's something that needs to be studied further.[62]

Well, as it turns out, it has been studied further. In 2003, the results of a study conducted at the Brookhaven National Laboratory comparing the effects of cocaine and Ritalin on the brain were published in the *Journal of Neuroscience*. The associate laboratory director for life sciences at Brookhaven National Laboratory, Nora Volkow, described the data from the study as clearly showing "that the notion that Ritalin is a weak stimulant is *completely incorrect*"[63] (emphasis added). As reported in the Brookhaven study, Ritalin has a stronger effect on the dopamine system than cocaine.[64]

This is significant because the dopamine system, according to doctors, is an area of the brain in which drugs such as cocaine and Ritalin have the most effect.[65] Apparently influenced by the benign image of Ritalin that has been cultivated within the medical profession, Volkow, a psychiatrist, described herself as "shocked as [expletive deleted]" that Ritalin had such a profound effect on the dopamine system.[66]

An article that appeared in 2003 in *American Journal of Psychiatry* gives more reason for concern regarding the use of Ritalin and other psychotropic drugs with children and adolescents. The study concluded that adolescents may be more susceptible to drug addiction than adults because of the stage of the development of their brain structure.[67] Moreover, the lead author of the study, who is also a psychiatrist on the faculty of Yale, R. Andrew Chambers, believes that far more research should be done specifically on the impact of psychiatric medicines on adolescents and their susceptibility to drug addiction.[68] Like the researchers in the Brookhaven study, Chambers also notes that addictive drugs and psychiatric medicines act on the same brain systems.[69]

HERE'S YOUR BRAIN ON RITALIN (AND SOME OTHER DRUGS)

Yet another cause for concern over "Ritalinizing" children was raised by a study of rats conducted by a research team led by Dr. William A. Carlezon Jr., an associate professor at Harvard Medical School and the director of the behavioral genetics laboratory at McClean Hospital, published in the December 15, 2003, issue of *Biological Psychiatry*.[70] In the study, juvenile rats were divided into a control group that received a placebo and another group that was given Ritalin.

The behavior of the rats as adults was then compared. The brains of the rats who had been given Ritalin as juveniles appeared to have been permanently altered. According to Dr. Carlezon, "Rats exposed to Ritalin as juveniles showed large increases in learned-helplessness behavior [determined by testing how quickly a rat under stress gave up on behavioral tasks] during adulthood, suggesting a tendency toward depression."[71] The researchers do not believe that the effects they observed are specific to Ritalin, but are rather a general reflection of how stimulant drugs affect developing brains — "early studies indicate that juvenile exposure to cocaine instead of Ritalin produces the same pattern of results."[72] While the results of rat studies are obviously not conclusive with respect to humans, the research by Dr. Carlezon's team makes it clear that very little is known about the long-term neurobiological consequences of exposing children to psychotropic drugs.[73] Nevertheless, the possibility that the promiscuous drugging of school children may lead to millions of adults who are depressed and who have little problem-solving ability is a disquieting prospect.

DRUG HIM OR LOSE HIM

In the face of clear evidence that ADHD may not exist, that ADHD is being diagnosed at levels that are obviously unreasonable, that Ritalin poses substantial risk of harm to children, and that, as a result of its prevalence in schools, Ritalin is being widely abused as a recreational drug, what are our highly trained educational professionals doing? *Threatening parents* who don't want to drug their children. Are you surprised?

As incredible as it may seem, school districts are beginning to threaten parents with the *loss* of their children if they don't want to medicate them. Here are just two examples:[74]

- A seven-year-old boy's parents were concerned about the side effects he was suffering from Ritalin. After the parents spoke to the school administrators about their decision to take their son off the drug, the school administrators called Child Protective Services alleging child abuse. As a result, the parents were placed on a statewide list of alleged child abusers and ensnared in a court battle to clear their names and keep their child.

- In another case, a mother decided to take her nine-year-old son off of a drug cocktail that included Ritalin, Paxil, and Dexadrine because they caused him to hallucinate. This led to the school district officials calling the police and Child Protective Services in an effort to enforce their preference that the boy be drugged.

According to observers, government schools "are increasingly using accusations of child abuse and neglect" if parents resist drugging their children.[75] David Lansner, a New York City lawyer who has seen cases similar to those described, reports, "The schools are now using child protective services to enforce their own desires and their own policies."[76] Similarly, Dr. Lawrence H. Diller has noted:

> It is no longer simply an issue of which school or class a child will attend. Instead, some parents are being threatened with the possibility of losing custody of their children if they refuse to comply with suggested treatment for an alleged medical condition [ADHD].[77]

One of the shocking aspects of these developments is that the government has traditionally respected parental decisions regarding medical treatment for their children unless the life of the child was in danger. In these cases, nothing of the sort is at stake. The government school officials in these instances simply believe that drugging the child is a better medical decision, and they obviously mean to have their way.

Change His Diaper, Then Give Him a "Hit" of Ritalin

School-age children and adults are not the only ones enriching the psychotropic drug industry.[78] Research done at the University of Maryland shows that the number of children ages 2–4 taking psychotropic drugs such as Ritalin, Prozac, Zoloft, and Paxil increased by 50 percent between 1991 and 1995.[79] Moreover, it is reported that over a quarter of a million pediatricians are prescribing Ritalin to children *under* age six.[80] Apparently, a lot of two-, three-, four-, and five-year-olds are showing unmistakable signs of ADHD. You know, stuff like not wanting to sit still, often not listening when spoken to, and having a short attention span. Do the pediatricians and psychiatrists have the vaguest idea what they are doing to these children? Of course not. In a February 23, 2000, article in the *New York Times*, Dr. Joseph Coyle, the chairman of psychiatry at Harvard Medical School, commented on the drugging of these very young children:[81] "These interventions are occurring at a critical time in brain development, *and we don't know what the consequences are*"[82] [emphasis added].

Evidently, elements of the medical research community wanted to remedy their lack of knowledge about how these drugs affect toddlers. This appears to explain a federally funded 72-week study on the effects of Ritalin on very young children begun in late 2001 in New York City by six medical institutions.[83] Most of the children were under five years old, with some of them being as young as age three.[84]

FROM THE FILM: "I'm afraid that it's doing enormous damage, particularly to boys in the schools."

According to reports, the children were started on small doses of Ritalin, and then the doses were increased to see how much they could tolerate.[85] After the children reached the maximum dosage they were able to tolerate, they were placed in a simulated classroom with one-way mirrors so that the researchers could study their behavior while being weaned off Ritalin.

If this sounds a bit like the kind of medical research performed in Eastern Europe by certain German medical professionals who "relocated" to South America in the mid- to late-1940s, don't worry. An official at one of the participating institutions (who, understandably, wanted to remain anonymous) avers that the study will enable doctors to "make intelligent decisions."[86] I guess we are supposed to feel better knowing that, after already drugging millions of toddlers and children, the psychiatric profession is now trying to figure out what it has been doing.

Where does the idea that toddlers suffer from ADHD and need to be drugged come from? Dr. Julie Mango Zito, the author of the

University of Maryland study, cites as a factor the increased reliance on daycare and the consequent need to have children "conform in their behavior."[87] This observation is confirmed by the New York City study in which some of the "research subjects" (aka "children") have been referred by schools.

Just in case you continue to be skeptical that our trusted professionals could really be doing this to children, consider that in 1994 over 3,000 prescriptions for Prozac were written for *children under 12 months old*.[88] And just exactly how does a psychiatrist or a doctor determine that a 10-month-old baby, for example, is depressed and is in need of Prozac? Do you think that there is a sound body of research indicating that it's just okey-dokey to give Prozac to infants? Do you think that anyone has the slightest idea what the long-term effects of giving Prozac to infants and preschoolers are?

PSYCHOTROPIC DRUGS AND CHILDREN: "READY, FIRE, AIM!"

When we get beyond the surface, it's clear that something very wrong is going on. Advocates of the ADHD diagnosis are still searching for a biological justification. That means that millions of children are being drugged to treat something that has not yet been shown to be a real disease, as distinguished from unruly or bad behavior. Worse, no one really knows what the true short-term or long-term effects of administering these drugs to children are. It is shocking that the drugging of millions of schoolchildren has been allowed to proceed without proof that there is a disease and, *especially*, without sufficient testing of the effects of these powerful psychotropic drugs on children. In fact, it is hard to think of a more egregious example of medical malpractice than to prescribe drugs to infants, preadolescents, and adolescents when the consequences to them in those particular stages of development are largely unknown.

When the legitimacy of the ADHD diagnosis is challenged, more than a few of its defenders resort to deriding the skeptics as "flat-earthers," "Scientologists," or "prejudiced." Some of the skeptics claim, on the other hand, that this ad hominem defense of the ADHD diagnosis reflects venality and professional arrogance. Perhaps, but I don't doubt that the name calling may also reflect, in some cases, a passionately held view that ADHD diagnosis is valid and that prescribing psychotropic drugs to, by some estimates, as many as 20 percent of our schoolchildren is somehow medically justified.[89] Still, those of us who are not psychiatrists might be excused if the votes, consensus letters, public relations efforts, and name calling that appear to be integral to establishing a psychiatric diagnosis strike us as resembling politics rather than science.

It is *possible* that among the children swept up in the very broad and subjective ADHD diagnostic criteria there may be some children that do have an organic problem that psychotropic drugs relieve [whether they do it safely is another matter]. Nor is it impossible for Ritalin and other psychotropic drugs to have some legitimate applications.[90] But no one now really knows whether that is the case with ADHD and children. Instead, schools and parents are medicating rather than disciplining, medicating rather than providing a stimulating environment, medicating instead of having recess, and medicating instead of correcting the institutionalized abuse of boys in government schools. The price of allowing schools to rely on "mother's little helper" to maintain order is likely eventually to carry a price tag that we can't even begin to comprehend.

"As Jazzed as Any Speed Freak"

There is ample scientific evidence to indicate that Ritalin is a very powerful drug with serious side effects. But what is it really like to be medicated with Ritalin? What is it like on the "inside"? Children, unfortunately, are not articulate or experienced enough to give us much insight into this question. But Walter Kirn, a professional writer, describes eloquently his experience with Ritalin after he had been diagnosed with adult "ADD." According to Kirn, the "Ritalinized" state of mind is far from benign — no matter how calm or in control the Ritalin user may *seem* to outside observers:

> I felt guilty each time I renewed my prescription, but like Ritalin's other effects, it didn't show. I felt guilty because the drug was so [expletive deleted] powerful — easily as euphoria-inducing as any illegal substance I'd ever tried. In fact, its effects were better. Cleaner. Tighter. Plus, compared to street drugs, the stuff was cheap. For the same amount cokeheads pay for one night's high, I could soar for a month, without fear of the police. Not that I didn't feel paranoid anyhow. During the eighteen months I took the drug, I rehearsed countless

times a scene in which a cop pulled me over for a traffic infraction, looked deep into my dilated pupils, then spotted the pill bottle on the seat beside me. "It's a prescription, officer," I'd say. And what could he do about it? Not a thing. There I am, as jazzed as any speed freak who's just put his girlfriend in the hospital after an all-night quarrel in a motel room, and yet I'm untouchable, innocent, free to go.[91]

Are you still wondering why Ritalin is being abused as a street drug or why it is being widely used as a recreational drug by teenagers? Kirn's experience with Ritalin also showed him how Ritalin could be prescribed to so many children: "It's no wonder, I thought, that parents and teachers love the stuff. . . . Forget how the little white pills make Johnny feel . . . they make the adults looking after him feel great."[92] Kirn ultimately took himself off Ritalin. Children don't have that option, even if they, like Kirn, could understand what is being done to them.

What Is Going On?

There is more to this controversy than mere institutional stupidity and professional cupidity, although they are present in good measure too. *Schools do have serious discipline problems*, and the reasons are many. Effective discipline of students, particularly the highly effective corporal variety, has been virtually eliminated from schools because of court rulings and biases against traditional discipline in schools of education and among some elements of society. For some of the same reasons, discipline is often largely absent in the home. This problem is particularly acute when fathers are absent from the home or uninvolved with their children. Many boys undoubtedly resent being treated as "disturbed" for no reason other than the fact that they are boys and are frustrated by the schools' failure to teach them how to read properly. Boys and girls alike are also doubtlessly bored by the thin intellectual gruel that government schools ladle out today. The increasingly politically correct curricula inflicted on children — often by marginally competent or incompetent teachers — also invite rebellion. Value clarification and other nonacademic curricula subtly undermine the authority of the teacher and school as well as that of parents, and the values of street gangs are present in schools as never before. For these and other reasons, government schools *are* difficult places to teach and to manage.

Viewed from this institutional perspective, ADHD and psychotropic drugs such as Ritalin are godsends. Faced with a severe break-down of discipline, many teachers and administrators undoubtedly believe that Ritalin and similar drugs are perhaps the only effective classroom management tools left to them. And what is even better, government schools can get *extra money* from the federal government for children diagnosed with ADHD, courtesy of the Individuals with Disabilities Act. Further, because the Elementary and Second-ary Education Act of 1965 brought an army of psychologists, psy-chiatrists, social workers, and psychiatric programs into government schools, in some sense it is probably natural now for many educators to see behavioral problems as medical problems. This may give you some insight into why Dr. Fred Baughman, a pediatric neurologist who is one of the more outspoken critics of the ADHD epidemic and Ritalin, believes:

> *Every child who goes to public school is at risk.* Psychology and psychiatry await. Teachers teach no more. They have become "diagnosticians."[93] [emphasis added].

By how does all of this look to schoolchildren?

Surely schoolchildren must view the situation as deeply ironic. They are told that they shouldn't use drugs (unless, of course, they have reached the opposite conclusion as a result of participa-tion in a program that taught them "critical thinking" or "values clarification"), and yet their schools have been turned into virtual pharmacies of psychotropic drugs that school officials are *urging* them to take. The ubiquitous presence of Ritalin and other psy-chotropic drugs, in turn, has created massive recreational abuse of these drugs in schools. Students may well be asking themselves why using drugs is bad if they use them to escape their problems for a while, but it's just fine if the school nurse gives them drugs so that teachers can escape from their ADHD, oppositional defiance disorder, or some other psychiatric mumbo jumbo diagnosis? Per-haps they are concluding that it is just a matter of whose problem counts.

By the way, if you think that it sounds as if the Cali drug cartel has infiltrated government schools, our highly trained educational professionals recommend that *you* seek a "medical evaluation."

Endnotes

Taken from *The Harsh Truth about Public Schools* by Bruce N. Shortt (Vallecito, CA: Chalcedon Foundation, 2004), used by permission from the Chalcedon Foundation, www.chalcedon.edu.

1. The lyrics, in part, go like this: "Kids are different today / I hear ev'ry mother say / Mother needs something today to calm her down / And though she's not really ill / There's a little yellow pill / She goes running for the shelter of a mother's little helper / And it helps her on her way, gets her through her busy day."

2. Psychotropic drugs are a class of drugs that act on the central nervous system to produce changes in thinking, feeling, and behaving. Jonathan Leo and David Cohen, "Broken Brains or Flawed Studies? A Critical Review of ADHD Neuroimaging Research," *The Journal of Mind and Behavior*, vol. 24, no. 1 (Winter 2003): p. 32, available online at http://psychrights.org/Research/Digest/NLPs/critical-reviewofadhd.pdf.

3. Because, historically, Ritalin has been the psychotropic drug prescribed in the vast majority of ADHD cases, the discussion of the general problem of schools drugging schoolchildren is discussed in terms of Ritalin, although the same or similar issues exist with respect to the use of other psychotropic drugs in connection with diagnoses of ADHD.

4. Ephrat Livni, "A Diagnosis Excess? A Lawsuit Alleges Attention Deficit Disorder is Over-Diagnosed," ABCNews.com, December 17, 2000. CHADD (Children and Adults with Attention Deficit/Hyperactivity Disorder), a non-profit organization of parents whose children are labeled with ADHD and which receives substantial funding from the makers of Ritalin and other similar drugs, promotes estimates that only 1.5 million schoolchildren take drugs for ADHD and seems to support the position that these drugs are generally under-prescribed. See Russell A. Barkley, Ph.D., *ADHD, Ritalin, and Conspiracies: Talking Back to Peter Breggin*, March 4, 1999, available at http://www.quackwatch.org/04ConsumerEducation/NegativeBR/breggin.html. Critics of the use of Ritalin-type drugs and ADHD as a medical diagnosis, such as Dr. Peter Breggin, argue that 8 million schoolchildren a year are being drugged.

5. This is based on a study conducted by Dr. Jerry Rushton of the University of Michigan, as quoted in "Ritalin and Prozac Combination used by more Children," *Reuters*, May 15, 2000.

6. "Ritalin: Violence Against Boys, Drug Is Being Used to Sedate Active Young Boys," *The Massachusetts News*, November 1, 2000, available at www.massnews.com/vioboy.htm.

7. Jane Marcus, "Schools Need to Crack Down on Ritalin Use," *The Baltimore Sun*, February 20, 2001.

8. "House Told Schools Overuse Mood Drugs," 7am.com News, June 16, 2003.

9. Ibid.

10. Kelly Patricia O'Meara, "Doping Kids," *Insight* magazine (June 28, 1999).

11. Ibid.

12. Peter R. Breggin, M.D. and Ginger Ross Breggin, "The Hazards of Treating 'Attention-Deficit/Hyperactivity Disorder' with Methylphendate (Ritalin)," *The Journal of College Student Psychotherapy*, volume 10 (2), 1995, p. 55–72.

13. Ibid.

14. O'Meara, "Doping Kids"; Breggin and Breggin, "The Hazards of Treating 'Attention-Deficit/Hyperactivity Disorder' with Methylphendate (Ritalin)," p. 55–72.

15. Marcus, "Schools Need to Crack Down on Ritalin Use."
16. As quoted in "Ritalin: Violence Against Boys, Drug Is Being Used to Sedate Active Young Boys."
17. Marcus, "Schools Need to Crack Down on Ritalin Use."
18. Ibid.
19. Ibid.
20. "Dealing and Stealing Ritalin," *Education Reporter* (February 2001).
21. Jonathan Riskind, "Schools Push Ritalin Panel Told," *The Columbus Dispatch,* May 17, 2000.
22. "Ritalin: Violence Against Boys, Drug Is Being Used to Sedate Active Young Boys."
23. Nadine Lambert, as quoted in "Ritalin: Violence Against Boys, Drug Is Being Used to Sedate Active Young Boys."
24. O'Meara, "Doping Kids."
25. Ibid.
26. As set forth in *Diagnostic and Statistical Manual of Mental Disorders* by the American Psychiatric Association. For a discussion, see Breggin and Breggin, "The Hazards of Treating 'Attention-Deficit/Hyperactivity Disorder' with Methylphenidate (Ritalin)," p. 55–72.
27. Ibid.
28. Ibid.
29. Breggin and Breggin, "The Hazards of Treating 'Attention-Deficit/Hyperactivity Disorder' with Methylphenidate (Ritalin)," p. 55–72.
30. Kristin Leutwyler, "Paying Attention — The Controversy Over ADHD and the Drug Ritalin Is Obscuring a Real Look at the Disorder and Its Underpinnings," *Scientific American* (August 1996).
31. Ibid.
32. Ibid.
33. See, e.g., Leutwyler, "Paying Attention – The Controversy Over ADHD and the Drug Ritalin Is Obscuring a Real Look at the Disorder and Its Underpinnings," and Barkley, "ADHD, Ritalin, and Conspiracies: Talking Back to Peter Breggin."
34. These articles are: "Ritalin Is Safe — and It Works," *The Detroit Daily News,* December 12, 2002; Robert McGough, "Attention-Deficit Gene Is Located," *The Wall Street Journal,* October 22, 2002, D-3; Michael Fumento, "Trick Question: A Liberal Hoax Turns Out to Be True," *The New Republic,* February 2, 2003.
35. See, e.g., Dr. Richard Bromfield, "Is Ritalin Overprescribed? Yes," drkoop.com, September 10, 1999, available at www.drkoop.com/news/focus/september/ritalin_yes.html; George Will, "Boys Will Be Boys or You Can Just Drug Them," *The Washington Post,* December 2, 1999.
36. Bromfield, "Is Ritalin Overprescribed? Yes."
37. In America, at least, the makers of drugs for ADHD are now beginning to market them to adults. As Sally Satel points out in a *Wall Street Journal* op-ed, "ADD Overdose?" July 24, 2003, A-14, there is a new epidemic of attention deficit disorder on the way. Satel believes that, although medical professionals will be "finding" that many adults are clinically mentally ill with ADD, much of the demand for these drugs will in fact be a demand for what Peter Kramer (author of *Listening to Prozac*) calls "cosmetic psychopharmacology." The object of cosmetic psychopharmacology is to make people who do not suffer from a mental disorder feel "better than well." Satel does, by the way, accept the validity of the ADHD diagnosis. Adult ADHD is diagnosed using a test in which the patient is asked how often he (1) has trouble wrapping up the final details of a project, (2)

has difficulty getting things in order, (3) has trouble remembering appointments or obligations, (4) avoids or delays starting tasks that require a lot of thought, (5) fidgets or squirms with his hands or feet when he has to sit for a long time, and (6) feels overly active and compelled to do things, like he is driven by a motor. If you answer "sometimes" with respect to (1), (2), (3) and answer "often" to any of (4), (5), and (6), "It may be beneficial for you to talk with your healthcare provider about an evaluation." In other words, you can probably get a medical professional to write you a prescription for Ritalin, Adderall, or some other psychotropic drug. Given that Ritalin, like caffeine, will help most people concentrate, and if Walter Kirn's "inside view" of what it is like to be on Ritalin is correct (see the end of the discussion of Ritalin in the text), we can expect that adult ADHD will become a growth industry. Popularizing the adult ADHD diagnosis presumably will also allow pharmaceutical companies to keep at least some of the children diagnosed with ADHD as customers for life. The test for adult ADHD is published by the World Health Organization. A copy of the test and an account of how adult ADHD is gaining ground as a diagnosis are provided in Robert McGough and Patricia Callahan, "An Illness That's Not Just for Kids Anymore," *The Wall Street Journal,* November 26, 2003, D1.

38. Breggin and Breggin, "The Hazards of Treating 'Attention-Deficit/Hyperactivity Disorder' with Methylphenidate (Ritalin)," p. 55–72.
39. Jay Joseph, "Problems in Psychiatric Genetic Research: A Reply to Faraone and Biederman," *Developmental Review,* 20, p. 582–593, 587.
40. Harvey McConnell, "ADHD Just Doesn't Add Up to Brit Psych Society," *The Medical Post,* January 21, 1997.
41. Ibid.
42. McConnell, "ADHD Just Doesn't Add Up to Brit Psych Society."
43. The *DSM-IV* does not say that ADHD is due to brain malfunction. Journals and textbooks do, however, express this view. See Fred Baughman, "The ADHD Consensus Conference: End of the Epidemic," quoting W.B. Carey (NIH), *Consensus Development Conference on ADHD,* November 16–18, 1998, available at www.home.att.net/~Fred-Alden/Es39.htm.
44. Dr. Fred Baughman, as quoted in O'Meara, "Doping Kids."
45. Dr. Peter Breggin, as quoted in O'Meara, "Doping Kids."
46. This view has been expressed, for example, by the president of The Citizens Commission on Human Rights, Bruce Wiseman. See O'Meara, "Doping Kids."
47. As quoted in O'Meara, "Doping Kids."
48. Dr. Russell Barkley headed the group that produced the letter, which is on the CHADD website.
49. Breggin and Breggin, "The Hazards of Treating 'Attention-Deficit/Hyperactivity Disorder' with Methylphenidate (Ritalin)," p. 55–72.
50. Ibid.
51. Ibid.
52. A January 26, 2004, story by David B. Rochelson in the *Harvard Crimson,* "Students Turn to Drugs to Study," reports on students' use of prescription drugs such as Ritalin and Adderall as "study drugs." According to the *Crimson,* many students believe that these drugs are far better than caffeine for enhancing study performance. According to one student interviewed by the *Crimson,* "It's helped me a lot.. . . I can sit down for more than three hours and it feels like ten minutes. . . . You don't necessarily have to have ADD for it to do something to you . . . especially if you snort it. . . . The thing with coffee is that your head is awake but your body isn't — it doesn't feel all that natural. . . . Ritalin is more like an all-over buzz."

53. D.J. Gottlieb et al., "Symptoms of Sleep Disordered Breathing in 5-year-old Children Are Associated with Sleepiness and Problem Behaviors," *Pediatrics,* October 2003, 112:870-877. This study involved a fairly large sample — 3,019 children.

54. See, e.g., *The Physicians' Desk Reference,* "ADHD May Be Overdiagnosed, Study Says," CNN.com, September 1, 1999, and Leutwyler, "Paying Attention — The Controversy Over ADHD and the Drug Ritalin Is Obscuring a Real Look at the Disorder and Its Underpinnings."

55. "Ritalin: Violence Against Boys, Drug Is Being Used to Sedate Active Young Boys."

56. O'Meara, "Doping Kids."

57. Ibid.

58. As quoted in Ephrat Livni, "A Diagnosis Excess? A Lawsuit Alleges Attention Deficit Disorder if Over-Diagnosed."

59. Breggin and Breggin, "The Hazards of Treating 'Attention-Deficit/Hyperactivity Disorder' with Methylphenidate (Ritalin)," p. 55–72.

60. "Ritalin May Change Brain Long-Term, Study Shows," Reuters News Service, November 11, 2001. See, also, Brendan McGarry, "UB Researcher's Findings on Ritalin Attract National Attention," *The Spectrum,* November 28, 2001.

61. "Ritalin May Change Brain Long-Term, Study Shows."

62. Dr. Jerry Rushton as quoted in "Ritalin and Prozac Combination Used by More Children."

63. As quoted in Kelly Patricia O'Meara, "New Research Indicts Ritalin," *Insight* magazine, July 22, 2003.

64. Ibid.

65. Ibid.

66. Ibid.

67. Robert McGough, "Brain Structure May Make Teens Addiction-Prone," *The Wall Street Journal,* June 6, 2003.

68. Ibid.

69. Ibid.

70. "Early Ritalin Exposure May Cause Long-Term Effects on the Brain," McLean Hospital — A Harvard Medical School Affiliate, December 12, 2004, available at http://www.mclean.harvard.edu/news/press/current.php?id=65.

71. As quoted in "Ritalin Use During Childhood May Increase Depression, Decrease Cocaine Sensitivity in Adults," press release by McLean Hospital, December 8, 2003, available online at http:/www.mcleanhospital.org/PublicAf-fairs/ritmod20031208.html.

72. Ibid.

73. It must be noted that the study also found that the rats that had been given Ritalin demonstrated a lower level of interest in cocaine than the rats in the control group. Note, however, that the University of California and University of Buffalo studies mentioned indicate that Ritalin may be a "gateway" drug for humans. Obviously, the differences in human and rodent biology may be such that all, some, or none of the findings from Carlezon's study may be applicable to humans.

74. Rick Karlin, "Ritalin Use Splits Parents, School," Albany, New York, *Times Union,* May 7, 2000.

75. Ibid.

76. Ibid., quoting David Lansner.

77. Lawrence H. Diller, M.D., "Just Say Yes to Ritalin," Salon.com, September 25, 2005.
78. It is estimated that Ritalin alone has added about $10 billion to the market capitalization of Novartis since 1991. See O'Meara, "New Research Indicts Ritalin."
79. "Into the Mouths of Babes — The Drugging of Preschoolers Is on the Rise, Study Shows," *Education Reporter*, April 2000.
80. Douglas Montero, "Studies on Ritalin Are 'Child Abuse,' " NYPost.com, December 3, 2001.
81. "Into the Mouths of Babes – The Drugging of Preschoolers Is on the Rise, Study Shows."
82. It appears that those who have prescribed Ritalin and similar drugs to children and adolescents have consistently done so without research to support their use. In an editorial in the January 2003 issue of *Archives of Pediatrics and Adolescent Medicine*, Dr. Michael Jellinek, commenting on a study in the same issue indicating dramatically increased use of Ritalin and other psychiatric drugs by children and adolescents between 1987 and 1996, expresses concern over increased prescription of psychiatric drugs to children *at a time when there was little research to support the use of these drugs with children.*
83. Montero, "Studies on Ritalin Are 'Child Abuse.' "
84. Ibid.
85. Ibid.
86. Ibid.
87. Julie Magno Zito, as quoted in "Into the Mouths of Babes – The Drugging of Preschoolers Is on the Rise, Study Shows."
88. Julie Magno Zito, et al., "Trends in Prescribing of Psychotropic Medications to Preschoolers," *The Journal of American Medical Association* (2000): p. 283.
89. This admittedly hard to believe estimate is from O'Meara, "New Research Indicts Ritalin."
90. For example, in a recent article it is reported that some geriatric specialists believe that Ritalin may relieve lethargy and depression in the elderly. Ritalin also has been used to combat the effects of strokes and brain injuries. Still, it appears that there are serious concerns about side effects. Christopher Windham, "Ritalin Shows Promise in Treating Lethargy, Depression in Elderly," *The Wall Street Journal*, July 17, 2003, D-1.
91. Walter Kirn, "Inside Ritalin," *GQ*, December 2000, pp. 297–301, at p. 300.
92. Ibid. Kirn also notes that if he had been given Ritalin in junior high he wouldn't have missed one dose. Why? As he explains: "They're uppers. Get it? Uppers. The act like downers on kids who truly need them, according to the experts, but what do they know? The experts are on the outside, looking in, monitoring behavior, not emotion. All they see are rows of little heads sitting obediently at little desks. The kids are the ones on the inside. It's different there — stranger, hotter, faster. I know," p. 301.
93. Fred A. Baughman, M.D., Jr., "The Totality of the ADD/ADHD Fraud," February 4, 1998, available at http://home.att.net/~Fred-Alden/Es5.html. A more recent work by Dr. Baughman on this subject is "Attention-Deficit Hyperactivity Disorder (ADHD) As Fraud," by Fred A. Baughman Jr. M.D., neurologist, pediatric neurology, published *La Catarsis de Quiron. Revista da Psicologia* 2(1), 2002, available online at http://psychrights.org/Research/Digest/ADHD/ADHDAsFraud.htm.

"Diverse weights and diverse measures, they are both alike, an abomination to the Lord."

— *Proverbs 20:10*

CHAPTER THREE

Dumbing Them Down

R.C. Murray

"I thought, This is not day care. I don't need to be reading stories to seniors."

R.C. MURRAY

R.C. Murray is a disabled veteran of the Army Infantry Paratroopers and a former public school teacher. He left his job as a technical writer for a satellite manufacturer to teach high school English, only to be told he could not expect, much less require, his students to read their literature assignments. After four years of fighting the public education system and having a stroke then a mini-stroke, Mr. Murray decided he was safer in the airborne infantry, and he left the classroom to return to technical writing. He has since dedicated his life to informing parents about what's really going on in public schools and exhorting them to seek better alternatives for their children's education. Mr. Murray is the author of *Golden Knights: History of the U.S. Army Parachute Team, Prole Nation*, and *Legally STUPiD*, from which this chapter was taken.

WHY JOHNNY DOESN'T HAVE TO READ

He was huge. In fact, he was so tall, I had to step back to look up into his weather-beaten face. His shoulders probably scraped both sides of a standard doorway. As the assistant administrator introduced us, I put out my hand and said, "Hello." With some hesitation, he put his own double-size hand out to meet mine. His dark, leathery brow seemed to constrict as he looked down at me. I guess he didn't know what to think of me. His big hand was strong and calloused. He must be a farmer, I told myself, sizing him up just as he seemed to be trying to figure me out. At that moment his boss came in the room.

She was a red lady. I say red because that's what I remember most about her. Her outfit was red, as was her hair. Her face was a flush red, too, like someone upset or embarrassed. And her eyes were red, a glowing angry sort of red. The look she gave her husband when she saw him shaking my hand said it all. He nearly jerked my hand off trying to get his back. Apparently seeing the instant tension, the assistant administrator asked the red lady and her subordinate to have a seat at the conference table.

"I'm sorry it had to come to this," she told the administrator without looking at me. "But since Mr. Murray is unwilling to work with us, we had no choice."

"Excuse me, ma'am," I spoke up, lifting a hand to the administrator as if to say I could speak for myself without his lawyering. "I'm not unwilling to work with any student or parent, but I cannot waive county policy."

"Really," she snapped, her red eyes turning on me.

It didn't work on me though. I wasn't her husband. In fact, I felt sorry for him. He just sat there, never saying a word. The administrator tried to ease the tension but with little success. She started talking about going to the school board before he could say much of anything. He knew the parental complaint had to do with their son getting a zero on his English III research paper because he failed to meet the minimum requirement of "four typed, double-spaced pages on a one-inch margin — top, bottom, and both sides." It was county policy, and this was my first year teaching. I certainly wasn't one to go against policy. Just so the administrator knew that the student and his parents were aware of that policy, I had brought a copy of the parental letter she had signed explaining the requirements for the research paper before our class began the assignment. I had also brought a copy of the county policy, so there would be no question about whether I had made up the requirements.

"I didn't know what that meant when I signed it," she admitted, trying not to look at her signature. Her husband reached for the letter to get a closer look, but she shoved it aside. "It's just like all them other things y'all're always sending home for us to sign. Yesterday, I had to sign something about Matt's tardies. And I just don't see why y'all gotta make such a big deal out that either. Ever'body's late once in a while."

At this point the administrator jumped into the verbal brawl. He explained to her our high school had to take tardiness seriously because too many students did not, that she just didn't realize what a disruption it was for the teacher to have students dragging into the classroom whenever they felt like it. He added that students who continued to be tardy would end up being suspended for a few days, and if she thought signing a Tardiness Notice was an inconvenience, having to come pick her son up from school and keep him home for a few days would be a greater inconvenience. He really tore into her, which caused her face to grow a darker shade of red. I was right proud of him and really appreciated his support.

"Well, I'm not here to argue 'bout that one right now," she conceded, raising her voice as she smirked at her speechless husband. "I'm here to get my son credit for what he done on his research paper."

"Ma'am," I said, pushing another document in front of her, "Matt only wrote two and a half pages, and that was at the wrong margins."

She glanced down at the incomplete research paper in front of her and turned up her nose at the big red "0" on the rubrics page.

FROM THE FILM: "For the reading test, she had to read to the student and then write down his responses, because he wasn't expected to write either."

I tried not to smile as I thought about the red ink zero and red ink note at the bottom of the page under Comments: "Does not meet minimum length requirements." And I thought she liked red. Finally, she lifted the rubrics cover sheet and looked at the short document her son called a research paper. There really was no room for argument. His paper was not only too short, it was bleeding with red ink that pointed out sentence fragments, run-ons, grammar errors, misspelled words, and incorrect citing of sources. She flipped the document upside-down and pushed it back across the table. It didn't matter to her. She wanted her son to get credit for what little work he had done and didn't care about policy.

"I reckon we're just gonna to have to go to the school board," she sulked.

The administrator placed both his hands in a "Whoa there" position. He said he didn't see any need for all that. He believed "we" could come to an understanding, that there was no need to involve the school board, that "we" could work something out. His support was gone. I could tell. In fact, he looked scared. And I was just getting started.

"I'm sorry," she went on, confident she had unnerved him, albeit not me. "You leave us no choice. And I just want you to know, we ain't the only parents taking issue with Mr. Murray."

"Excuse me," I said, my own face now getting red. I could feel my blood pressure rising. "And what's that supposed to mean?"

"Just what I said," she chirped sarcastically. "We ain't the only parents that ain't satisfied with you. And a lot of yur students feel the same way. They know ya play favorts in yur class."

"What?!" Now my blood was boiling. Her husband looked nervous. It's not a pretty thing to see a man that big look for a place to hide.

FROM THE FILM: "They were supposed to do writing assignments in what is called group learning. They put one "motivated child" with three or four "diverse learners." The gifted student will actually do all the work, but everybody gets the same grade."

"You heard me," she went on. "I've heard how yur willing to help certain . . . certain ethnic students but not reg'lar students like our Matt."

I knew what she was saying now and what she was up to. I was being accused of reverse discrimination. She was referring to Matt and three or four other Rebel flag T-shirt-wearing, cowboy belt buckle, race car fans whose idea of help was to waive reading and writing assignments and just talk about NASCAR, hunting, and fishing. Now, I like these things myself, but I didn't teach NASCAR, hunting, and fishing; I taught English. The "ethnic" students she accused me of favoring had asked me for instructional help, not waivers. I didn't do waivers.

I stood my ground and invited her to go on to the school board. I told her and the administrator if the school board saw fit to fire me for doing my job then I could go back to technical writing and quality assurance or teach in a Christian school where standards were not so relative. The administrator wasn't at all for that. He suggested she wait and let him talk to the head of the English Department then he'd get back with her. She agreed. I didn't.

The following morning, I was called to another meeting, this time with the same administrator and the English Department chair. She seemed apologetic when I came in the room. I didn't like the feel of it. On his desk was a copy of the county policy on research papers. I didn't like the looks of it.

"Mr. Murray," she said, taking a deep breath, looking at me then the administrator then back at me, "I realize you didn't know it, but the county policy on research paper requirements has never been approved by the school board. So it's not really an official policy."

"What?!" I asked, my voice inflected. "You mean I was told to follow a policy that wasn't a policy at all?"

"I'm afraid so," she told me, sighing. "And because of that, I can't stand behind you if Matt's parents go to the school board."

The administrator seconded that motion. Now here I was, a brand-new teacher, being left on my own to face the school board for having done what I was told to do. What a deal! And they wonder why there's a teacher shortage. But she and the administrator did try to apologize. As it turned out, he used to be an English teacher himself. Between them there was probably 40 years teaching experience. But neither of them had ever known of a single parental complaint about the policy before now. It was just "so unfortunate" the first time someone complained, a new teacher was the one forced to make a humiliating compromise or face the wrath of the school board.

"I had 17 students who got zeroes for not writing their papers to the standards of the county policy," I told them.

That was okay. I only needed to change Matt's grade, to give him credit for what little work he'd done, and thereby satisfy his mother

— I mean, parents. But I couldn't do that. If one student would not be required to adhere to the policy, whether it was an official policy or not, it seemed to me no student should have to adhere to it. No student should be assessed by a different standard than his peers — that's just plain wrong. That evening as I re-graded 17 research papers, I understood why students like Matt put forth so little effort in the classroom. It was okay for him and millions like him to be stupid. They have legal permission to be stupid — permission from their parents, permission from administrators, the school board, and other politicians, and permission from teachers' unions.

I realize there may be a lot of folks who take great offense at the notion that school children would be called stupid by a teacher, someone entrusted with filling their young minds with knowledge and preparing them for college and the workplace. However, for those who are willing to read just a few more lines, please indulge me a moment with an explanation of what I mean by "stupid."

Mere ignorance and stupidity are not the same. Ignorance is simply a lack of knowledge. We're all ignorant about something, some of us more than others. And unless we seize an opportunity to learn about those things, we will remain ignorant about them. Stupidity, on the other hand, is a matter of the will. When someone refuses to learn, that person is exercising his free will. He is willingly putting his mind in "mental darkness," a thing Frederick Douglass vehemently denounced as the worst thing about slavery.[1] And because such a person is willingly ignorant (or as creation evangelist Dr. Kent Hovind would say, "dumb on purpose"), it's only right to say he is stupid. Likewise, a society that accepts willful ignorance, mediocrity, and failure in its public schools is also stupid.

Since the National Commission on Excellence in Education submitted its 1983 report, *A Nation at Risk: The Imperative for Education Reform*, those most responsible for the "tide of mediocrity" uncovered in the report[2] have gained an even stronger hold on public schools by continuously renaming their same failed teaching strategies as "reform." But America's education problems require more than reform that reduces low tests scores or teacher shortages. These are just symptoms of the real problem that money alone won't fix. We've lost our will to learn. Oh, we talk about learning all the time, but talk is cheap. Real knowledge is just about as hard to find in public school classrooms as wisdom is among education leaders. Reading and writing skills have been sacrificed in favor of so-called technological skills, producing a generation that's technically proficient, but one that cannot think. And someone wants it this way.

Let me show you what I mean.

DUMBING THEM DOWN WITH . . .

Whole Language Reading/Learning

Students who are taught using phonics are required to learn 44 basic sounds of the English language — each letter of the alphabet, long and short vowels, and groups of letters (i.e., ch, ph, th, str, etc.). Phonics can help students develop a reading vocabulary of 24,000 words by the end of the fourth grade. By contrast, students who are taught using the whole language method learn to memorize words on flash cards and other media. By the end of the fourth grade, these students may have memorized as few as 1,500 words — words selected by those who would limit and control their vocabulary. So why do we use whole language?

Modern deconstructionists say that some kids — those whose low-income parents that have little education and therefore don't speak proper grammar or enunciate words correctly — have difficulty enunciating some words phonetically. The elitists know about this missing language skill but argue for a curriculum and teaching strategies that take advantage of and perpetuate this weakness. Rather than teach these kids and all others how to properly enunciate vowel sounds, read, write, and speak proper English, about 75 percent of our schools still use the whole language method.

To add insult to injury, whole language curriculum costs nearly eight times as much as phonics. For this reason alone, I can see why there is opposition to going back to phonics. Some greedy devils are getting rich off the destruction of our country, one mind at a time.

Holistic Grading

People typically don't like it when someone lies to them. Yet allowing a child to believe he has written a wonderful report or essay when his paper is slam full of grammar, word usage, spelling, punctuation, and sentence structure errors is the same as telling that child an absolute lie. It gives the child a false sense of self-esteem, and it sets him up for failure down the road.

When kids started doing poorly on writing tests, elitists devised a new way to grade these exams, a way that ignores the rules of grammar in favor of the total impression of quality — whatever that's supposed to mean. Writing skills haven't improved, but students now feel better about their writing.

But the fact is, the rules of grammar really do matter. Intergenerational communication is continuing to break down at an alarming rate — maybe we can't even communicate now, particularly with some elitists.

By the way, holistic grading is another clever ploy by the same deconstructionists who gave us whole language reading.

Learning Disability Labels

From 1989 to 1996 there was a 50 percent increase in the number of students labeled as having a learning disability — that's over the course of less than a decade. One should question what might have been the cause of this increase, especially since most of the children who received these labels were minority children.

Students get labeled by being tested, and based on the results of these tests, any special education teacher can make a life-changing decision that the student's low score is the result of a learning disability. He is then labeled as such and protected from teachers who might try to teach him to learn something. Motivation problems are always ruled out. It is assumed that every child wants to learn.

This fallacy and the probability the kid scored low because of missing core knowledge — knowledge that is missing because of multicultural teaching strategies, constant excuses, and the simple fact the child has never been required to learn — leads the evaluators to determine the child is disabled and needs a label that legally allows him to be stupid.

Again, I realize that's a cold way to say it, but I think this ridiculous concern for self-esteem has created a school system that pumps kids up with a false sense of self-worth when, in fact, their academic achievements don't support their phony pride. Besides, why is pride considered a good thing in the first place? After all, "Pride goes before destruction, and a haughty spirit before a fall" (Prov. 16:18). Unless we turn around public education very soon, the next proud but academically stupid generation will lead us to our fall.

Learning Style Labels

I prefer eastern North Carolina pork BBQ or my wife's Southern fried chicken to a piece of broiled fish. I prefer collard greens boiled with ham hocks and just a touch of hot sauce to steamed broccoli. I prefer my mama's homemade pecan "wedding" cookies or a thick slice of my aunt Pearl's homemade pound cake to a bowl of Jell-O, even if it includes a whipped topping. I prefer all of the above, but I've learned the hard way that my preferences can kill me. That's why I had a stroke at 48.

Many students today prefer to be read to rather than read for themselves. Many students today prefer to work in a group and dump the responsibility for completing projects on someone else, like an Accelerated Gifted (AG) student, who's been forced into the group via "mixed ability grouping." Many students today prefer to draw pictures or cut out paper dolls relating to some theme in a major piece of literature or historical event rather than sit down and analyze that literature for its literary devices, allusions, symbolism, and overall artistic merits. Most students today would prefer to do anything but be actively engaged in real learning, but one day their lack of core knowledge will kill their chances of getting into a good college or getting that good-paying job. We can help kids now by feeding them the facts and knowledge they really need, or we can let them do what they prefer and program them for failure.

FROM THE FILM: "Now, when you walk through a high school or elementary school, you will see pictures all over the place. Forty years ago, you would see essays, reports all over bulletin boards with a big A+. Not anymore."

Learning style labels are some of the latest reform measures ransacking our classrooms. The theory is that each of us has a unique way in which we prefer to learn, some visually (reading), some audibly (hearing), and some kinesthetically (touching). Teachers must prepare lesson plans with these diversities in mind and thereby show movies, play games, or just have their students surf the Internet. Even though little or no real learning of anything takes place in the classroom, everyone's diverse preference about learning is considered, which is held as far more important than actual learning.

As with whole language, somebody is making lots of money off of this strategy that essentially leaves children — particularly those of low-income families — in mental darkness. Teachers must either be allowed to teach students what they need to succeed in college or the workplace, or we must accept the fact that the next generation will feel really good about themselves, but they'll be too stupid to run this country anywhere but into the ground.

Group Learning

Mixed ability grouping seeks to pair up one AG (motivated) student with three or four "diverse learners" (unmotivated students). The class is given their assignment and the AG student in each group does all the work, but everybody in the group gets the same grade. Basically, group learning removes the stigma of getting caught cheating by making it legal to cheat.

Despite all the rhetoric published by socialistic constructivists and psychologists, learning is not a collective process. It is a personal process that must take place within the individual's mind. It is a process that can be aided by others, most particularly teachers — as opposed to facilitators.

Group, or cooperative, learning has to be one of the most Orwellian terms in modern education. The group cannot learn for the individual, and the only real cooperation taking place is the teacher cooperating with the deconstructionists' agenda, all the while compromising their integrity by failing to actually teach their students.

Thematic Visualization

The concept of thematic visualization can be traced back to those same brilliant folks who gave us learning style labels and is linked to the concept to follow — block scheduling. Deconstructionists like supporting each other's progressive crimes as they tend to have the same objective — a socialist America.

The concept is simple: most kids don't like to read, but they love to play; so let them play and claim they're actually learning. Reading can be hard work, particularly when you've avoided it all the way to high school. So, rather than require that poor, struggling kines-thetic learner to read for himself, the teacher reads to the whole class. When the reading is finished, students are woken up and asked to set aside the letter to their boyfriend or the conversations they were having during the reading, so they can be told about the wonderful game they're about to play. It better be wonderful though. Don't try to trick them into learning anything!

After about 20 or 30 minutes of playtime, students are "engaged" in a special artistic project. They are asked to draw or cut out paper dolls or in some other way visually express how they feel about some theme or a character in the piece of literature or historical doc-ument that was read. For example, instead of requiring my students to read Arthur Miller's *The Crucible* then making them take notes as I analyzed the play with them, I could try thematic visualization. My classroom would have been filled with paper dolls of witches and color pictures of stick figures wearing Puritan era costumes (though my students would have known nothing about this great play).

Kids love to draw. You can see their artwork everywhere — bath-room walls, billboards, the sides of buildings. You'll rarely get a lot of fuss about having to draw. But if you were to ask them to read the assignment themselves and take notes as you analyze the literature with them, you'll get a lot of flak, some of it from the students, but most of it from administrators, parents, and school board officials. They really don't care that students aren't going to be assessed on standardized tests for their reading comprehension or writing skills by drawing pictures or cutting out paper dolls. Teachers who force their students to read and learn how to analyze literature are going to get below standard reviews from their administrators, even though they may have higher standardized test scores. Test scores, they say, only represent one aspect of what a child is learning. What's really important is how the child feels about learning, even if the child isn't learning anything at all.

Block Scheduling

Block Scheduling is where a course normally taught over two semesters in 50-minute classes, five days a week, is now taught in only one semester in 90-minute classes, five days a week. Right off the top, you have to realize you're losing about 10 percent of your instruction time because 36 weeks times 50 minutes comes to 150 classroom hours, but 18 times 90 minutes comes to only 135 hours in the classroom. Some might say, so what? To that, I ask, have you ever dealt with public-schooled teenagers? Do you know anything about their attention spans?

You can teach most of them two 20-minute lessons in one 50 minute class period. On a normal schedule, this allows you five minutes at the beginning and at the end of class for administrative matters (i.e., taking roll, collecting homework, etc.). Supposedly, Block Scheduling allows you to have four 20-minute lessons in one 90 minute class period. But that assumes these teenagers can pay attention through 80 minutes of straight instruction. Sure, you can still get the two lessons in, but after that, you've lost them. So with Block Scheduling, you have 40 minutes instruction time that's essentially wasted every class period. You may get a few AG types to stay awake or on task, but most of them are long gone after the first 40 minutes, some way before that. So, instead of 135 classroom hours per semester, you're really getting about 75 classroom hours with Block Scheduling — that's half of what they could have maybe learned.

Teachers then have to decide what core knowledge to leave out of their lesson plans. Students think they get by with shorter, easier requirements, but in reality, they're being cheated out of 50 percent of what they should be getting from that course. It's like paying $100 for a pair of shoes but only getting one shoe.

Why would anybody in his right mind want to sacrifice this much instruction time? The answer is money. Block scheduling is cheaper because you can get more students through a particular course with fewer teachers, and real teachers are not that easy to come by these days. Here you have a very good reason for adopting a new strategy. You have the always important dollar to save, and you have an opportunity to get more kids through a class who might ordinarily fail that course because so much knowledge would have to be learned, but now the course has been shortened — dumbed down even more than it was already.

Legally Stupid

Because stupid people are easily led (or misled), it's important for those who would rule over us to deconstruct the language and math skills of as many people as possible. And because they're doing it with permission of parents, school boards, and all levels of the government, they're doing it legally.

Education involves academic as well as moral and spiritual training. Until the mid-19th century, most Americans received their academic, moral, and spiritual training at home and/or through the local church-run, one-room schoolhouse, not government schools. And back then this nation was over 90 percent literate — and very eloquently literate, compared to today's standards. Since 40 percent of today's public school graduates can only be described as functionally illiterate, I think we need to return to what used to work quite efficiently. And we need to do so right now. Every parent needs to be reminded of their job as a teacher, and every local church needs to be willing to accept its responsibility as a school, as well as house of worship. We can go back to what worked for the first 200 years of American history, or we're going to become just another faded chapter in world history.

Socialist and atheist John Dewey called it cooperative intelligence. Other like-minded deconstructionists, including Piaget, Vygotsky, and Erikson, called it discovery or student-centered learning. Extremists like John Holt called it unschooling. The very idea that students should be allowed to learn what they want to learn, when they want to learn, and how they want to learn, if they want to learn at all, is what opponents like Samuel L. Blumenfeld call a fraud; E.D. Hirsch calls it a knowledge deficit. John Taylor Gatto, Charles Sykes, Charlotte Iserbyt, and Maureen Stout call it dumbing down. I call it just plain stupid. If you agree to even a small degree, make a decision to do something about it right now — not regarding the 50 million other children attending government schools, but regarding your own children.

Endnotes

Taken from *Legally STUPiD: Why Johnny Doesn't Have to Read* by R.C. Murray (Spring Lake, NC: Peach-Pine Publishing, 2007), used by permission from Peach-Pine Publishing, P.O. Box 271, Spring Lake, NC 28390,www.voicefromthepews.com.

1. Frederick Douglass, *Narrative of the Life of Frederick Douglass, An American Slave* (Boston, MA: 1845; Reprinted ed. Harvard, 2009), p. 85.
2. U.S. Department of Education, "ED Publications," http://www2.ed.gov/pubs/NatAtRisk/risk.html (accessed January 13, 2012).

"Foolishness is bound up in the heart of a child. . . ."

— *Proverbs 22:15*

CHAPTER FOUR

Discipline Discipleship

Sarah LaVerdiere

"The public school system culture as a whole is overwhelmingly anti-Christian."

SARAH LAVERDIERE

Sarah LaVerdiere is a former public elementary school teacher who became a homeschooling advocate after her very first day of working in the classroom. Her short career began as a fulfillment of her four-year scholarship obligation with the state of North Carolina. But in October of 2010, she was ultimately forced to resign by her school district due to their "concern that [her] Christian views would influence the students and their parents." Mrs. LaVerdiere is now a stay-at-home mom and is currently writing a book about her experiences in public education and graduate school to warn Christian mothers about the harmful effects that public schools have on their children. She and her husband, Chuck, plan to homeschool their own children, starting with their firstborn who arrived in August of 2011. The following excerpts are taken from Mrs. LaVerdiere's upcoming book, *The Christ-Absent Classroom.*

Discipline Discipleship

To best understand a person's view of the world, it is insufficient to only hear what they profess to believe with their mouth — much more importantly, one must observe how that person acts. In a similar manner, examining the curriculum of your child's school is only a small part of the picture when it comes to grasping how dedicated to certain values and beliefs the school is, values and beliefs that are taught to your child not only by direct instruction but also by example.

The word *discipline* means "training that corrects, molds, or perfects the mental faculties or moral character."[1] In this way, whoever disciplines — or disciples — your child defines the very morals they believe your child should have. Therefore, it is important to take a close look at how public schools discipline, because it reveals how they view the nature of the child and because it is partly by these methods that public schools have been so successful at discipling students away from the values and beliefs of their parents.

Over the past several decades, school discipline systems have gone through major changes, reacting to the public's adoption of new beliefs about how behavior is learned. There are no more rulers striking rebellious knuckles; you will be hard pressed to find a paddle hanging on the wall of any principal's office — in fact, corporal punishment in schools is outlawed in the majority of American states — although at one time, these things were widely accepted as the norm for dealing with misbehaving students.

My point is not to argue that if only kids were getting their knuckles bruised in school again, everything would be fixed. Instead, it is to note that today's absence of "traditional" disciplinary methods is in no way an indication that there is now a total absence of discipline in the schools. In actuality, a new discipline system has been implemented that is based on Darwinist behaviorism — and is diametrically opposed to the truths found in God's Word.

A Brief History of Behaviorism

Like many modern-day philosophies, the foundational concept behind behaviorism has its root with the ancient Greeks who worshiped human reasoning. Aristotle (ca. 350 B.C.) was the first on record to describe the mind (which he defined as the part of the soul that knows and thinks) as "a writing tablet on which as yet nothing actually stands written."[2] To Aristotle, the human soul was like a chalkboard that was written upon only by what one actually thought. And until a person had any thoughts, his soul remained blank; it was a *tabula rasa*, or blank slate, as it would be named by various medieval thinkers who would later build upon Aristotle's idea.

But the modern "blank slate" view of the human soul comes more distinctly from Enlightenment philosopher John Locke, who wrote in his *An Essay on Human Understanding* (1690):

All ideas come from sensation or reflection. . . . Let us then suppose the mind to be, as we say, white paper, void of all characters, without any ideas; how comes it to be furnished? . . . To this I answer, in one word, from experience; in all that our knowledge is founded, and from that it ultimately derives itself.[3]

In this influential essay, Locke argued that the only way to gain knowledge was by sensory perception. His view — now known as Lockean empiricism — held that humans were not born with any natural inclinations whatsoever. There was no inborn sense of morality, or conscience; there was no natural inner knowledge of the existence of God; no sin nature; nothing — just blankness.

Related to Locke's assertions was the research of Ivan Pavlov (1927), whose experiments on dogs paired the ringing of a bell with the feeding of food, which confirmed that dogs could be trained to salivate when a bell was rung, even if no food was present. It was thought that this "conditioning" effect could be exploited and used to psychologically manipulate human behavior.

Later, B.F. Skinner's theory of radical behaviorism (1974) proposed that humans were deterministically controlled by their various responses to external stimuli.[4] Meaning, there was no such thing as free will; a person could only do what his brain told him to do in reaction to specific things that happened to him. Essentially, radical behaviorism asserts that human beings are soulless, input/output computers with given reactions for various conditions. We are all just robotically climbing up the evolutionary ladder into the future.

FROM THE FILM: "What the public school system has done is taken Christ out of the morals, so they have taken the foundation that the morals are based on away. I can't tell the students about God. I can't give Him glory for anything."

These theories may come across as abstract, but today they are quite popular and guide much of how our society views the process of learning behaviors. However, these ideas cannot stand up to basic philosophical criticism, and they are heavily flawed when considered in light of biblical truth.

UnLocke-ing Behaviorist Theory

A reasoned argument against behaviorism, particularly Lockean empiricism, is that it is based on the assumption that human beings can trust their senses to give them accurate information about the world around them. According to Locke's theory, truth may only be established by making observations of the natural world using human perceptions. Locke must have sensed this concept to be true because, according to him, sensing is the only way to know anything. One of the problems with this theory is that we cannot always trust our senses. Perhaps you can recall a time when you saw someone from across a room, yet as you approached them to say 'hello,' you realized that it was not the same person you thought it was. Your sense of sight was not reliable in this case. And because we can't always trust our senses, Lockean empiricism is fallacious.[5]

Without acknowledging the all-knowing God of the Bible – the standard of truth – one cannot account for knowledge, let alone decide if the soul is blank at the time of conception (Prov. 1:7, 9:10). As Christians, we can account for knowledge because we know from God's revealed Word that human beings are created in His image with the ability to reason (Gen. 1:26; 1 Pet. 3:15). Only because God's creation is orderly and He omnipotently maintains

FROM THE FILM: "If I talk about my faith the way I want to, I know that I'll lose my job. I'd probably be out of here that day."

it day to day, can we make reliable observations about how His creation works (Gen. 8:22; Heb. 1:3).

In this way, Locke, Skinner, or anyone, for that matter, cannot make up philosophically sound theories to account for their views of human learning without first acknowledging the existence of the Christian

God. Now that we have established this, let's go to His revealed Word as the ultimate standard of truth about all things, including whether or not human beings are born with certain behaviors.

In the Book of Romans, Paul declares that men know things in their heart of hearts because God has made specific knowledge manifest there. It is man, in his sinfulness, who deceives himself and outwardly denies the things that he knows to be true about God because he loves his sin more than he loves the truth about his need for repentance (Rom. 1:18–20). Here is indication that knowledge is put in us by God; that we do not learn everything we know from experience as Locke suggested.

Secondly, concerning humanity's sin nature, Paul wrote that by Adam's disobedience all of mankind was made sinners (Rom. 5:12, 19) — but does this include children? Yes. Remember, David lamented that he was born in iniquity, and it was in sin that his mother conceived him (Ps. 51:5). There is no escaping the sinful nature that we all inherit. These passages clearly indicate that from the moment a human life begins, the soul is tarnished, not "blank."[6]

Finally, Jesus stated that it is not external things that defile a man, but it is from out of man's heart that evil thoughts, murders, adulteries, fornications, thefts, false witness, and blasphemies proceed (Matt. 15:19). All the wickedness of every horrific sin you can imagine is bound up in the heart of man, and it is only by God's grace that our evil is constrained to the extent that it is on a daily basis.

Having worked closely with babies and young children since I was 12 years old, I have personally witnessed the foolishness of the behaviorist position — it doesn't take a psychoanalyst to explain the "Terrible Twos." This stage is a prime example of the rebellious, sinful nature of the child upon whom we put cute labels to disguise the wretchedness of their misbehavior.

As the mother of an eight-month-old girl, I can testify that even little babies have sin natures. Where did my daughter learn to impatiently scream herself red in the face when she was just a few months old? Who taught her this behavior? From what experience did she learn this? My husband and I don't even have a TV in our home, so I know it wasn't from that! She learned this from the father of the human race — Adam — whose sin has affected us all by innately branding our hearts with an inward desire to rebel against our Creator.

But when you disregard the truth of God's Word and take the doctrine of original sin off the table, you are left open to all sorts of silly theories about how humans learn behavior and what we know, or rather don't know, when we are born.

So what is the point of examining all this madness? Because your child's school is likely implementing a disciplinary system that is either directly based on or heavily influenced by behaviorist ideas. And the effects of daily subjection to this type of humanistic indoctrination can be extremely damaging to your child.

Positive Behavior Interventions and Supports (PBIS)

The discipline system in more and more public schools today is formally known as Positive Behavior Interventions and Supports (PBIS). Based on Skinner's theory of human behavior, PBIS operates on the assumption that children will behave properly if all the conditions around them are just right. It follows that without these positive conditions children cannot be expected to behave, and the fault of their misbehavior must only be attributed to their negative environment, not to the children themselves. PBIS goes so far as to say that consequences for misbehavior actually *contribute* to behavior problems because negative consequences give attention to and thus support negative behavior.

As the name suggests, teachers at PBIS schools are told that their disciplinary measures should only consist of support for positive behavior. Because of this, there is a heavy reliance on the use of public praise and rewards to incentivize desired behaviors. Common activities such as walking through the school's halls without yelling, sitting quietly in class during a lesson, or not being disruptive in the cafeteria are frequently rewarded with stickers or colorful, laminated pieces of paper with the school's mascot on them. These tokens are collected by each student and cashed in for prizes or used in a school-wide raffle at the end of the quarter.

When students do exhibit misconduct — such as speaking out of turn in class — teachers are instructed to praise and reward other students who are sitting quietly and not draw attention to the student who is misbehaving. Another tactic teachers could use would be to find something the misbehaving student is doing correctly at the time of their misbehavior and praise him for that. For example, if a child is interrupting in class, he might be praised and rewarded for sitting still in his chair while the teacher ignores his interruption.[7]

As with all false doctrines, PBIS's flaws are demonstrated by the inconsistency of its application. The same school systems that matter-of-factly declare that *"negative consequences detract from children's ability to follow the rules"* are also drug-free zones and have zero tolerance policies toward violence. So which is it? Isn't expulsion for violent behavior or selling drugs on campus a negative consequence? To be consistent, PBIS schools would have to overlook this misbehavior and only focus on rewarding those who are not being violent or bringing drugs to school.[8]

THE NEGATIVE EFFECTS OF POSITIVE BEHAVIOR SUPPORTS

I am familiar with the PBIS system because I taught in two schools that embraced this absurd philosophy, and I was required by my school district to use the system in my classrooms. Through my direct experiences, I made various observations about the effects that this system had on my third and fifth grade students.

Entitlement Mentality

PBIS teaches children that they have a right to a reward for exhibiting basic appropriate behaviors. They learn to be self-centeredly focused on what they will receive from every situation. I saw this sense of entitlement most clearly when I once asked a student to complete a simple task, only to have the young boy look up at me with a greedy grin and say, "What are you gonna give me?" He was deciding if he would obey me based on the appeal of a reward.

I also witnessed this conditional obedience when ice cream parties or extra recess were on the line near the end of each quarter. In the schools where I taught, students could use their rewards/tokens to attend special events — such as getting out of class to watch a movie— by cashing in however many tokens were required to attend those events. Near the end of the quarter, students would act in an acceptable manner until they had received just enough tokens to get the reward they desired — then they would stop behaving. Because there are no negative consequences in PBIS, the tokens could not be taken away from them. Under PBIS I saw no true changes of heart, only increases in manipulation.

Biblically, there is a place for rewarding good behavior. The Lord does indeed bless obedience (Deut. 28:1–14), and it is good to model this reality to children. The difference with PBIS, however, is that God desires obedience that is from the heart, not done for public recognition (Matt. 6:1–4, 15:8).

I believe the sense of entitlement that PBIS instills in children will be a considerable problem for our society as they grow into adults that continue to expect rewards for exhibiting standard moral behavior. The influence of socialism in our country has already produced many individuals who demand that the world provide them with a living, as demonstrated in part by the recent Occupy Wall Street movement. If my generation, which grew up getting trophies even when we came in last place, acts in such a way, what will tomorrow's high school graduates do after they have grown up under an even more committed behaviorist system? Remember, the Bible tells us that children will not depart from the way they are raised (Prov. 22:6).

Socially Unfit

Another concern is that these future graduates of PBIS schools will be unprepared to enter society — particularly college or the work force — because they lack the necessary social skills even though the stated purpose of our public education system is to teach children how to successfully function as adults. Parents send their children to public schools believing that their children will graduate prepared to succeed in the world. However, the schools' systems of behavior management do not even prepare children to function in American society, much less succeed. The child who has been given constant behavior supports and praise for basic proper behavior from kindergarten to 12th grade will be ill-equipped to live in the real world where the social environment is not continually adapted to meet his specific needs.

Basically, PBIS-trained children become adults who are unprepared to handle life outside of public schools and are especially unprepared to be hardworking citizens, who, in order to make a living, need to do things on a daily basis that are beyond the basic expectations of society's standards of behavior — they will have to *work*, not simply exist without getting into trouble, to get their reward (paycheck, college diploma, etc.).

FROM THE FILM: "Teachers who are homosexuals, radical environmentalists, and atheists are given free rein to pervert the mind of your child, and are given special protection by the same public school system that is all too eager to attack Christian educators."

Consider how different the typical work environment will be for these children when they have to function in a setting where they are not continually rewarded for showing up on time or completing basic tasks. When's the last time a boss commended his employee by saying, "Thank you so much for submitting your report fully completed," especially if the report was turned in a week late?

And what about encounters with law enforcement officers? When a police officer sees someone speeding, does he ever pull over a law-abiding driver to say, "Thank you for driving the speed limit and using your turn signal so well!" in the hopes that the law-breaking driver will see that good drivers receive special attention? Of course not; he pulls over the speeder and gives him a ticket with a fine and a court date — a direct consequence for breaking the rules.

PBIS: The Anti-Gospel

God gives us clearly stated commands throughout His Word, and there are punishments for breaking those commands. "The wages of sin is death" (Rom. 6:23), and to help man better understand this reality, God established the family, civil, and church governments each with the authority to punish evil within its respective jurisdiction. By undermining the relationship between law and consequence, PBIS removes the picture of "sin leading to death" that God has given us as a means of turning man toward Him in repentance. In this way, PBIS's approach to consequences is a denial of the very foundation of the gospel of Jesus Christ.

My greatest concern about PBIS is that children who receive no consequences for their misbehavior and are continuously praised for their good behavior are given a great stumbling block when it comes to recognizing their own sinfulness and their dire need for a Savior. Instead, PBIS children are trained to view themselves as naturally good people.

It is always miraculous when the Lord, by grace, calls a man's soul, dead in his sins and trespasses, into His fold by causing him to hear the Word of life (Ezek. 37:1–14). But if admitting you have a sin problem is the first step to having it fixed, the false sense of inner goodness that PBIS establishes in children may prove to be their greatest obstacle in coming to repentance and forming a relationship with Jesus Christ — the only One who can save them from their sins.

By far, the most devastating effects of PBIS are on your child's soul.

Conclusion

It is imperative for children to understand that we live in a fallen world where every child of Adam is a natural-born sinner. One of the most important responsibilities Christian parents have is to explain this reality to their children, pointing them daily to the depravity of their hearts by consistently disciplining them according to biblical standards and telling them that their only hope for eternal life rests upon the mercy of a holy God who requires repentance and trust in the atoning, substitutionary sacrifice of His Son Jesus Christ.

As a parent, you know your child's heart better than anyone. No school teacher or administrator can determine the motives for obedience inside this heart more accurately than you. When the Lord blessed you with a child, He also gave you the precious responsibility to disciple your little one in a way that is guided by His Word. As our Lord Jesus, the great teacher, taught His disciples, you are called to teach your children (Deut. 6:7). It is your role as a Christian parent to give your children *training that corrects, molds, and perfects their mental faculties and moral character* in a way that glorifies the King of kings.

Endnotes
Taken from *The Christ-Absent Classroom: 10 Things Every Christian Mother Should Know about Her Child's Public School Education* by Sarah LaVerdiere (not yet published), used by permission from the author.

1. "Discipline," *Merriam-Webster.com*, December 27, 2011, http://www.merriam-webster.com/dictionary/discipline.
2. Aristotle, *On the Soul (De Anima)*, DA III.4, 430a1-2.
3. John Locke, *An Essay Concerning Human Understanding*, bk. II, chap. 1 (1690; reprint edition, London: Tegg, 1841), p. 51.
4. B.F. Skinner, *About Behaviorism* (1974; reprint edition, London: Penguin, 1993), p. 59.
5. For more information regarding the presuppositional approach to defending the Christian faith, see the book *Always Ready* by Dr. Greg Bahnsen (Nacogdoches, TX: Convenant Media Press, 1996).
6. Also, "There is none righteous, no, not one" (Rom. 3:10).
7. For more information on Positive Behavior Interventions and Supports see www.pbis.org and *Creating the Culture of Positive Behavior Supports* video: http://www.pbis.org/swpbs_videos/pbs_video-creating_the_culture.aspx.
8. Further inconsistency can be seen by the way school districts handle misbehaving teachers. For instance, teachers who express Christian beliefs will be terminated instead of receiving praise for something else they are doing right.

"So everyone who acknowledges me before men, I also will acknowledge before my Father who is in heaven, but whoever denies me before men, I also will deny before my Father who is in heaven"

— *Matthew 10:32–33*

CHAPTER FIVE

On Trial for Christ:
A Teacher's Testimony
Robert Ziegler

"I was going to teach in my classroom in a way that if God was my supervisor He would be pleased with me."

ROBERT ZIEGLER

Robert Ziegler is a Summa Cum Laude graduate of Bethel College with a BS in math education. Immediately out of college, he took a position in a public school where he was fired for proclaiming God's Word in his classroom. He continued in education by working for two private Christian schools — the last as K–12 principal — before resigning in 2009. Mr. Ziegler has not lost his zeal for God's Word or for working with parents and their children. He is currently laboring to meet the biblical qualifications for becoming a pastor with hopes of one day shepherding a flock toward godliness in all areas of life, including education. The following article was written by Mr. Ziegler for the *IndoctriNation* book.

A Decision to Become a Teacher

It was the spring of 2000, nearing the completion of my sophomore year of college. I spent the remaining nights of that school year lying awake, meditating on what I was going to do with my life. I loved to learn, and nearly all subjects proved interesting to me.

I had enrolled in college to become an engineer, but by my second year I was a pre-med major — and I still wasn't settled. Romans 12:1 was at the forefront of my mind, and presenting my body as a living sacrifice seemed to be all that I desired. I was zealous for the Lord Jesus Christ, and I wanted to be used by God, a vessel of honor who would serve as a great influence for the glory of His name.

In those days, my perspective on what a man could do with his life was somewhat limited. I had spent 15 of my first 20 years on this earth in school and the rest on our family farm or playing sports. I recognized the impact that school had on the young people around me, and the thought of becoming a teacher began to resonate in my mind. Where else could I spend so much time with people at an influential age where it would actually be my job to do so? Where else could I influence so many people on a daily basis? With my limited perspective, I found no other answer to those questions, and decided that one day I would teach in the classroom.

And so it was a major in mathematics that finally won me over, and I devoted the rest of my college education to earning a degree that would qualify me to teach at the high school level. To me, math was a testimony that if a man began with sound presuppositions, thought logically about each step, and rightly applied principles and laws, then he could solve a problem and arrive at the correct, objective answer. The order, logic, and beauty of such complexity in solving tough problems not only proved to be challenging, but it was something I began to love.

As my final years of college passed, I became thoroughly convinced that a career in teaching was a suitable fit for me. Because of my previous successful experiences in teaching younger students, youth groups, and coaching basketball camps, I was confident in my ability to teach. I saw my own achievements in high school as providing a foundational understanding of what it would take for other students to do well, and I reasoned that such wisdom would prove beneficial to my future students.

Finally, I believed that the transition from being a Christian student to a Christian teacher would be a minimal change. I had known many teachers who professed belief in Christ. I was convinced that if they were able to be faithful in their walks then it would be possible for me to do so as well.

Transition into Teaching

As my college career neared its end in the spring of 2003, I began to look for available positions at public schools in Nebraska. While attending a job fair at a central Nebraska university, I scheduled three interviews in three days. I finished those interviews with three job offers, which led to a long weekend of deliberation.

The school I chose was in a south suburb of Omaha. It was the least appealing job going into the interviews, but it became clear to me that small-town Nebraska values were still recognized in this large suburban town. My meetings with the school's administrators demonstrated this feeling, and it was they who eventually won me over.

These five gentlemen, many of whom were well established in the system, had worked together for years, and a few of them were from small towns just like mine. In fact, the head principal reminded me of my own grandfather, both honorable men worthy of respect. I was taken in and looked after as a new part of their staff, and my respect grew for these men as I witnessed their kindness, hard work, pleasantness, common sense, and high standard of professionalism. Being with them brought back memories of the family farm where my grandfather and father had cultivated the same kind of working environment.

FROM THE FILM: "Can we profess Christianity and at the door of the public school leave His name behind in everything we do?"

Summer came and went, and I eagerly began my new job. But my dreams of having great influence quickly waned as the reality of my new duties settled in. Only the fraternity of teachers can truly identify with the challenges of that first year as they are so uniquely sketched in memories. In my best words, I was wet behind the ears in an unfamiliar city, and totally unfamiliar with the encompassing weight of everything involved with teaching Algebra I and II to high school sophomores, juniors, and seniors.

Therefore, much of my energy was devoted to daily lesson planning as I was teaching subject matter from unfamiliar books. I devoted what energy I had left to the tedious duty of grading the work of 120 students. And to further complicate the situation, many of my students were identified as having either learning or behavioral disorders. In spite of all this, I made every effort to develop meaningful relationships and to see each student succeed. However, that year could best be described as simply keeping my head above water and just watching how the whole system worked.

As that year ended, I looked back, feeling like I had never even stopped to sleep, and it consequently felt like the entire school year had taken place during one long day.

The summer would give me time to breathe. With one season under my belt and having familiarized myself with my duties and all the associated challenges I would face the following year, I determined to use the summer to improve my teaching abilities.

THE SUMMER OF 2004

While growing up, I was trained by my grandparents, parents, coaches, and pastors to understand that a good man was to have the attitude summarized by Colossians 3:17: that whatever he did was for the glory of God. I was also taught that a good man should strive to be the best in all that he put his hand to and that the best work did not come about without preparation.

That training drove how I spent my summer. My zeal for the Lord was still as strong as it had been when I made my decision to teach, and after being on my own with the opportunity to establish a household and a reputation, I knew that it was time to become the best in my profession.

During the days, I worked for a carpenter framing new construction projects, but my free time was devoted to prayer and Bible study as I purposed to specifically study passages related to teaching and education. Oddly enough, even though I had received a degree from a private Christian college, I do not recall my professors referring to God's Word as a text for training my classmates and me as future teachers. Here are a few passages that I meditated on that summer.

- Whoever therefore breaks one of the least of these commandments, and teaches men so, shall be called least in the kingdom of heaven; but whoever does and teaches them, he shall be called great in the kingdom of heaven (Matt. 5:19).

- It would be better for him if a millstone were hung around his neck, and he were thrown into the sea, than that he should offend [entice to sin] one of these little ones (Luke 17:2).

- We will not hide them [teachings] from their children, telling to the generation to come the praises of the LORD, and His strength and His wonderful works that He has done (Ps. 78:4).

- All Scripture is given by inspiration of God, and is profitable for doctrine, for reproof, for correction, for instruction in righteousness, that the man of God may be complete, thoroughly equipped for every good work (2 Tim. 3:16–17).

- My brethren, let not many of you become teachers, knowing that we shall receive a stricter judgment (James 3:1).

- But shun profane and idle babblings, for they will increase to more ungodliness. And their message will spread like cancer (2 Tim. 2:16–17).

- Casting down arguments and every high thing that exalts itself against the knowledge of God, bringing every thought into captivity to the obedience of Christ (2 Cor. 10:5).

By the end of the summer, the Lord had strengthened me in faith, knowledge, wisdom, and love for my brethren.

Four principles related specifically to teaching guided me as to how God would be glorified by my work:

First, as James instructed, greater condemnation is reserved for false teachers than for others. Although the passage is unclear as to exactly what that greater condemnation is, the degree of its severity can be understood from Luke 17:2, where it would be better to have a millstone hung around one's neck and be thrown into the sea than to lead a little one to sin. These verses influenced me in two ways. One, they led me to a better understanding of the immense responsibility that comes with being a teacher, and to seek the Lord more diligently for His ways as to how not to fall into that condemnation. Second, it forced me to think about why greater condemnation is reserved for teachers. As I read further in James 3, I found the chapter was not so much about the greater condemnation of teachers as it was about the tongue and the words that proceed from the mouth. The tongue, being such a great member of the body, as it functions to bless or curse, is associated with teaching because it is the primary duty of teachers to proclaim words that communicate truth.

The second principle God brought to my attention that summer was the clear differences between the teacher and the student. The classroom was my sphere, small though it was, to steward for the glory of God. Like Adam in the garden with Eve, he was ultimately responsible for what took place there, and I would be held responsible for what would take place in my classroom. As a student, I was not responsible for what was taught, the standard of behavior, how the classroom was managed, or what discipline was needed to train in the fear of the Lord. Although responsibilities come with being a Christian student, I began to realize it was in no way comparable to those of a teacher.

Third, Christianity cannot be lived simply by acting like a Christian while never verbalizing one's beliefs, which is often referred to as "lifestyle evangelism." On the contrary, Christianity is not simply a verbal profession without any good works — fruits of true faith (James 2:18). The Christian walk involves both speaking truth and doing good works.

Finally, a good teacher teaches the law of God as directed by Jesus in Matthew 5:19. I was not to hide those teachings from the next generation (Ps. 78). I was to shun worthless talk and teachings and replace them with truth.

With a deeper understanding of God's will in my profession, I was focused and excited for what the new school year would bring.

The 2004 School Year

Prepared with what to expect, I had an arsenal of lesson plans and a yearly schedule already worked out, and I set out to accomplish the tasks that come with a new school year. I became familiar with approximately 125 new students, learning their names faster than the previous year. I studied their habits and observed their strengths and weaknesses to determine how I could best help each one of them. I tried to learn about their home lives and what problems they were dealing with. I made fewer mistakes, resulting in my classes running much more smoothly.

What a change from the year before! Then, my mind was focused on simply getting the lessons taught, but now I was able to see more of what was really going on in my classroom — and God began to manifest new things to me.

From day one, I had tried to implement high standards of behavior in my classroom. I expected honesty, respect, wholesome words, hard work, order, love for one's neighbor, no complaining, and general pleasantness — basically, an atmosphere that was based on external obedience to the law of God.

But the Lord began to show me how a large number of my students actually perceived my standards. Although they were learning right behaviors, they saw the origins of those behaviors wrongly — many of them believing that the standards were coming from me. Because of this, I was concerned that they essentially believed man to be the highest authority in life, deciding what is right and what is wrong for himself. Many of them only obeyed the rules out of fear of punishment, living in fear of man. Frankly, this disturbed me.

My desire to set godly rules without speaking about the Source of those rules resulted in great misunderstandings of what I believed, what they perceived I was teaching, and, most importantly, the everlasting truths those rules were meant to represent. Essentially, the way I was teaching them was leading them to error, and I recognized that it was my responsibility to correct that error.

Around that same time, I noticed that certain students were struggling to behave properly, especially those identified as having behavioral problems. I saw some success, but it was often mixed with great failure and, therefore, great disappointment. By God's grace, I realized that I had been overlooking some foundational principles. External obedience to God's law does not get a man closer to God. In fact, a man is still in bondage to sin despite all the good he might try to do as the Bible teaches that true freedom is only found after repentance to God and faith in the Lord Jesus Christ.

I realized that while growing up, being book smart was not necessarily what made me successful at school or successful at anything.

Much should be attributed to the godly character the Lord had given me that allowed me to stay focused in class, desire to work hard, do all things in an exemplary way, have peace when trials were in my life through problems at home or with friends, love the subjects being taught because they spoke of my Creator, and have joy knowing my sins were forgiven. Such is true freedom.

I knew that if I was to be the best steward of my classroom I would have to teach my students the one thing that could help them desire to obey and do the works of a good student. Only then would they have the strength to obey the rules from their hearts and have peace in the midst of their messed-up worlds.

I needed to give my students the gospel of Jesus Christ and opportunities for them to hear and believe. If I was to be a Christian teacher, I would need to teach my students that Christ is the cornerstone of learning.

I began to think of the doors that might be opened if I would only begin to teach the way I knew I should. At the time, I did not know the extent that public schools had taken to eradicate all forms of Christian speech, but I was familiar with the popular interpretation of the phrase "separation of church and state." While I didn't know exactly what would happen if I began to speak freely about my faith, I knew that it would not go unnoticed.

FROM THE FILM: "[I was charged with] insubordination, unprofessionalism, and neglecting my duties as a teacher. And so many things were said about why they were terminating me, but I believe it simply came down to Jesus."

I could not identify with this dilemma because I had no previous experience with such a situation. As a student, I was never punished for my view that truth aligns itself with the Word of God. I was at times looked at funny and perhaps mocked or jeered, but I had never had so much on the line.

Now, as the Lord's ambassador, I was His servant carrying His banner. The way I would speak in my classroom would either be a blasphemous, empty profession or glory for His name.

But my mind was entangled as I considered that many teachers before me had made long-lasting careers in public schools as professing Christians. So for a time I held my tongue in situations that came up that required me to speak the truth of God, all while recognizing that if the same situation would have occurred in any other place, I would have spoken up.

Trying to pinpoint why I initially held back is hard to discern, but I believe it was due to conflicting concerns that made me unsure about the right thing to do. I knew that if I trusted Scripture alone, my responsibilities as a teacher were clear. But I also wanted to be in complete compliance with my principals, honoring them as my superiors by submitting to them as authorities whom God had placed over me. To my shame, I now believe that I let the fear of man and what might happen to my career restrict my actions.

As I wrestled in prayer and searched for wisdom, time passed, and I felt sick every day. I do not consider myself to be an expert on what it means to grieve the Holy Spirit, but during that time it sure felt like that's what I was doing. I believe the words of Jeremiah give the best description of what was going on inside me:

> Then I said, "I will not make mention of Him, nor speak anymore in His name." But His word was in my heart like a burning fire shut up in my bones; I was weary of holding it back, and I could not (Jer. 20:9).

Like Jeremiah, I too could not hold back any longer.

I do not remember all the details of what took place in my classroom, but I do know that because of some foolish action taken by one of my students in front of the whole class, I was given a clear opportunity to speak the truth to them.

And from that time on, I would not hold back. I spoke God's Word as it pertained to my students' everyday actions and situations that would surface in my classroom. Sometimes it was along with a discipline situation, but many times I taught proactively, addressing problems before they arose. I did not always quote Scripture to them, but I drew mightily from its principles.

I made certain to correct my previous errors, and my students soon understood that all authority in existence is passed down from God Himself. I made certain that they understood that the most powerful man in the world is not the one who makes the rules, and that right and wrong do not originate with man but with God. As I corrected their misunderstandings about where I stood, I felt like I was not playing the hypocrite anymore; it was what I believed, and it was my responsibility as a Christian teacher to communicate these things to them.

In the meantime, I did consider how I could honor my administrators whom I so loved. Sometime shortly after I started to speak freely in the classroom, I went to the head principal's office and told him what I was doing with my classes. There was no action taken against me, but I knew that if there were to be any complaints from students or parents, I would be on my own.

All this had transpired within the first and second quarters of the school year.

I am unaware how much time passed between talking to my principal and when he called me into his office to notify me of a complaint that had been filed. As a result of this complaint, I was explicitly and clearly warned about teaching the truths of God in my classroom.

Shortly after this, another complaint was filed, and I was warned again, with it now clear that my job was in jeopardy.

The concept of "lifestyle evangelism" arose again in my mind. Was I to obey my principals in this matter, drop the issue, and let my deeds be unaccompanied by a verbal testimony in my classroom? While working in this position, was it my responsibility to explicitly teach the truth of God's Word as I believed it in conjunction with my algebra courses? Would it be an offense toward God if I did not?

Peter and the Apostles' response to the high priest in Acts 5 held my answer:

> And when they had brought them, they set them before the council. And the high priest asked them, saying, "Did we not strictly command you not to teach in this name?

And look, you have filled Jerusalem with your doctrine, and intend to bring this Man's blood on us!" But Peter and the other apostles answered and said: "We ought to obey God rather than men" (Acts 5:27–29).

With that decision squarely determined, I knew that I still had not explicitly articulated the gospel to my students. Knowing what was transpiring and that there was a real possibility that I would lose my job, I spent much of that weekend praying, talking to my dad, and poring over more Scripture to prepare myself for another week.

I walked back into school that Monday and did something I had never done before — I shared the gospel with my first-hour class and explained why it was so important to all aspects of life. I was planning to start each of my classes that day in this way, but before I had a chance to speak to my next class, I was summoned to the principal's office. Someone had immediately reported me to them, and I was told that I would not be allowed to go back into my classroom. They were giving me the day off to consider what would transpire if I continued down this path and did not recant.

I think I cried. I loved my principals. I loved my students. I loved my job. And I felt that Christ was the answer to the problems we were dealing with in the school.

That day I went home and talked things over with many people who I knew would try to give me godly advice. However, I believed firmly in my heart what was required of me. I went in the next day dressed and ready to go to class, but I told my principals I could only teach one way, and I tried to explain to them all that God had shown me in His Word regarding teaching. They were not swayed, and I was put on suspension, during which time I could decide to either voluntarily resign my position or be terminated.

Besides handling questions from my family and friends and dealing with the media, I didn't have much to do during the following weeks except make a decision. I was free to resign, but if I did that I would not have an opportunity to talk with the school board, where my status as an employee ultimately rested. If I refused to resign, I would have a chance to convince the board of my case and there was a possibility I could keep my job. However, if the board were to decide against me, I would be terminated.

Making this decision was probably the toughest part of the whole ordeal. I was committed to the school, to my job, to the community, and to the contract I had signed stating that I would teach the entire year. For these reasons, I felt it was my responsibility to face the school board personally.

DECEMBER 22, 2004

We gathered downtown at the administration building nearly two months after I was suspended. It was the first time I had seen many of my associates since my last day at school that Monday. There were a lot of people in attendance, and news cameras were the first things I saw as I walked through the door. I was nervous.

My courageous sister accompanied me from my apartment to the board meeting. When we arrived, she was seated with the rest of my family, and I was led to a side office to wait alone.

My nervousness subsided as I was strengthened by a piece of Scripture that I began to trust in during the weeks leading up to the trial. Repeating it to myself made me feel at peace and confident that by His power I would be able to handle anything that transpired during the hearing:

> Now when they bring you to the synagogues and magistrates and authorities, do not worry about how or what you should answer, or what you should say. For the Holy Spirit will teach you in that very hour what you ought to say (Luke 12:11–12).

To my surprise, the attorney representing the district came and personally told me that he was going to give me as much time as I needed near the beginning of the trial to say whatever I wanted to say. How great an opportunity to speak freely without being pressed and questioned like I had expected!

Proving Himself faithful, the Holy Spirit directed my words with power, love, and a sound mind as I declared the goodness of His name while telling the school board all that God had shown me about the responsibility of teachers. In the very midst of that trial, I felt at peace regardless of the outcome.

At one point, one of my principals read a statement to the effect that if I would have only stopped saying the name "Jesus," I would have been accepted back into the classroom. What peace I had to know that all this simply came down to Jesus' name! And what a joy it was to know that I had not denied Him.

I was terminated by a unanimous vote of the board, but I felt like I was walking away from that trial with a mighty victory.

I praise God for the simple things He taught me during those first two years of teaching and for what He has continued to teach me since then.

As I write this article, that school board meeting was seven years ago almost to the day. My prayer is still that I will continue to offer my body as a living sacrifice, and that I will grow in obedience, doing all things for the glory of God.

*"No one can serve two masters;
for either he will hate the one
and love the other, or else he
will be loyal to the one and
despise the other . . ."*

— *Matthew 6:24*

CHAPTER SIX

A Tale of Two Masters:
Parents or the State —Which Does Your School Board Serve?

Karl Priest

"Public schools cannot be monitored, they cannot be redeemed. I was there for thirty-four years, and I'm telling you, you need to get your children out, they are in danger."

KARL PRIEST

Karl C. Priest grew up in Charleston, West Virginia. After service with the navy, he obtained a teaching degree and a master's degree in education administration. He worked as a principal and teacher for over 34 years in West Virginia public schools. After retirement he became the West Virginia State Coordinator for Exodus Mandate and now encourages parents to place their children in homeschools or Christian schools. Mr. Priest also has an active ministry demonstrating how insects proclaim the wonders of God's creation. He has been married to Melody since 1972 and they have two adult children—Aaron Caleb and Noel Faith. The following excerpts are taken from Mr. Priest's book *Protester Voices*.

THE GOOD, THE BAD, AND THE UGLY

In 1974, an event occurred in Kanawha County, West Virginia, that has been referred to as the first shot in the cultural war. Christians and their conservative allies objected to anti-Christian and anti-American textbooks that were being used to instruct children in the public schools. Their protest shut down the state's largest school system (about 45,000 students) along with many major businesses and the bus system of Charleston. At least four neighboring county school systems were also affected.

The protest garnered national attention as it was covered by all three national television news sources, many major newspapers from coast to coast, as well as mainstream media in other countries.

Conservative activist Connie Marshner said, "The first inkling that most of the nation had anything resembling a parents' rights movement came in late 1974, when the Kanawha County (West Virginia) textbook controversy made front-page headlines."[1]

A headline of major significance read: "Kanawha County Textbook War Was Pivotal to Life in America Today — Events Called Omen of 'Rightward Shift' from '60s Liberal Radicalism." That article was written by Professor Carol Mason, a prominent critic of the protesters. Dr. Mason was quoted as saying, "Without a doubt, the textbook controversy heralded the post-1960s rightward shift in American culture and politics."[2]

I was a young Christian in 1974, had been married two years, had an infant son, and had just completed my second year as a public school teacher. There were many legitimate reasons for me not to get involved with the protest. My wife and a toddler deserved all the time I could give them. Both my parents were elderly. There was a very real possibility that my job would be in jeopardy. But what was going on in Kanawha County motivated citizens — especially Christians — to step up and speak out. I could not remain silent.

The event in which I became involved has been called both the "Textbook Controversy" and the "Textbook Protest." I call it the "Textbook *War*" because that is what it was — war: "A concerted effort or campaign to combat or put an end to something considered injurious,"[3] and it was "active hostility or contention; conflict; contest: a war of words."[4]

***

Liberals have aggressively protested many things that offend them. They have violently reacted to several forestry and fishing activities. They have viciously tried to impede important scientific investigations that use living creatures (unless they are human embryos). In May of 2009 in West Virginia, 17 liberal protesters were arrested for obstructing the free enterprise of mining coal.[5]

Honest liberals know that there is no ultimate compromise with those who have values and viewpoints different than theirs. They will fight for their pantheistic or atheistic religious dogma and their socialistic political agenda. Regarding the public school curriculum in 1974 (and to this day), liberals and conservatives have two opposing worldviews, and neither wants the other to control the upbringing of their children.

FROM THE FILM: "Lots of memories here. This is where the peaceful protesters were arrested."

During the Textbook War, a profound editorial appeared in a newspaper in the nearby community of Hurricane, West Virginia. Author Cookie Allen concluded with a premise of "no compromise" in response to the November Kanawha County Board of Education decision that involved putting into the classroom some of the books that could be used with parental permission. The editorialist pointed out that the protesters could not be "half-Christian and half-atheist, half-moral and half-immoral, and half-patriotic and half-unpatriotic."

He took the "intellectual elite minority" to task:

> You (liberals) actually seem to think that you are so much better than a coal miner who disapproves of the school books his children will be required to read. . . . At least these "uneducated" ones don't try to impress anyone as you intellectuals try to do with your self-assumed superiority. . . . I don't care for the attitude of those who attempt to make the children of others study subject matter that the children's parents find objectionable.[6]

I couldn't say it any better than that.

Compromising Christians were chastised, too. Allen pointed out that some Christians were so confused that they could not discern evil, and the blame was laid on the pulpits of the pastors who saw nothing wrong with taking the name of God in vain as long as it was done "in context."

The editorial articulated an argument echoed by conservative commentators to this day: *No school board has the right in any way to cause children to question the beliefs of the children's parents.* Now, many people have come to realize what the protesters proved in 1974 is true today: Christians cannot compromise.

A *Charleston Daily Mail* article lamented the bad national press making West Virginia look unsophisticated — even backward. The article was quite ironic because the protesters were widely derided locally in print and in political cartoons that portrayed them dressed as grim Puritans.

In January of 1975, nationally syndicated columnist Jeffrey Hart revealed media hypocrisy and bias against the protesters. He pointed out how the media had conveyed the image of the protesters as "ignoramuses and religious nuts." Hart said that the *Washington Post* had printed some innocuous lines from a poem from one of the protested books while omitting "more lurid" lines.[7]

"Pro-bookers"[8] laughed at the poor grammar of some protesters, even though the offending books ironically stated it was fine to use nonstandard English. Although protesters used colloquial language — like anyone in casual conversation — they were not stupid.

Protester Mick Staton was a bank officer and leader of the breakaway segment of the textbook review committee. He said that he was offended by the "persistent references to the low intelligence quotients of protesters." Especially irksome was a critic who, Staton said, "seems to equate firm convictions and absolute moral values with low intelligence."[9] Staton offered to compare his IQ with that of the critic. A few years after the protest, Staton was elected to the U.S. House of Representatives.

FROM THE FILM: "By September, when school opened, the protests had grown so strong that the school system was shut down for a few days, the parents kept their children out."

The protesters were Norman Rockwell Americans. The over-whelming majority of them were peaceful, and their actions were honorable. Unfortunately, the minuscule minority who were violence prone were the ones who received nearly all of the attention. There was violence (property damage from gunfire and car bombs) directed *toward* the protesters. That violence was seldom mentioned by the media.

Mothers were a strong and vital segment of the protester population. They were vital in picketing, organizing, and many other valuable activities. Many of them were jailed. When the school superintendent threatened truancy arrests, nearly 300 mothers stood outside the courthouse holding signs such as "My Kids Are Out" and "My Kids Are Not in School" and dared the sheriff to arrest them. Many of those ladies were wearing the protesters' trademark red, white, and blue armbands.

Many of the protesters made sacrifices to protect their children. One family canceled their newspaper subscription and was willing to cancel their phone service in order to pay tuition for their children to attend a Christian school. I can think of no families that exemplified the protesters better than the McGraws and the Boyers. During the protest, social workers were sent to homes to investigate parents who were withholding their children from school. The Boyers had five children, four of whom were school age. The father faced four warrants and went to jail. Attorney James McKenna of the Heritage Foundation represented Mr. Boyer in court and got an innocent verdict. The McGraws twice endured prosecution for truancy. Those families sacrificed to keep their children in Christian schools.

There were dozens of arrests for picketing incidents, including violation of a September 18, 1974, injunction prohibiting more than five protesters on school property. Judge John Goad, who issued that order and jailed the protesters, lost his re-election bid.

The protesters were ridiculed for not being able to understand satire and other figurative language. Reality reveals a different picture. One photo shows a protester holding a sign that said, "What happened to Mary had a Little Lamb? Now it's Mary had a Little Shiv." She was next to another protester with drawings of monkey heads under the "Hear, See, and Speak No Evil" labels. Other protester signs read, "Today's Education is not a Journey, but a Bad Trip," "More Pearl S. Buck, Less Eldridge Cleaver," and "Even Hillbillies Have Constitutional Rights." I wish I had a collection of all the wit that was displayed on protester signs.

One criticism of protesters was that they did not actually read the books. One may wonder how many of the pro-bookers read the Bible that they frequently criticized.

By the Numbers

Around 8,000 people attended a rally and heard protest leaders speak in early September of 1974. At least 12,000 people signed a petition listing their educational values and asking the board of education not to purchase the offensive books.

Between one and two thousand people attended the June 27, 1974, three-hour board of education meeting where the books were approved by a 3-2 vote. The spectators were overwhelmingly against the books. The auditorium and hallway were packed. Most of the folks held umbrellas and stood outside the open first-floor windows in a heavy downpour. The board of education should have realized that the taxpayers and parents of the school systems' students were bothered about the books! The protesters naively thought the board would be responsive to the thoughts of thousands of its constituents.

Fifty thousand flyers containing information about the books were distributed. Several churches paid for newspaper ads appealing to the board to hear the people and not use the textbooks. There were even many teachers who objected to the books.

There were two large protest marches. On October 28, 1974, approximately 4,000 protesters marched about three miles from downtown Charleston to the capitol building. The *Charleston Gazette* reported on the march and stated that the marchers stretched for several city blocks. There was joyous singing of Christian choruses. I walked in that march.

As a propaganda ploy, a reporter wrote that we had been asked to march three to four abreast and spread out. I don't remember such an instruction. I remember a *Gazette* reporter walking with me and my wife for a short distance while she interviewed us. I have not found any record of her using anything we said. After all, my wife was articulate and soft-spoken, and I was a college-educated teacher and did not fit her narrow-minded concept of a Bible-believing fanatic.

The board of education thumbed their noses at the citizens who had elected them. It is understandable that the people got angry.

FROM THE FILM: "Even if parents could be in every classroom all day long, they would still not be able to stop the onslaught that has occurred since 1974."

In January 1975, the protesters began to vigorously lobby the state legislature, but only one insignificant bill related to the protest was passed during the entire session.

At one point during the protest some local political officials seriously studied the possibility of secession by the eastern end of the county.

Roll Call

The protesters were often accused of not having read the books or overreacting to what they had read. But they were the ones who originally put the books on display in key locations throughout the valley and encouraged the public to read them for themselves.

The following is my analysis of offensive material from the grade school English *Communicating* textbook series.[10]

It is easy to see what bothered the protesters in that day and age.

The First Grade Book begins with a thread of depressing, bad examples to indoctrinate the children in negativism. I did not take detailed notes of the books from this grade level but did record the following: "(There is) story after story of examples of people with low standards."

The Second Grade Book has a significant amount of material about violence, death, and other negativity. Here are a few examples:

- One story is a classic folk tale of the "Turtle Who Couldn't Stop Talking." The traditional story teaches a lesson and explains why the turtle shell has the appearance of having many pieces. In the *Communicating* book, the turtle "fell dead at the feet of the children" and contains a cartoon of the turtle falling in the view of happy children (p. 48 and 49).

- The adaptation of *The Adventures of Pinocchio* opens with the killing of the cricket.

- Those in favor of keeping the books in the schools claimed the series was not religious in nature, but the last line of the "Chain Rhyme" exercise is, "If a wind bothers you show it to God."

- One page alone is enough to cause concern. Page 96 contains a segment called "Telling Your Own Story." It is a series of four photos that show a boy setting off a false fire alarm and hiding behind a tree to watch the fire truck pass.

Protester-friendly school board member Alice Moore provided more information about the second grade book:

> This book, in the teacher's manual, suggests the children debate whether it was right for Jack to steal from the giant. That is a classical tool for indoctrinating in moral relativism. Who wants their seven-year-old defending stealing under any circumstances? "Pupils on a team can debate such questions as whether Jack was right to steal from the giant in *Jack and the Bean Stalk* or what difference, if any, there is between a poor man and a rich man stealing."

> "During a unit on myth, children might be asked to play two opposing gods and debate the kind of world they are about to create. Or one child might play a god and another child could be one of the god's creatures. They would then debate the kind of world the god created. The latter approach, of course, opens up avenues of discussion about authority figures, group dynamics, point of view and perspective and the golden rule" (p. 8, Teacher Notes). These writers obviously have no problem with religion in school, just so it is not the religion of the Christ.

> Consider the following questions asked of children. Do you think this might be a little invasive of family privacy or encourage a child to ponder the fairness of his parents?

1. Have you ever disobeyed your parents and been punished? Why did you disobey them? What happened? Were you sorry? Why or why not?

2. Have your parents ever punished you because they thought you had done something wrong when you hadn't really done it? What happened? How did you feel?

3. Do you think you tend to be a good or bad child? Why?

There is a poem on page 25 where the child fills in blanks in a poem:

The _____ was so bad
It killed my _____ (the only word that fits is "dad")
And that was that
For my dad and his car.

That is not a very pleasant suggestion for a second grader. Additionally, the book is replete with angry parents and bad behavior, especially stealing.

The Third Grade Book — In my 1974 notes I cited over two dozen instances of negative components. The book contains several instances of violence and death, and many depressing and bad examples.

This book is an excellent example of how the Bible was undermined by the *Communicating* textbooks:

- On page 66, a boy who is cheating says, "Oh, I hope and pray...." That comment may seem innocuous and is susceptible to scoffing by those who were in favor of keeping the books in the schools. But after reading the story, students are to be asked if cheating "is just a bit bad? ... Is it (based upon) the intention you have ... that is wrong?" On page 76, the children are asked to tell when cheating is right.

- Religious themes are prevalent throughout the *Communicating* series. On page 84 a little green man is asked if his name is Nicodemus or Methuselah — both well-known biblical names. Under "Telling Your Own Fable" (p. 130) the children are presented with an idea of "Treat others as you want to be treated." That is obviously a sneaky attempt to equate the historical comment of Christ with a fable. There are versions of that precept in non-Christian religions, but that particular way of saying it is strictly from the mouth of Jesus Christ (Matthew 7:12 and Luke 6:31).

- On page 130, an American Indian myth about the "Great Spirit" is followed by asking the children, "If you were a god, would you walk around the earth checking on people?"

- Magic and miracles (in a negative context) are discussed on page 133, and four scenarios involving "gods" are provided for discussion.

- A section on "Telling Your Own Myth" (p. 142–143) asks, "Why do we have pain?" and "Why do so many animals eat meat?" Then children are instructed to "Imagine a time when man did not have pain. Next, imagine that some kind of god walked among men and something happened. Maybe a man did something bad or made a bad mistake. Because of this the god punished men. . . ." Children are asked to make up myths about "Why do men tell lies?" and "Why don't all men speak the same language?" The children are guided with "Maybe these pictures will suggest some more ideas for the myth." The pictures are of a zebra, elephant, and giraffe. Those could be construed to be "Just So Stories" (in the mode of Rudyard Kipling) like how the zebra got his stripes, or they could be connected to the factual biblical account of Noah and the ark. The teacher notes refer to the "god of work" as an idea to answer the question, "Why do roses have thorns?" Refer to Genesis 3:17–18 for the answer to that question — and that explanation is not a myth.

- On page 227, children are told to "Tell this myth, but use a god in your story." On page 232, "The children are encouraged to tell their own myths using gods."

- The most obvious example of an attack on the Bible is where the children are asked to compare the fable "Androcles and the Lion" to "Daniel in the Lion's Den" (p. 38). The latter story is a fact as recorded in the Bible (Daniel 6:4–27). In the *Communicating* book, the teacher is supposed to ask a student to tell the story of Daniel in the Lion's Den and "If it is told in any detail, you could then discuss the similarities between that story and 'Androcles and the Lion.' "

- In the teacher notes evolutionism predominates. "We don't know how or when man first used language . . . a million years ago for an educated guess" (p. 118–120). Actually, we do know from the Bible why there are many languages (Genesis 11:9). But any reference to that explanation is censored in public schools to ensure that the evolutionism indoctrination will be passed on to the young children. Beginning with including man as another animal (such as bees) with "complex communication systems," the teacher is instructed:

> You may wish to say something about the origin of language. However, this topic will not make a good assignment for children because most encyclopedias present theories that are no longer taken seriously. If you discuss the subject, you should begin by saying that we don't know how or when man first used language. Recorded history is only four or five thousand years old. And man has had language ever so much longer — a million years for an educated guess. . . .

The Fourth Grade Book has a depressing overall theme with an abundance of death:

- There is an exercise called "Telling Your Own Story" (p. 113) with two story starter photos. One shows three boys shoplifting fruit at an open-air market. The other photo shows two boys stealing hubcaps.

- On page 178 the children are asked to "Pretend you don't like living the way you do, so you run away."

- A lengthy story features children from a poor neighborhood who are gang members. They risk injury and damage to parked cars while they play a game of "walking the plank." Even more alarming, they use clothes lines and rope to run between the fenders and door handles of vehicles parked along both sides of the street. "The result was a Traffic Tieup with such splendid honking and shouting that two squad cars of armed and helmeted policeman were sent rushing to 94th Street" (p. 93). The same page displays a sketch of the traffic snarled due to the ropes crisscrossing the street, angry motorists, dismayed policemen, and snickering boys. The main theme of this particular story is how the residents resent new neighbors who try to beautify the outside of their building. The young thugs take it upon themselves to vandalize the improvements made by the new neighbors. The vandalism occurs with the implicit approval of the adults who watch the kids in action (while some shoot dice). The book from which the story was adapted has a positive ending, but it was edited out of the *Communicating* selection. I grew up in a tough neighborhood that was once referred to as "the South Bronx of West Virginia" by the media. The kids of areas like that do not need examples of criminal and dangerous activity in their literature.

- Page 102 has a series of values questions. Teachers were just beginning to institute their training in values clarification — a strategy for moral relativism and situation ethics.[11]

- Religion is prevalent in the fourth grade book. The opening story is about sons who bring their father back from the dead. Excessive alcohol consumption is alluded to in the sentence, telling that the people "drank much palm wine. Everyone was happy" (p. 7). The third story features some Brahmans: "Usually they are very religious. . . ." One selection is about a boy playing with frogs. The way he does it is called "a game for a God" (p. 81).

- "An Indian Myth" (p. 195) is pure New Age religion with the main character doing things "that only a god can do" as the grandson of the female "Earth." The introduction tells the students that other stories tell how he came back to earth (after dying) and gave immortality to his people.

- A selection on capital letter usage has "The men are members of the unitarian church, so they are unitarians" (p. 340). Note: Unitarians were the main foes during the evolutionism battles in Kanawha County.[12]

- Pages 218–219 instruct the students to tell their own myth. The students are told that a story they had previously

read "is a way of talking about and explaining very serious matters — what happens after death, the struggles
between good and evil, and so on. Such questions have
absorbed men everywhere. And you will find that it's fun
to try to be a myth-maker and make up a story about our
origin. . . . a. Think of a god — maybe 'Big Bear, the Sky
Man.' b. Think of a son or daughter of your god. c. Where
does evil come from? Why are some people so bad? d. You
could have a war between your son-of-god or daughter-
of-god and evil. How does the encounter change the lives
of people?" Next the students are told to "Pretend you
are God. What would you do to make the world a better
place?"

- There are two poems that are prayers (ps. 265–267). One
  is by a monkey and the other is from a mouse. The monkey prays, "Dear God, why have you made me so ugly?
  . . . Could You not, one day, let someone take me seriously,
  Lord?" The mouse asks, "Dear God . . . Who made me but
  You?" Two of the questions students are to answer are, "If
  you were a monkey, what do you think you would pray
  for?" and "Does the monkey in the poem pray for the same
  thing that you would?" (Both questions are repeated regarding the mouse.) Notice the negativity toward God conveyed
  in those items.

The Fifth Grade Book opens with "all the different peoples of
the world have myths. These ancient stories were created in order
to explain the world in which people lived, so myths often became
part of the religions of the people" (p. 12). That is correct, but one
only has to become familiar with atheistic attacks on the Bible to
see this strategy of call-ing the Bible a book of mythology.

FROM THE FILM: "We won the battle back
then, we got the books out. But that was only
temporary."

- The Sun (a male) is called the "Person Above All" on page 27.

- This book has "Lord, will you let me into your paradise?" asked by a flea (p. 50). The children are asked, "What would you have the Lord say?"

- There are references to witches, Catholics, Buddhists, Easter, gods, El Diablo, and the continuation of violence and negativity.

The Sixth Grade Book has "to hell with you" (p. 206) and uses "good God" as an exclamation (p. 261). "For heaven's sake" is on page 23.

- My notes indicate a sarcastic selection containing "The sins of the father are visited on the child even to the third and fourth generation." Compare that to Exodus 20:5 from the Bible.

- Children are asked to make up their own myth that is based upon "In the beginning of the world God wanted to create men, but he was afraid that men would cause trouble. What would happen to convince God that he should create man?" (p. 158).

- In a legend, students read that they "committed the soul to God" and "he died in hope of heaven" (p. 287). On page 40 students read "God's love" and "devil." "Biblical stories," "myths," and "legends" are used in the same sentence on page 87.

- There are magic and spirits (p. 27); the phrase "Holy Roller" (p. 1); references to the Garden of Eden (p. 11 and 15); and more of the negative aspects that permeate the rest of the *Communicating* series. With an understanding of the humanistic philosophy that was becoming prevalent in the early 1970s, it is easy to see that the thread woven throughout these textbooks could be perceived as a real plan to undermine the values of the protesters and, in effect, to destroy the Judeo-Christian foundation of America.

Conclusion

During the protest, secret radical groups were formed. Relationships were often negotiated with street elements, which sometimes conducted violent actions — often without the protester's approval. A streak of conservatism remained a hallmark of the protesters.

Not all the demonstrations remained peaceful. One building was pulled down and the resulting jumble of wood was used for a great bonfire. The protesters also organized demonstrations, enforced boycotts, and occasionally resorted to violence to advance their agenda.

Shocked? Would you want to have tea with people like that? If not, then you would miss the company of Samuel Adams, Paul Revere, and other early American patriots (protesters) and "Tea Partiers." The preceding two paragraphs are my paraphrase of "Sons of Liberty."[13]

According to Harry Stout, professor at Yale University, "Angry colonists were rallied to declare independence and take up arms because of what they heard from the pulpit."[14]

The Textbook War was also about religion — the protesters' religion versus the pro-bookers' religion. There cannot be any compromise between two diametrically opposed belief systems.

The 1974 Kanawha County Textbook War was the first call for Christians to remove their children from the public schools. Many people in 1974 thought they could reform the public schools. History has proven them wrong.

THEN AND NOW:
THE TEXTBOOK WAR CONTINUES

Twenty-five years after West Virginia's Textbook War, Kanawha County parents were still battling their school board over the content of books assigned to their children. In 2000, parent Brad Liston went to a board meeting to protest the content of a sexually explicit book that had been assigned to one of his daughters as homework. The book is so graphic, Mr. Liston was asked to stop reading it, igniting an argument between the board members. Televised broadcasts of the school board meeting were censored with "bleeps" over some of the offensive things Mr. Liston read from the book. Mr. Liston told the board, "There are parts in this book where if there were illustrations, you all would be arrested for distributing pornographic material to the children."

Endnotes

Taken from *Protester Voices: The 1974 Textbook Tea Party* by Karl Priest (Poca, WV: Praying Mantis Pub., 2010), used by permission from Praying Publishing, www. insectman.us.

1. Connie Marshner, as quoted in Carol Mason, "Reproducing the Souls of White Folk," in *Hypatia: A Journal of Feminist Philosophy* 22:2 (2007): p. 98–121.
2. Tom Breen, "W.Va. Textbook Protest Marked Pivotal Movement," *Associated Press*, August 21, 2009.
3. "War," TheFreeDictionary.com, February 13, 2012, http://www.thefreediction-ary.com/war.
4. "War," Dictionary.com, February 13, 2012, http://dictionary.reference.com/browse/war.
5. Staff Reports, "17 Arrested in 3 Mining Protests," *Charleston Gazette*, May 24, 2009.
6. Part of a two-full-page ad placed by the *Business and Professional People's Alliance for Better Textbooks* in both Charleston newspapers on November 14, 1974. Mr. Allen's piece originally ran in the *Hurricane Breeze* as an editorial.
7. Jeffrey Hart, "Our Blushing Media," *Cumberland News*, January 30, 1975.
8. "Pro-bookers" is simply a brief label for those who supported keeping the offensive books in the schools. Perhaps a more accurate title for them would be "the anything goes except Judeo-Christian concepts crowd."
9. "Textbook Foe Airs Challenge," *Charleston Gazette*, November 15, 1974.
10. I obtained two of the protested books from a member of the Teachers' Chapter of the *Business and Professional People's Alliance for Better Textbooks*, and the rest of the comments were copied from my original 1974 notes.
11. For more on "Values Clarification" see chapter 15 of this book (from Dr. Erwin Lutzer).
12. Unitarians claim to be Christians, yet they deny the divinity of Christ. They actively promote liberal, humanistic agendas and have been involved in guiding government schools since their founding. Notable examples include the Harvard Unitarians who worked with the Owenite socialists to form America's first compulsory, government schools in Boston (1819); and Unitarian minister Dr. Charles Francis Potter's advising of Clarence Darrow during the Scopes "Monkey Trial" in Dayton, Tennessee (1925). Potter would later join John Dewey as one of the original 34 signers of the Humanist Manifesto (1933).
13. U-S-History.com, "Sons of Liberty," http://www.u-s-history.com/pages/h635.html (accessed February 13, 2012).
14. "How Preachers Incited Revolution," *Christianity Today*, http://www.christiani-tytoday.com/holidays/fourthofjuly/features/50h010.html (accessed February 13, 2012).

"Unless the Lord builds the house, they labor in vain who build it."

— *Psalm 127:1*

CHAPTER SEVEN

Educational Monopoly

Neal McCluskey

"Government education doesn't have competitors. The Department of Education doesn't have any competitors."

NEAL MCCLUSKEY

Neal McCluskey is the associate director of The Cato Institute's Center for Educational Freedom. Prior to arriving at Cato, he served in the U.S. Army, taught high school English, and was a freelance reporter covering municipal government and education in suburban New Jersey. More recently, he was a policy analyst at the Center for Education Reform. His writings have appeared in such publications as the *Wall Street Journal, Baltimore Sun,* and *Forbes.* In addition to his written work, Mr. McCluskey has appeared on C-SPAN, CNN, the Fox News Channel, and numerous radio programs. He holds undergraduate degrees from Georgetown University in government and English, a master's degree in political science from Rutgers University, and is a Ph.D. candidate in public policy at George Mason University. The following is taken from Mr. McCluskey's book *Feds in the Classroom.*

ENFORCE THE CONSTITUTION

The powers not delegated to the United States by the Constitution, nor prohibited by it to the States, are reserved to the States respectively, or to the people. — Amendment X, Constitution of the United States

On May 11, 2004, U.S. secretary of education Rod Paige gave the opening address at a Cato Institute event commemorating the 50th anniversary of *Brown v. Board of Education.* He lamented the Jim Crow era of his youth and hailed the Supreme Court decision that officially declared unconstitutional the "separate but equal" doctrine that mandated so much separation and so little equality between the races. "I was a junior at Jackson State when I heard the news that the Supreme Court exposed the lie of segregation," he recalled. "The case sent seismic shock waves throughout the country. . . . Justice was truly blind."[1]

Paige was right to hail *Brown* as the moment in American history when the federal judiciary at long last removed the state-fastened bars that had denied so many children access to the best American public schools. But, of course, Paige was not speaking as a historian or a civil rights crusader but as the secretary of education — a political appointee — and his remarks soon turned to advocacy of the "cornerstone" of his boss's administration. Despite *Brown*, "It's clear that after 50 years, we still have a lot of work to do," Paige lamented. "Our education system does not provide a quality education to all. . . . That is why the No Child Left Behind Act is so important. It goes beyond *Brown* and says that every child deserves a quality education."

With that statement, Paige leapt from what the Constitution requires to what it strictly prohibits. This chapter shows clearly that no matter what politicians tell us, neither the legislative nor executive branches have constitutional authority to make education policy.

Two Popular—but Unconstitutional— Federal Education Models

For most of American history, elementary and secondary education has been a family, local, and state affair. The federal government only assumed a substantial role in schooling after passage of the Elementary and Secondary Education Act (ESEA) in 1965, and even with an investment that reached more than $66 billion in 2004, federal policy makers still paid homage to local control. "I can assure you this administration understands the importance of local control of schools, that we don't believe in the federalization of the public school system, that one size does not fit all when it comes to education," George W. Bush told the National Conference of State Legislatures (NCSL) in March 2001.[2]

Nearly four years after Bush's remarks, in February 2005, NCSL's task force on No Child Left Behind (NCLB) made clear that Bush's words rang hollow:

> The Task Force is greatly concerned about the extent to which the federal government seems indifferent to . . . a shift of local control of schools to the control of state education agencies and the U.S. Department of Education, and incentives that encourage action contrary to the law's stated goals.[3]

What was the urgent mission that precipitated the sudden change to federal control? The federal government itself, it turns out, cannot even answer that, asserting that its mission is to promote "educational excellence" across the land while somehow simultaneously serving as little more than an education safety net. Unfortunately, this is just the kind of confusion one should expect in federal policy, because the foundation upon which policies should be built — the powers delegated to Washington by the Constitution — provides no support for an educational role. And the contradictions between stated missions are just the beginning of the problem: while the government couches its roles in at least somewhat limiting terms, in reality the scope of "acceptable" federal activities has become almost boundless.

FROM THE FILM: "It's a major error when people are not happy with what the Department of Education does, and they say, 'I have to try and change this thing,' because it's almost impossible to change it."

The safety net role could be dubbed the "emergency response model." As explained on the U.S. Department of Education's website, "The historical development of the federal role in education," has been "as a kind of 'emergency response system,' a means of filling gaps in state and local support for education when critical national needs arise."[4] Of course, how one defines "critical national needs" is quite variable. The term "emergency," however, can be defined, allowing us to establish at least some kind of boundary for acceptable federal activities under this model. We'll use Webster's definition, which calls an "emergency" "an unexpected situation that requires prompt attention."[5] This definition suggests that the federal government ought to grapple only with education problems that are both unexpected and demand an immediate response.

The second role the federal government has established for itself is much more expansive than the emergency response model, though it too comes from the Department of Education, which asserts that the federal government must "promote educational excellence throughout the nation."[6] This latter model, of course, opens up an almost limitless horizon for intervention, justifying any initiative politicians in Washington proclaim will make schools "excellent."

Amazingly, the feds have enacted numerous programs and initiatives transcending even the near limitless boundaries they have set for themselves. The following sections briefly discuss some of the most outlandish federal programs, first looking at a few of the federal initiatives that exceed even the boundless "national excellence" model, then noting some that violate the more constrained "emergency response" mission.

Beyond National Excellence

- *Exchanges with Historic Whaling and Trading Partners*: According to the Department of Education, this program "supports culturally based educational activities, internships, apprenticeship programs, and exchanges for Alaska Natives, Native Hawaiians, and children and families of Massachusetts."[7] Congress appropriated almost $38 million for this far-from-national program between 2002 and 2006.[8]

- *Cooperative Civic Education and Education Exchange Program*: This program is intended to make ostensibly "exemplary curricula and teacher training programs in civics, government, and economics developed in the United States available to educators in eligible countries," with the goal of helping recipients build American-style institutions.[9] This might meet the "educational excellence" requirement — though given the performance of our elementary and secondary schools, it's doubtful — but on an international, not national scale. This program has received nearly $110 million since 2002.[10]

- *"Dramatic Results" and "Storybridge" Projects funded through Arts in Education Model Development and Dissemination*

Grants Program: The Arts in Education program seeks to strengthen arts learning in K–12 schools,[11] a goal that enjoys, in principle, both a national scope and a target of excellence. At least two of the program's grantees, however, fail utterly to provide an "excellent" product. The first is a partnership between the Long Beach Unified School District, Cal State University at Long Beach, and an agency called Dramatic Results, which runs a program that explains "how to use basketry to provide quality arts instruction and how to integrate basketry into the academic curricula to strengthen instruction in math."[12] This partnership literally teaches basket weaving using federal dollars. The second program, "Storybridge," is a partnership between Stagebridge, "a nationally acclaimed theatre of seniors," and the Oakland Unified School District. It is designed to bring "storytelling, oral history, and intergenerational theater by senior citizens to at-risk, low-income urban elementary students."[13] Neither oral storytelling nor "intergenerational understanding" is in any way related to educational excellence. Moreover, a district such as Oakland, California, which the state had to take over in 2003,[14] would be much better served applying the time and money spent on Storybridge to teach basic reading and writing. Together, Dramatic Results and Storybridge have received nearly half-a-million dollars.[15]

EMERGENCY RESPONSE

There are, as one might expect, many more outrageous federal programs than those above. But, as mentioned, "national excellence" can justify just about anything. The emergency response model, however, cannot. Given its narrower focus, there should be little surprise that many more federal programs are wholly illegitimate under this model than under educational excellence. Below are just a few of the major violations:

- *Reading First and Early Reading First Grants*: Reading First is intended to ensure "that more children receive effective reading instruction in the early grades."[16] Early Reading First is its preschool partner. According to the education department, both were established by President George

W. Bush "because of compelling evidence that too many young children do not master reading."[17] This evidence, however, was not new information demanding an immediate federal response: educators have known since at least 1955, with the publication of Rudolph Flesch's *Why Johnny Can't Read*, that many students suffered from poor reading skills.[18] Moreover, states had caught on long before the federal government: Virginia, West Virginia, Rhode Island, and Alabama all had instituted statewide reading improvement programs years before Reading First came along.[19] Nonetheless, since 2001 more than $6.8 billion has been expended on these two efforts.[20]

- *Improving Teacher Quality State Grants*: This was added to the ESEA in 2001 but there was nothing new that year either about the excessive number of educators who were either unqualified to teach the subjects they were assigned or who were simply ineffective in the classroom. Studies dating back to at least 1994 made the connection between student achievement and such qualities as teachers' verbal abilities and content knowledge, and found teachers sorely lacking,[21] and *A Nation at Risk* identified teacher-quality problems more than 20 years ago.[22] As of 2006, the federal government had expended more than $17.4 billion on these grants.[23]

- *Enhancing Education Through Technology (Ed-Tech)*: There was no technological crisis in America's schools in 1995, the year this program was started. Nonetheless, the program was created to integrate technology in learning and "assist all students in becoming technologically literate by the end of eighth grade."[24] Far from confronting a technology emergency, in fact, the research organization Public Agenda has consistently reported that while professors and employers find the math and writing skills of America's high school graduates atrocious, "Very large majorities of both . . . rate the computer skills of the young people they come in contact with as excellent or good."[25] This program seems to be treating an American educational strength, not a weakness. Nonetheless, it has received nearly 5.7 billion since 1997.[26]

- *Grants for State Assessments*: Perhaps the most visible of NCLB's changes is the requirement that states set academic standards for all children in grades three through eight and create assessments to determine whether students are meeting those standards. These grants help pay for the development and dissemination of the assessments.[27] Again, this program does not address an emergency. Even if one considers a lack of state assessments to be dangerous, the federal government got into the game far too late for its initiatives to be considered "immediate action." Moreover, states have been creating standards and assessments since as far back as the "minimum competency" movement of the 1970s.[28] Between 2002 and 2006, Congress appropriated almost $2.4 billion for these grants.[29]

FROM THE FILM: "Everything that's done is generally for the benefit of the politicians, and that usually means the most powerful special interests — those people who are most motivated to be in the politics and who can most easily organize."

All of these programs highlight a clear trend in federal education policy: When responding to shortcomings in America's schools, the federal government is always a follower, never a leader. Indeed, NCLB mainly took standards and testing reforms that individual states had been developing for years and imposed them everywhere, only with significant new regulations and perverse incentives that pushed states such as Michigan to lower their own relatively rigorous standards.

Because it has no clear mission, the federal government has constantly taken states, schools, and taxpayers down treacherous paths and into dead ends. All the way back in 1959, Admiral Hyman Rickover explained that America's educational failure was attributable, at least in part, to the U.S. Office of Education reflecting "only one educational philosophy [progressivism]."[30] Since then, many federal programs have embraced fads that have produced no rewards, including programs for metric education, consumer education, class-size reduction, and character education.[31] As Diane Ravitch, who headed the Education Department's Office of Education Research and Improvement (OERI) in the early 1990s, explained at an April 2003 Harvard University conference, "My impression, based on the last 30 years, is that the federal government is likely to be hoodwinked, to be taken in by fads, [or] to fund the status quo with a new name."[32]

Finally, in addition to leading the nation's schools down too many primrose paths, federal policy makers have bungled their one clear self-proclaimed mission, to fill in the "gaps in State and local support for education." Comparing U.S. Census Bureau's ranking of states based on their 2000 poverty rates to its 2001 ranking of federal per-pupil financing, for instance, reveals at best a weak correlation between poverty and federal education dollars:[33] Alaska was the number-one recipient of federal funds per pupil in 2000–2001, yet it had the 9th lowest poverty rate. North Dakota received the 4th largest amount per student, but ranked only 21st for poverty. Despite being 8th overall for poverty, Alabama placed only 22nd in federal funds received. Finally, New York and North Carolina tied with the 17th highest poverty rate, but came in 17th and 36th, respectively, in federal education funding, a difference of $153 per pupil.

Of course, politicians are not concerned primarily with a program's success. What is important to them is that they create programs that appear to do something about educational shortcomings. It is a reality clearly reflected in politicians' aversion to having their pet programs seriously evaluated, their overwhelming tendency to proclaim that their policies are successes in the absence of proof, and the continued growth in federal control of education despite the fact that nothing but academic stagnation has accompanied federal expansion. Oh, and there's plain old pork: President George W. Bush tried unsuccessfully to cut the absurd Exchanges with Historic Whaling and Trading Partners program since the beginning of his administration, but it was protected by Senator Ted Stevens (R-AK), who as chairman of the Senate Appropriations committee for most of that time wasn't going to let anyone keep the program's dollars out of his state.

What the Constitution Actually Says about Education

No matter how the federal government has defined its mission, it has exceeded its own mandate. Many programs have had little national applicability or have failed to encourage excellence. Most have simply picked up on innovations developing in the states and imposed them on the entire nation. And throughout it all, educational performance has been stagnant. If only politicians and the public had not abandoned the Constitution: the founders knew what they were doing when they gave the feds no power over America's schools, and, indeed, reserved all nonenumerated powers either to the states, should the people choose to give it to them, or to the people themselves.

That all rights ultimately belong to individuals underlies the philosophy that shaped the Constitution. Because of their convictions that individuals are born with innumerable rights, the framers struggled to give to the federal government only those powers it must have, leaving all others to the states and, especially, the people. "[The framers] viewed natural rights as liberty rights — a concept of rights that, paradoxically, is both limited and limitless," explains constitutional scholar Randy Barnett. "They incorporated this view of rights into the text of the Constitution."[34]

Where in the Constitution are the "natural" rights of individuals protected? Most immediately, in Article I, Section 8, where the only powers that the federal government may legitimately exercise are enumerated, including the authority to coin money, regulate commerce with foreign nations, raise and support an army and a navy, and declare war. It is here that the framers, had they intended to give the federal government authority over education, would have explicitly ceded that power to it. Of course, they did no such thing, automatically leaving the states and the people with power over education and prohibiting the feds from exercising it themselves.

But what of the "general welfare" clause that precedes the list of powers in Article I, Section 8, and is often cited by enthusiasts of federal education activism as empowering federal intrusions in America's schools? Doesn't it confer upon Washington the right to govern education? Were one not to delve too deeply into the meaning of the Constitution's words, it would certainly seem reasonable to interpret promoting the general welfare as justifying federal involvement in the nation's classrooms. But one must delve deeply, because it turns out that such an interpretation is in direct conflict with the restriction of federal powers to those specifically enumerated in the

Constitution. It is also a misreading the framers addressed: Because the general welfare clause precedes the list of enumerated powers in Article I, Section 8, Madison makes clear in *Federalist* no. 41 that the general welfare is composed only of *those specific powers identified after the clause*: "For what purpose could the enumeration of particular powers be inserted, if these and all others were meant to be included in the preceding general power?" Madison asks. "Nothing is more natural nor common than first to use a general phrase, and then to explain and qualify it by a recital of particulars."[35] The general welfare clause explains why the federal government has been given enumerated powers but does not itself confer any power.

In addition to the clear restriction of powers to those enumerated in Article I, Section 8, the Bill of Rights re-emphasizes the framers' intent to give only specific powers to the federal government and leave all others with the states and people. The Bill's last two amendments make this clear. The Ninth plainly asserts that individual rights are not restricted to free speech, religious freedom, or the others explicitly mentioned in the first eight amendments, but are almost limitless: "The enumeration in the Constitution, of certain rights, shall not be construed to deny or disparage others retained by the people." The Tenth reinforces the Ninth by setting strict limits on the federal government, unambiguously declaring, "The powers not delegated to the United States by the Constitution, nor prohibited by it to the States, are reserved to the States respectively, or to the people." Finally, the Fourteenth Amendment, added after the Bill of Rights, expands the protection of individual rights by empowering the federal government to protect individual liberty from state-level intrusions, declaring that "no State shall make or enforce any law which shall abridge the privileges or immunities of citizens of the United States."

In light of the federal government's strictly constrained authority, and the absence of enumerated power over education, what, if anything, can Congress or the president legitimately do in our schools? The answer appears to be "nothing," an appearance that largely reflects reality; the federal government may undertake no endeavor intended to either advance or control American education. In other words, it can do nothing "for the sake of education."

The federal government can, however, influence education, but only if it does so either in pursuit of its legitimate powers or to ensure that state governments do not violate individual rights. That essentially limits Congress to dealing with education as it pertains to its power "to raise and support Armies" and "provide and maintain a Navy." It also gives the federal government one jurisdiction, Washington, DC, over which it has a constitutional right to do almost anything; while saying nothing about

FROM THE FILM: "You have to pay for this, and so for someone to use private education or to homeschool, they have to say I'm going to give up that [tax supported] 'free' education and then I'm going to pay twice for it."

education, Article I, Section 8, gives the federal government full jurisdiction "over such District . . . as may . . . become the Seat of the Government of the United States."

Ironically, it is from the nation's capital that one often hears the loudest demands for local control, as occurred when Congress debated a school-choice program for Washington in 2003. "There's a lot of hypocrisy to put vouchers in the District when these members have school districts just like the District of Columbia in their states," DC congressional delegate Eleanor Holmes Norton declared in reaction to federal efforts to establish a voucher program in the District. "They ought to be voting for vouchers so that their low-performing school districts can be getting federal money, but they're not. Vouchers can't win nationally, so they shouldn't win locally."[36] Local control is guarded very jealously in the one place where the federal government actually has a right to interfere.

While the federal government's jurisdiction over the District of Columbia is clear-cut, its educational role in relation to its responsibility to support a military is less clear. When it comes to K–12 education, the "national defense" argument for federal involvement has both legitimate and illegitimate manifestations.

First, the legitimate. The U.S. Department of Defense (DOD), through the Department of Defense Educational Activity (DODEA), runs schools for children of service members and others connected to the DOD both in the United States and abroad. Domestic DOD schools fall under the Defense Domestic Dependent Elementary and Secondary Schools (DDESS), which enrolled almost 26,000 students in April 2005. Overseas schools are run by the Department of Defense Dependents' Schools (DODDS), which enrolled nearly 69,000 students in 2005.[37] Assuming that the Constitution does not prohibit the federal government from stationing U.S. military personnel overseas, it is certainly reasonable to believe that the government may legitimately provide educa-tion for the children of service members and civilian employees in overseas assignments who likely do not have access to American-style schools. Whether similar schools need to be provided domesti-cally is more debatable, but providing them is probably not uncon-stitutional consider-ing that many military installations are both expansive and remote.

FROM THE FILM: "As recently as 1996, the Republican Party was still saying in their platform [that] the Department of Education is unconstitutional and needs to be eliminated."

The other, broader national defense justification for federal inter-vention in education is the assertion that America requires a well-educated citizenry to compete with other nations militarily, and this has produced illegitimate interference. Perhaps the best example of this reasoning was clamoring for improved education after World War I in reaction to many draftees requiring remedial training in reading and writing before they could move on to combat training. The other well-known argument was made after the launch of *Sput-nik*, which generated demands for America's education system to produce more scientists and engineers in order to compete with the Soviets, resulting in passage of the National Defense Education Act (NDEA).[38]

Today, these grounds for federal control seem shaky at best. The assertion that the federal government ought to be involved in Ameri-ca's schools in anticipation of needing a well-educated populace for a national draft, for instance, is a serious stretch. For 30-plus years our military has been an all-volunteer force and is considered the best in the world. No draft seems either imminent or desirable. Moreover, the Constitution's wording that the federal government may "raise and support Armies" and "provide and maintain a Navy" cannot be reasonably interpreted to allow the federal government to dictate education policy for civilians based on the assertion that educated citizens make good soldiers. Congress and the president may assemble, arm, and pay an army and navy, but it has no right to dictate school curricula or standards in anticipation of having to draft soldiers, sailors, airmen, and marines.

The contention that the federal government needs to take charge of America's schools to ensure the nation's international competitiveness — as President George W. Bush suggested in introducing the "American Competitiveness Initiative" in his 2006 State of the Union address — is even further divorced from constitutional reality. Aside from the fact that the United States has arguably the most dynamic economy in the world as a result of its decentralization and freedom, there is simply no wording in the Constitution that would brook the federal government assuming control of the schools to ensure "competitiveness." Proponents of such a reading of the Constitution might point to Article I, Section 8, in which the federal government is empowered to "provide for the common defense." They would, however, be wrong: like the general welfare clause, the common defense clause *precedes* the enumeration of specific powers and by itself confers no power at all.

In addition to controlling the education of students in Washington, DC, and providing education for children connected to the military, the federal government through its legislative and executive powers has only one proper function: enforcing prohibitions on race-based and other legally mandated discrimination. This does not mean the federal government may prohibit private behavior — nowhere in the Constitution is such power found — but thanks to the Fourteenth Amendment it must prohibit government from violating individual rights.

Overall, the executive department is empowered by the Constitution to enforce the laws.[39] Within the executive branch, the task of enforcing federally protected civil rights in education falls primarily to the education department's Office for Civil Rights (OCR), the mission of which "is to ensure equal access to education and to promote educational excellence throughout the nation through vigorous enforcement of civil rights."[40]

Ironically, even though OCR executes almost the only constitutionally legitimate function in the Department of Education, it seems to have become an afterthought as the federal mission has evolved from preventing de jure discrimination to promoting educational "excellence." Indicative of this trend is the change in OCR's funding: While total, inflation-adjusted appropriations to the Department of Education increased by about 159 percent between 1980 and 2005, funding for OCR actually *decreased* slightly.[41] This does not necessarily indicate that OCR cannot do its job. It does, however, illustrate both how much the federal government's priorities have changed over the years and how far it has exceeded its rightful purview.

FEDERAL "SOLUTIONS":
DESTROYING THE CONSTITUTION TO SAVE DEMOCRACY

"America's public education system is critical to our economy and is also the foundation of our democratic rights and freedoms," claims *Getting Smarter, Becoming Fairer: A Progressive Education Agenda for a Stronger Nation*, a 2005 report from the Center for American Progress (CAP) that concluded that America's education system is failing and solutions must be found.[42] Unfortunately, CAP thinks it knows where to find them: "In the past, when urgent national needs for education improvement became clear . . . the federal government led the way. The federal government will need to lead again."[43]

Championing such a "solution" to our educational woes is far too common. Despite public schooling's shameful legacy of discrimination, coercion, strife, and even bloodshed — not to mention its academic problems — the myth that it is the bedrock of our "democracy" continues to be perpetuated. Meanwhile, the true safeguard of Americans' liberty and success, the Constitution, is ignored by those who wish not only to perpetuate public education but to cement government's grip on all children and all schools by putting them under control of one entity: the federal government.

Freedom, of course, does not come from majority rule but from protecting the liberty of individuals. As Madison observed in *Federalist* no. 47, "The accumulation of all powers . . . in the same hands, whether of one, a few, or many, and whether hereditary, self-appointed, or *elective*, may justly be pronounced the very definition of tyranny" [italics added].[44] The Constitution, and the powers it both distributes and restrains, is what protects us from such oppression. Those who call for greater federal control over education to safeguard democracy are in fact sowing the seeds of our freedom's destruction.

They are also raising the stakes in the culture, curriculum, and religious wars that have set Americans against each other for centuries. Right now, states and communities across the country are being torn asunder by struggles for control of ever-larger, more centralized public school systems, which everyone must support but which only the most politically powerful can control. Federalizing education only raises the scope and stakes of the conflicts to the federal level, embroiling all Americans in battles over evolution, religious expression in schools, reading and math curricula, school uniforms, multiculturalism, and the endless issues on which all, or even most, people will never agree. If education is federalized, all Americans will be forced to entrust their children to a single system dominated by whatever faction can bring the most raw political force to bear, the very opposite of the liberty our system of government was designed to protect. We ignore the Constitution at our peril.

CONCLUSION

What we need is not a greater federal presence in our classrooms but one that is much smaller. Unless we want to see a disastrous escalation in the math, reading, cultural, religious, political, and countless other "wars" already besetting our public schools, we must demand that Congress and executive authorities halt their campaigns to control an educational process in which they have no authority to interfere. Voters must demand that the U.S. Department of Education be dismantled, that tax dollars used for federal education programs be returned to taxpayers, and that parents' rights to provide and administer their own children's education be restored. Finally, they must demand that the federal courts have an obligation to safeguard the people against unconstitutional predations of government, corral the federal beast, and force it back into its cage. Only when the federal government once again obeys the Constitution will educational liberty and excellence be rekindled.

Endnotes
Taken from *Feds in the Classroom: How Big Government Corrupts, Cripples, and Compromises American Education* by Neal McCluskey (Lanham, MD: Rowman & Littlefield Publishing Group, Inc., 2007). Used by permission. www.rowmanlittlefield.com.

1. Rod Paige, "Prepared Remarks of Secretary Rod Paige on the 50th Anniversary of *Brown v. Board of Education* Decision," *Cato Institute*, May 11, 2004, www.cato.org/research/articles/paige-040511.html.
2. *United Press International*, "Bush Emphasizes Local Control Over Education," NewsMax.com, 3 March 2011, www.newsmax.com/archives/articles/2001/3/2/164233.shtml.
3. National Conference of State Legislators, *Task Force on No Child Left Behind: Final Report*, February 2005, 11.
4. U.S. Department of Education, "The Federal Role in Education," *Overview*, www.ed.gov/about/overview/fed/role.html?src=ln, accessed August 30, 2005.
5. *Webster's II New Riverside Dictionary, Revised Edition* (Boston, MA: Houghton Mifflin Co., 1996), p. 226.
6. U.S. Department of Education.
7. U.S. Department of Education, "Exchanges with Historic Whaling and Trading Partners: Purpose," Find Programs, www.ed.gov/programs/whaling/index.html, accessed August 30, 2005.
8. U.S. Department of Education, *ESEA 66-2007 PB*. This Excel document is available upon request from the Budget Office, U.S. Department of Education.
9. U.S. Department of Education, "Cooperative Civic Education and Economic Exchange Program: Purpose," Find Programs, www.ed.gov/programs/cooped-exchange/index.html, accessed August 30, 2005.
10. U.S. Department of Education, *ESEA 66-2010*.
11. U.S. Department of Education, "Arts in Education Model Development and Dissemination Grants: Purpose," Find Programs, www.ed.gov/programs/artsedmodel/index.html, accessed August 30, 2005.
12. U.S. Department of Education, "Arts in Education Model Development and Dissemination Grants Program: Awards." Find Programs, www.ed.gov/programs/artsedmodel/artsdemo2003abstracts.pdf, accessed August 30, 2005.
13. Ibid.
14. Larry Slonaker, "Oakland's Ailing Schools Come Under State Control," *Mercury News*, June 3, 2003.
15. Funding data reported via e-mail by Paul Edwards, education program specialist, U.S. Department of Education, March 29, 2004. Information reported in response to a Freedom of Information Act request.
16. U.S. Department of Education, "Reading First: Purpose," Find Programs, www.ed.gov/programs/readingfirst/index.html, accessed August 30, 2005.
17. U.S. Department of Education, "Reading First" *Fiscal Year 2006 Budget Summary*, p. 22.
18. Diane Ravitch, *Left Back: A Century of Battles Over School Reform* (New York: Touchstone, 2000), p. 353–356.
19. Virginia Department of Education, "Virginia's Early Intervention READING Initiative," www.pen.k12.va.us/VDOE/Instruction/Reading/readinginitiative.html, accessed August 30, 2005; West Virginia Department of Education, "Reading for All," wvde.state.wv.us/reading/index.html, accessed August 30, 2005; Rhode Island Department of Education, "Rhode Island Reading Initiatives," www.ridoe.com/standards/reading/RIReadingInitiative.htm, accessed 30 August 2005; A+ Education Foundation, "The Alabama Reading Initiative: Literacy for All," www.aplusala.org/initiatives/ari/ari.asp, accessed 30 August 2005.
20. U.S. Department of Education, *ESEA 66-2007 PB*.

21. J. Whitehurst, "Research on Teacher Preparation and Professional Development," presented at the White House Conference on Preparing Tomorrow's Teachers, March 5, 2002, www.ed.gov/admins/tchrqual/learn/preparingteachersconference/whitehurst.html.

22. Paul E. Peterson, editor, *Our Schools and Our Future: Are We Still at Risk?* "What Has Changed and What Has Not," by Caroline Hoxby (Stanford, CA: Hoover Institution Press, 2003), p. 92.

23. U.S. Department of Education, *ESEA 66-2007 PB.*

24. U.S. Department of Education, "Enhancing Education through Technology (Ed-Tech) State Program: Purpose," Find Programs, www.ed.gov/programs/edtech/index.html, accessed August 30, 2005.

25. Jean Johnson and Ann Duffett, *Where We Are Now: 12 Things You Need to Know about Public Opinion and Public Schools,* Public Agenda, 2003, p. 22, http://www.publicagenda.org/reports/where-we-are-now.

26. U.S. Department of Education, *ESEA 66-2010.*

27. U.S. Department of Education, "Grants for State Assessments: Purpose," Find Programs, www.ed.gov/programs/gsa/index.html, accessed August 30, 2005.

28. Paul E. Peterson and Martin R. West, editors, *No Child Left Behind? The Politics and Practice of School Accountability,* "Refining or Retreating? High-Stakes Accountability in the States," by Frederick M. Hess (Washington DC: Brookings Institution Press, 2003), p. 69–71.

29. U.S. Department of Education, *ESEA 66-2007 PB.*

30. U.S. House Subcommittee of the Committee on Appropriations, *Review of the American Educational System.* 86th Cong., 2nd sess., February 3, 1960.

31. U.S. Department of Education, *Appropriations for Programs Authorized by the Elementary and Secondary Education Act, 1966–2006.*

32. Diane Ravitch, "Recycling Reforms," *Education Next* (Winter 2004): p. 40.

33. Comparison uses U.S. Census Bureau, *Public Education Finances 2001,* "Table 11. States Ranked According to Per Pupil Elementary-Secondary Public School System Finance Amounts: 2000–2001," www.census.gov/govs/school/01fullreport.pdf and *Ranking Tables: 2000,* "Percent of People Below Poverty Level," www.census.gov/acs/www/Products/Ranking/C2SS/R01T040.htm.

34. Randy E. Barnett, *Restoring the Lost Constitution: The Presumption of Liberty* (Princeton, NJ: Princeton University Press, 2004), p. 53–54.

35. Madison, *Federalist* no. 41, p. 263.

36. Sylvia Moreno, "House Panel Approves Plan for DC Vouchers," *Washington Post,* July 11, 2003.

37. U.S. Department of Defense Education Activity, "Enrollment Data," www.dodea.edu/schools/, accessed August 31, 2005.

38. Wayne J. Urban and Jennings L. Waggoner Jr., *American Education: A History,* third edition (Boston, MA: McGraw Hill, 2004), p. 329.

39. U.S. Constitution, Art II, § 3.

40. U.S. Department of Education, "Office for Civil Rights: Overview of the Agency," www.ed.gov/about/offices/list/ocr/index.html?src=oc, accessed August 31, 2005.

41. U.S. Department of Education, "edhistory.xls," www.ed.gov/about/overview/budget/history/edhistory.xls. Inflation adjustment calculated using Bureau of Labor Statistics, "Implicit Price Deflators for Gross Domestic Product," October 28, 2005.

42. Task Force on Public Education, *Getting Smarter, Becoming Fairer: A Progressive Education Agenda for a Stronger Nation,* Center for American Progress and the Institute for America's Future, August 2005, p. 67.

43. Ibid., p. 67.

44. Madison, *Federalist* no. 47, p. 301.

"He who is not with Me is against Me, and he who does not gather with Me scatters."

— *Luke 11:23*

CHAPTER EIGHT

Seperation of School and State

Howard Phillips

"The federal government's involvement in schools is totally unconstitutional."

HOWARD PHILLIPS

After graduating from Harvard College in 1962, Howard Phillips worked as chairman of the Boston Republican Party from 1964 to 1966. As director of the U.S. Office of Economic Opportunity, he fought to end the use of federal funds as ideological patronage for the radical Left. In 1974, Phillips parted ways with the Republican Party and became chairman of The Conservative Caucus (TCC), a nonpartisan, nationwide grassroots public policy advocacy group. TCC has led campaigns to end judicial tyranny, eliminate the graduated income tax, terminate federal subsidies to ideological activist groups, and dramatically reduce federal taxes, spending, and regulations. Recent TCC campaigns have opposed President Obama's radical agenda, socialized medicine, abortion, and special rights for homosexuals. Mr. Phillips and his wife, Peggy, have 6 children and 18 grandchildren. The following is a transcript of remarks made by Mr. Phillips before the Separation of School and State Alliance.

THE SEPARATION OF SCHOOL AND STATE

Nineteenth-century theologian R.L. Dabney got it right when he observed, regarding conservatives:

This is a party which never conserves anything. Its history has been that it demurs to each aggression of the progressive party, and aims to save its credit by a respectable amount of growling, but always acquiesces at last in the innovation.

What was the resisted novelty of yesterday is today one

of the accepted principles of conservatism; it is now conservative only in affecting to resist the next innovation, which will tomorrow be forced upon its timidity and will be succeeded by some third revolution to be denounced and then adopted in its turn.

American conservatism is merely the shadow that follows radicalism as it moves forward towards perdition. It remains behind it but never retards it, and always advances near its leader. This pretended salt hath utterly lost its savor: wherewith shall it be salted?

Its impotency is not hard, indeed, to explain. It is worthless because it is the conservatism of expediency only, and not of sturdy principle. It intends to risk nothing serious for the sake of the truth, and has no idea of being guilty of the folly of martyrdom.

It always — when about to enter a protest — very blandly informs the wild beast whose path it essays to stop, that its "bark is worse than its bite," and that it only means to save its manners by enacting its decent role of resistance. The only practical purpose which it now serves in American politics is to give enough exercise to Radicalism to keep it "in wind," and to prevent its becoming pursy and lazy from having nothing to whip.[1]

Professor Dabney's comments certainly remain applicable and relevant today.

When President Jimmy Carter proposed creation of the Federal Department of Education in the 1970s, much Republican rhetorical bombast ensued.

Indeed, Ronald Reagan made the very existence of the Department of Education an issue in his 1980 presidential campaign.

The Republican platform that year said:

Next to religious training and the home, education is the most important means by which families hand down to each new generation their ideals and beliefs. It is a pillar of a free society. But today, parents are losing control of their children's schooling. . . .

The Republican Party supports deregulation by the federal government of public education, and encourages the elimination of the federal Department of Education.[2]

However, during the Reagan years, funding for the Department of Education increased from $14.6 billion per year in 1980 to an annual $21.5 billion appropriation at the end of Mr. Reagan's tenure on January 20, 1989.

Under George H.W. Bush, federal funding for education increased to $25.8 billion.

During Bill Clinton's presidency, federal education funding skyrocketed to more than $70 billion for a single year, according

to a study prepared by Jim Jacobson and Mike Hammond for the National Center for Home Education. (The U.S. Department of Education's published budget accounted for only $33 billion of that estimated $70 billion in federal education assistance.) When Republicans gained control of both Houses of Con-

FROM THE FILM: "Even when the states are in charge, they have permitted horrible things to go forward. They are truly indoctrination academies."

gress in the 1994 midterm elections, GOP leaders had spoken seriously of abolishing the Education Department. They then went on to give Mr. Clinton more than he asked for, appropriating all the money needed for the very programs which they had decried.

With the advent of the No Child Left Behind Act of 2001, George W. Bush partnered with Ted Kennedy and hand delivered liberals their long-time dream of federally controlled classrooms via standardized testing. Under Bush, federal funding for education increased from $42.2 billion in 2001 to $54.4 billion in 2007.

Through the American Recovery and Reinvestment Act of 2009, President Obama piled on a staggering $176 billion to the Department of Education's budget from 2009 to 2011. The Education Department's budget is expected to top $71 billion in 2011 alone, all under the approving, watchful eye of Republicans who are all too eager to increase federal funding with the hopes of appearing "pro-education" to the average American voter.

Once a principle is conceded, the question is not *whether* defeat will be experienced, but rather *when* and to *what* extent.

Conservatives, especially the Republican variety of conservatives, tend to assume that, when a skirmish is lost, the supposed principle on which it was being waged need, be surrendered forever. In other words, once the federal government puts its nose in the tent, it can never be pushed out. The liberals make no such strategic concessions. For them, every step backward is followed by an attempt to take at least two steps forward.

On the other hand, the Republicans seem never willing to attempt recovery of lost ground, but are instead content to argue about how much of the remaining turf will be shared with the adversaries of those whom they purport to represent. They constantly argue that they cannot make big changes all at once — but that is precisely what the liberals do.

For the liberals, the statists, the socialists, and the democratic fascists — all of whom favor more government control and less personal liberty — incrementalism is merely a tactical ploy that they use to achieve their objectives circuitously without having

FROM THE FILM: "The government schools are doing their best to train future generations to be servants of the state, to adopt the ideology of dependents."

to change either destination or direction.

The Republicans foolishly believe that resorting to incrementalism, even when they have the power to achieve a complete turnaround, offers some kind of victory, when really all that they are doing is temporarily slowing the growth of liberal programs — without in any way challenging their permanence or legitimacy.

Once having surrendered the principle, they lack the moral and political confidence to subsequently reassert it. There is no hill they seek to take, because fighting for that hill might place at risk their political lives — which they value far more highly than any political principle.

The fact of the matter is that, constitutionally, there is no proper role whatsoever for the federal government in education, except with respect to the armed forces of the United States and occupied territories. Indeed, the First Amendment to the Constitution stipulates that "Congress shall make no law respecting an establishment of religion, or prohibiting the free exercise thereof." Inevitably and inescapably, every educational institution is an establishment of religion, however that word "religion" may be defined.

In the 18th century, the authors of the Constitution understood religion to mean "the duty which we owe our Creator." *Webster's Collegiate Dictionary* (fifth edition) characterizes religion as "one of the systems of faith and worship." The compact edition of the Oxford English Dictionary carries this definition: "devotion to some principle." Indeed, the *Oxford Dictionary and Thesaurus*, published in 1996, asserts simply that religion is "a thing that one is devoted to." It further stipulates that to educate is to "give intellectual, moral, and social instruction."

Religion is, in fact, a system of ideas concerning the nature of God and man.

One can argue that, for some, the advocacy of homosexuality has become a system of faith and practice. The same can be said of environmentalism, which, carried to extremes, can take the form of "earth worship." Feminism, Nazism, and communism are all ideologies or systems of faith and belief.

Professor Robert H. Nelson wrote in *Forbes* magazine:

> The problem is that many public schools have been teaching religion for years without calling it that. In their recent book, *Facts Not Fear*, Michael Sanera and Jane Shaw studied 100 children's books on the environment being used in schools. What did they discover? That many of the books advocate a kind of salvation through environmental activism.

Is this religion? Of course it is. Roger Kennedy, until recently the director of the National Park Service, has said, "Wilderness is a religious subject" that should be "part of our religious life." John Muir, the founder of the Sierra Club, believed that in the wilderness people find "terrestrial manifestations of God. . . ."

The environmental gospel teaches that excessive consumption is bad for the soul, that a new reverence for the earth is required and that the people of the world must repent of their wasteful ways. Recycling has become an environmental religious ritual, analogous to keeping kosher kitchens or eating fish on Friday.

Whether values are taught in the name of old or new religions, they are still religious values, not facts. . . .

The Christian right and other religious groups complain that under current court rulings . . . they are being discriminated against. Indeed they are. Why should separation of church and state apply to historic Jewish and Christian teachings but not to education in newer and more modern gospels? The use of public schools to require that students learn an environmental state religion is as clear an infringement on religious liberty as requiring that they learn Catholic doctrine. [3]

When Jefferson wrote in the Virginia Declaration of Religious Liberty that "to compel a man to furnish funds for the propagation of ideas he disbelieves and abhors is sinful and tyrannical," he was asserting the principle of liberty of conscience which is implicit in and fundamental to the plain text of the First Amendment to the Constitution.

All education is essentially, inescapably, and inevitably religious, in that it must carry with it presuppositions about the nature of God and man. Those presuppositions, in the early days of the American Republic, were explicitly Christian. Now, they are increasingly humanistic and antinomian.

That is why we must be thankful for the straightforward language of the First Amendment to the Constitution which forbids Congress from making any law, whether to raise revenues or expend them, in support of a religious establishment, even as it prevents Congress from interfering with the free exercise of religion.

Personally, I reject the "doctrine of incorporation," which wrongly asserts that the First Amendment applies to state governments, as well as to the Congress.

But, if I were to join those liberals who argue thus, my case would be even stronger, deducing as it would that the Federal Constitution prohibits any expenditure of public funds, even by state and local governments, in support of educational establishments, since they are, in fact, religious establishments — institutions which indoctrinate in the context of their preferred presuppositions.

The notion of religious "neutrality" is a myth. There is no middle ground on the question of biblical reality. Either God's word is true, or it is not. All subsequent conclusions must be based on one or the other of these prepositions.

Either man is a created being "endowed by his Creator with certain inalienable rights" or man is an historical accident — an evolutionary entity who exists by random selection, without moral order, discernible origin, or ultimate purpose.

When biblical presuppositions are rejected, the door is opened for, at first, the official "toleration" of and very soon thereafter, the advocacy of all that which God condemns — from sexual promiscuity to abortion to homosexuality, and, of course, in all cases, the eventual rejection of all legitimate, ultimate, God-ordained authority.

Because law is "the will of the sovereign," so long as the United States has a political system that recognizes that God's creatures owe a duty of stewardship to their Creator, and that we have a right and duty to hold accountable those to whom we delegate political authority (so that we may conscientiously exercise our stewardship), then concepts of national independence are viable and understandable.

But, when the chain of accountability of civil government to the citizen is broken and constitutional limitations, such as those proscribing congressional action with respect to any establishment of religion, are ignored, then the biblical common law system that defines our liberties is easily rejected in favor of the globalist nostrums of "world citizenship," which are now increasingly part of government-funded educational curricula.

The real issue is not *whether* education shall be religious, but rather on *which* religious premises our system of education shall be based.

Because I favor civil liberty and have wanted my own children to be educated in the context of a Christian worldview, I must reject any law that propagates faiths alien to my own and that obliges me, through compulsory taxation, to subsidize the propagation of those other hostile faiths, even as such law places bounds on the advocacy and exposition of that which my family and I believe.

After all, children are not the property of the state, and God assigns parents primary and ultimate responsibility for the nurture and admonition of their progeny.

If anyone needs evidence that questions of religion are inescapably intertwined with issues of education, he need look no further than the unceasing stream of headlines that highlight all the latest controversies of megalomaniacal federal judges ignoring both the First Amendment and the Tenth Amendment to the federal Constitution, as they seek to impose their own will, to deny the teachers, administrators, parents, and students of this country their constitutional right to the free exercise of their religious faith.

FROM THE FILM: "To honor God and His Son, we must remove our children from the government schools. For the family to be a strong institution, mom and dad have to play the leading role in the education of their children."

These violations simply underscore the necessity of not obliging any citizen to subsidize with his taxes official hostility to what such citizens understand to be true education and true religion.

But, despite the failure of Republicans at the White House and on Capitol Hill to make good their promises, there is hope, for the Constitution makes clear that no funds may be disbursed from the federal treasury, except by a presidentially signed congressional appropriation, or an overridden presidential veto of such an appropriation.

No president can veto a zero. So whenever Congress has the discernment and the courage to end the federal role in education, it can do so by appropriating zero funds for such purposes.

Failing that, we must await the election of a president morally and openly committed to veto any and all appropriation measures that reach his desk, including even a single cent for the unconstitutional provision of federal tax dollars to establishments of religion — at any and all levels, whether such appropriations include funding for the Elementary and Secondary Education Act or subsidies, direct and indirect, to colleges and universities, which have all too often become institutions of anti-Christian indoctrination.

By saying yes to liberty of conscience, we must say no to federally subsidized and regulated establishments of religion.

Endnotes

Taken from remarks by Howard Phillips before the Annual Conference of the Separation of School and State Alliance on November 22, 1997 (updated September 30, 2011), taken from The Conservative Caucus. Used by permission from The Conservative Caucus, 450 Maple Ave. E., Vienna, VA 22180, www.conservativeusa.org.

1. Robert Lewis Dabney, *Discussions*, Vol. IV: Secular (1897; reprint edition, Harrisonburg, VA: Sprinkle Publications, 1994), p. 496.
2. "Republican Party Platform of 1980, Education," adopted by the Republican National Convention on July 15, 1980, online by Gerhard Peters and John Woolley, *The American Presidency Project*, http://www.presidency.ucsb.edu/ws/?pid=25844, accessed July 4, 2012.
3. Robert H. Nelson, "Religion as Taught in the Public Schools," *Forbes* (July 7, 1997), http://www.independent.org/printer.asp?page=%2Fnewsroom%2Farticle.asp?id=2700.

". . . Christ, in whom are hidden all the treasures of wisdom and knowledge."

— Colossians 2:2–3

CHAPTER NINE

Early American Education

Roger Schultz

"The founders were convinced that for a country to be successful it had to be virtuous."

ROGER SCHULTZ

Dr. Roger Schultz is the dean of the College of Arts and Sciences at Liberty University. He previously served as chair of the History Department at Liberty, and has taught at Virginia Intermont College, the University of Arkansas, and Oak Hills Christian College. As a specialist in American religious history, he is interested in the interaction of religion and culture. His recent work deals with Christians in the American Revolution, biblical principles of government, and American fundamentalism. His essays and reviews have appeared in numerous publications and have been translated into Hungarian and Spanish. Dr. Schultz frequently preaches in local churches and speaks at academic and Christian conferences. The Schultzes have nine children — five of whom are Liberty alumni and two are current Liberty students. The following is taken from an article written by Dr. Schultz that was published in the Chalcedon Foundation's *Chalcedon Report* magazine.

A CHRISTIAN AMERICA: EDUCATION AND THE FOUNDERS

Consider the following college mission statement: "Every one shall consider as the main End of his life and studies, to know God and Jesus Christ, which is Eternal life. John 17:3"[1] Match that statement with the correct school. The choices are (1) Liberty University, (2) University of California-Berkeley, (3) Duke, (4) Harvard, or (5) Bob Jones University. The correct answer is Harvard College, and the statement is taken from the college's first laws of 1646.

Did anyone guess Duke? In 1924, when James Duke transformed Trinity College into the university that bears his name, the bylaws of the act of endowment included the following mission statement: "The Aims of Duke University are to assert a faith in the eternal union of knowledge and religion set forth in the teachings and character of Jesus Christ, the Son of God. . . ."[2] (That 1924 mission statement is still displayed on a monument in front of the beautiful Duke chapel.) As late as the 1920s, American higher education still formally stressed its Christian character.

Liberty University has an excellent doctrinal statement. It affirms the inerrancy of Scripture, a literal six-day creation, justification through faith alone, and the necessity of salvation through Christ. But the doctrinal fidelity that makes Liberty exceptional today was commonplace in early American institutions.

America has a great Christian heritage. Early American education, which was fundamentally Christian, is an excellent example of that heritage. Unfortunately, that commitment to Christ-centered education has been lost and needs to be recaptured.

The desire for godly education was a consuming passion for the Puritans. It was one of the reasons for their exodus from England. In his 1629 justification for leaving for New England, John Winthrop points (among other factors) to problems in the schools:

> The fountains of learning and religion are so corrupted most children (even the best wits and fairest hopes) are perverted, corrupted, and utterly overthrown, by the multitude of evil examples and the licentious government of those seminaries, where men strain at gnats and swallow camels . . . but suffer all Ruffian-like fashion and disorder in manners to pass uncontrolled.[3]

It is worth noting that, in part, the Puritans fled England because of crummy schools! Colonial higher education reflected this Puritan passion for Christian education. Harvard was chartered in 1636, primarily to train clergymen, and had as its motto "Christ and Church." Virtually all of the Ivy League schools shared this early commitment to a Christian education. Princeton, the Presbyterian college in the colonies, counted revivalists Samuel Davies and Jonathan Edwards among its earliest presidents.

The commitment to religious education in the colonial period started with the youngest students. The *New England Primer* was the Puritan book used to teach generations of Americans to read. The Primer taught the ABCs: each letter of the alphabet was associated with a biblical character or a scriptural lesson, and a corresponding doctrinal truth was anchored in the mind with a rhyme. A was for Adam; there was a woodcut of Adam and Eve; then the rhyme, "In Adam's fall, we sinned all." In addition to learning the alphabet, children were instructed in sound Augustinian theology. C was for Christ, and with the saying, "Christ crucified for Sinners Dy'd," children were exposed to biblical soteriology. There were many reminders of human mortality in the *Primer*. G was for Glass (Hourglass), and "As runs the Glass, Our life does pass."[4] Y was for Youth — and then there is a woodcut of a skeleton nailing a little kid with an arrow — "Youth forward slips, Death soonest nips."

FROM THE FILM: "When the Puritans came to America, they said one of the reasons why they left England was so that they could have stronger training for their children."

My favorite is U was for Uriah (the Hittite). The slogan goes, "Uriah's beauteous wife made David seek his life." The attached picture shows King David leering down on the nubile Bathsheba, which was the precursor to his adultery and his conspiracy to murder Uriah.[5] Sin, death, betrayal, adultery, and murder — who needs TV? It is all in the *Primer*. It is saucy stuff — especially for those of us who grew up with the sanitized and conformist Dick and Jane readers. The Primer was profoundly philosophical as well. It included theological lessons, prayers, and catechisms. The first question of the Shorter Catechism, for instance, asks, "What is the chief end of man?" That is a heavy teleological question for a five-year-old; it asks about purpose in life and the very reason for existence. The answer: "to glorify God and enjoy him forever."

In the 19th century, the *McGuffey Reader* largely replaced the *New England Primer*. Between 1836 and 1920 some 120 million copies of the *Readers* were sold, putting it in the class with the Bible and Webster's Dictionary.[6] McGuffey (1800–1873) was a Presbyterian clergyman, a professor of ancient languages, president of Miami University, and, at the time of his death, the professor of moral philosophy at the University of Virginia. His *Readers* projected a specifically Christian and largely Calvinistic worldview, although later editions of the *Readers* were less theologically inclined and more moralistic. The *Readers* include religious lessons (to say your prayers, to be thankful to God, etc.), stories about the natural world and historical figures, and strong endorsements of moral behavior. Children are taught the Golden Rule, the virtue of honesty, and respect for authority. Other stories warned about the cruelty of torturing animals, the evil of being mean to others, or the dangers of becoming a drunkard (temperance was an important issue for McGuffey). These largely religious texts were widely used in public schools.

The first national act to endow public education was the Ordinance of 1785, dealing with western lands. One section (section 16) in every township — that is, one square mile in every 36 square miles of territory, or roughly 3 percent of all western land — was set aside to support public schools. The rationale for this endowment was important: "religion, morality, and knowledge, being necessary to good government and the happiness of mankind, schools and the means of education shall forever be encouraged."[7] Let it be noted that the first national educational endowment was specifically to encourage religion and morality.

FROM THE FILM: "Many people are familiar with the *New England Primer*, which taught children how to read with ABC lessons tied to the Bible. So, when you learned your 'A,' you didn't learn about apples, you learned about Adam."

In the 19th century, almost all of the nation's colleges had religious roots and denominational affiliations. Many of those colleges sprang from evangelical bodies that had arisen during the great religious Awakenings. In southwest Virginia and northeast Tennessee, for instance, with which I am most familiar, the first colleges had strong ecclesiastical ties. Virginia Intermont College, for example, got its start when Reverend Harrison traveled through southwest Virginia with John the Baptist (the name of his horse), sharing his vision of a Baptist institution of higher education.[8] But he certainly wasn't unique in combining a passion for education with the Christian faith.

Before the 20th century, Christianity had a natural and critically important role in American education. But then something happened. Schools and colleges lost the spiritual vision and religious commitment that characterized early generations.

What happened? In *The Soul of the American University*, George Marsden points to the sweeping trends of secularization. And he poses this historical question:

> Why were the fledgling universities of the late nineteenth century, despite their founders' expressed commitments to Christianity, designed in a way that would virtually guarantee that they would become subversive of the Christian heritage of learning?[9]

A good question, indeed.

Cultural historian Daniel Boorstin argues that pragmatism and raw economics diluted the religious focus of American colleges. Struggling Christian institutions, to remain solvent, were forced to appeal to the community and attract a broader constituency, a process that muted their theological distinctives. "To make their colleges appeal to everybody," Boorstin continues, "to people who believe anything or nothing, the denominations themselves became powerful breeders of 'Nothingarianism,' which some observers said was the truly dominant American sect."[10]

The 19th-century Princetonians offered a sharper criticism of the direction of American education. In his 1886 *Evangelical Theology*, A.A. Hodge writes:

> If every party in the state has the right of excluding from the public school whatever he does not believe to be true, then he that believes the most must give way to him that

believes least, and then he that believes least must give way to him that believes absolutely nothing.

"A compulsory and centralized system of national education, separated from religion," Hodge continues in this excellent analysis, would be an instrument for atheism and nihilistic ethics.[11]

Rousas Rushdoony notes that education has become a "messianic and utopian movement." It is an inherently religious part of a statist worldview. "The state has become the saving institution," he argues, "and the function of the school has been to proclaim a new gospel of salvation."[12] Education will invariably reflect a culture's core values, base convictions, and our true religion.

Evangelical Christians should be both encouraged and forewarned by the testimony of the past. Like their Puritan ancestors, they should flee the "disorderly" and "licentious" educational establishments of their day. True education will always be Bible-based and Christ-honoring. Like previous generations, we should cultivate institutions of higher education that are truly committed to the glory of Christ and the good of His church.

Endnotes

Taken from "A Christian America: Education and the Founders" by Roger Schultz, from the *Chalcedon Report*, March 2003, used by permission from the Chalcedon Foundation, P.O. Box 158, Vallecito, CA 95251, www.chalcedon.edu.

1. Quoted in George Marsden, *The Soul of the American University* (New York: Oxford, 1994), p. 41.
2. Ibid, p. 322.
3. Jack Greene, editor, *Settlements to Society, 1607–1763*, "Reasons to be Considered for Justifying the Plantation in New England," by John Winthrop (New York: Norton, 1975), p. 63; spelling modernized.
4. Woodcuts and lessons varied with the editions of the *Primer*. Examples included come from *The New England Primer* (Boston, MA: 1777; reprint ed., Aledo, TX: Wallbuilder Press, 1991).
5. Jerome Reich, *Colonial America*, 2nd edition (Englewood Cliffs, NJ: Prentice-Hall, 1989), p. 225.
6. John Westerhoff, *McGuffey and His Readers* (Milford, MI: Mott Media, 1982), p. 14.
7. Malcolm Rohrbough, *The Trans-Appalachian Frontier* (Belmont, CA: Wadsworth, 1978), p. 48. The purpose statement was added to the 1787 version of the Ordinance.
8. Hendrika Schuster, "When John the Baptist Traveled Our Roads: A Tale of Virvinia Intermont College," *Bulletin of the Historical Society of Washington County, Virginia*, Series II (1998) 35:1–6.
9. Marsden, *Soul of the American University*, p. 31.

10. Daniel Boorstin, *The Americans: The National Experience* (New York: Vintage, 1965), p. 154.
11. A.A. Hodge, *Evangelical Theology* (1890; Carlisle, PA: Banner of Truth Trust, 1976), p. 242–244, http://www.scribd.com/doc/30740731/03-MAR-CR-Proof.
12. Rousas Rushdoony, *The Messianic Character of American Education* (Nutley, NJ: The Craig Press, 1979), p. 4.

"Remember the days of old, consider the years of many generations. Ask your father, and he will show you; your elders, and they will tell you. . . ."

— *Deuteronomy 32:7*

CHAPTER TEN

A Firm Foundation —
A Brief Survey of the Faith of America's Founding Fathers

John Eidsmoe

"If you really study and work hard, you might be able to . . . remotely approach the level of academic sophistication of the farmers of colonial America."

JOHN EIDSMOE

Colonel John Eidsmoe holds five degrees in law, theology, and political science. He currently serves as professor of constitutional law and related subjects at the Thomas Goode Jones School of Law at Faulkner University in Montgomery, Alabama, where he received the Outstanding Professor Award in 1993. A constitutional attorney and lieutenant colonel in the U.S. Air Force Reserve, he has also taught church history and other subjects in various seminaries and has produced a 12-part video series titled *The Institute on the Constitution*. His books include *The Christian Legal Advisor*, *God and Caesar*, and *Columbus and Cortez*. The following excerpts are taken from Col. Eidsmoe's book *Christianity and the Constitution*.

THE FAITH OF OUR FOUNDING FATHERS

"It is really an assembly of demigods," Thomas Jefferson wrote to John Adams.[1] Later Jefferson added, "A more able assembly never sat in America."[2] Nor, we may add, has a more able assembly ever sat since.

Most of America's great minds assembled as the Great Convention in Independence Hall in Philadelphia on May 14, 1787, to propose changes in America's plan of government. The men were hopeful; they intended to pool their learning and wisdom, draw from the best of past governments and thinkers, and perhaps try a few new ideas. They had experienced tyranny under Great Britain with a government that was too powerful. They had fought a major war to be freed from that oppression. They had experienced anarchy under the Articles of Confederation that created a government that was too weak, and the nation had nearly collapsed as a result. So they hoped to formulate a system of government powerful enough to prevent anarchy but appropriately restricted to prevent tyranny.

Right from the beginning, the convention was beset with problems. First, the convention was without funds. The delegates who came did so at their own expense. Second, the convention began with only 7 of the 13 states represented, some by a partial delegation. Finally, 12 of the 13 states were represented. Rhode Island chose not to participate. How could a new nation be formed with so little cooperation and enthusiasm?

It soon became apparent that those present were by no means of one accord. Alexander Hamilton, the distinguished and brilliant New Yorker, distrusted the masses and wanted a strong central government. In contrast, Roger Sherman of Connecticut and others, strong defenders of states' rights, didn't trust a central government. Delegates from the large states, like James Madison of Virginia, wanted proportional representation in Congress. Men like William Patterson of New Jersey felt smaller states would be abused by the larger states unless each state had an equal voice in Congress.

There was also the underlying issue of slavery. Some northern delegates totally opposed slavery and wanted it abolished. Other delegates morally opposed slavery but were slaveholders themselves. Some delegates defended slavery as an institution and declared that the South would not ratify the Constitution if it contained anti-slavery provisions.

Debating this point and that, the convention dragged listlessly on. It passed some measures, defeated others, referred some matters to committees, and then seemingly lost sight of them. The state delegations were unwilling to compromise; each wanted its own way. A discouraged George Washington, the convention chairman, wrote a friend saying that he doubted the convention would ever agree on a new plan of government.

On June 28, 81-year-old Benjamin Franklin, the oldest delegate at the convention, delivered what was probably the most famous speech of the entire meeting. He noted that "the small progress we have made after 4 or 5 weeks [was] melancholy proof of the imperfection of the Human Understanding." Rather than mere human understanding, the delegates needed something more: "the Father of lights to illuminate our understandings"! He reminded the delegates that during the War for Independence they had prayed regularly to God in that very hall: "Our prayers, Sir, were heard, and they were graciously answered." All of them could remember God's intervention on their behalf, and to that intervention they owed their victory over Great Britain:

> And have we forgotten that powerful friend? or do we imagine that we no longer need his assistance? I have lived, Sir, a long time, and the longer I live, the more convincing proofs I see of this truth — that God governs in the affairs of men. And if a sparrow cannot fall to the ground without his notice, is it probable that an empire can rise without his aid? We have been assured, Sir, in the sacred writings, that "except the Lord build the House they labour in vain that build it." I firmly believe this; and I also believe that without his concurring aid we shall succeed in this political building, no better than the builders of Babel.[3]

Franklin then suggested daily prayers, led by one or more Philadelphia clergymen. How was Franklin's suggestion received? Did the delegates become conscious of their need for God's help? Did they turn to God and implore His assistance? Was God present at the Great Convention in Philadelphia? Did He intervene and forge unity out of discord? Does the U.S. Constitution bear God's imprint, reflect His wisdom and His precepts?

What can be concluded about the faith of America's founding fathers? Let us consider the religious beliefs of a representative dozen of the Great Convention's delegates, a balanced representation of Federalists and Republicans spanning a geographic cross section of New England, Middle Atlantic, and Southern states.

Eight of these 13 men — John Witherspoon, Alexander Hamilton, John Jay, Samuel Adams, Patrick Henry, Roger Sherman, Charles Cotesworth Pinckney, and George Washington — were Christians. It is likely Gouverneur Morris was also a Christian. John Adams, a strong Congregationalist/Puritan in his early years, liberalized his beliefs in the 1800s but could still be considered a Christian. James Madison is an enigma; he was an orthodox Christian in his early years, but in later years he was silent about his religious beliefs. Ben Franklin was a deist in his early years but moved toward faith in a God who answers prayer and guides human history, though he still had doubts about the divinity of Christ. Thomas Jefferson could probably be classified as a deist in his early years, but in later years moved toward Unitarianism; unlike the deists, he recognized a God who answers prayer and intervenes in human affairs. He called himself a Christian, using a liberal definition of the word, but did not consider Jesus Christ to be the second person of the Trinity.

How do their political and religious beliefs relate? Some think the Republicans and Antifederalists, influenced by free thinkers and rationalists, were less likely to be Christians than the Federalists. However, there were Christians in both groups. It is difficult for 20th-century conservatives to identify strictly with either position.

If Washington, Hamilton, Jay, Morris, John Adams, and Pinckney are broadly categorized as Federalists; and Witherspoon, Madison, Samuel Adams, Franklin, Jefferson, Sherman, and Henry are classified as Republicans, the following chart can be drawn:

	Strongly Christian	Probably Christian	Probably Not Christian
Federalist			
George Washington	X		
Alexander Hamilton	X		
John Jay	X		
Gouverneur Morris		X	
John Adams		X	
Charles C. Pinckney	X		
Republican			
John Witherspoon	X		
James Madison		X	
Samuel Adams	X		
Benjamin Franklin			X
Thomas Jefferson			X
Patrick Henry	X		
Roger Sherman	X		

Four of the six Federalists were Christian and two were probably Christians. Four of the seven Republicans were Christian, one was probably Christian, and two were probably not Christian.

While Christians predominated in both groups, they came to different conclusions concerning government matters. Their basic worldview was the same, but they differed in opinion as to how to apply that worldview in establishing America's political system.

FROM THE FILM: "I require my students to read the Federalist Papers...they'll say 'this is the hardest thing I have had to read....' Then I tell them...it was written for a very elite audience – the farmers of Colonial America!"

The founding fathers (with the partial exception of Thomas Jefferson, who was not at the convention) held a low view of human nature; they agreed with the biblical view of the sinful nature of man. But this view of human nature led them to different political applications. Alexander Hamilton and Gouverneur Morris distrusted the sinful nature of the masses and believed a strong central government was necessary to keep the masses in check. Patrick Henry and Samuel Adams distrusted the sinful nature of the rulers and feared that a strong central government would become tyrannical. Rev. Witherspoon, through his student James Madison, suggested the solution that was finally adopted: prevent any one individual or group from becoming too powerful by separating power into legislative, executive, and judicial branches, with each checking and balancing the others. The following conclusions emerge about the religious beliefs of the founding fathers:

- Each of them professed and exhibited a deep faith in God. They believed not only in a God of creation, but also in a God who is active in human history. Franklin and Jefferson came to that belief later in life; the other 11 held that belief throughout their lives.

- At least 8 and probably 11 believed Jesus Christ is the Son of God. One of these 11, John Adams, questioned, but he affirmed a belief in Jesus' resurrection and apparently believed Jesus was more than a man. Madison believed in the Trinity early in life, but his later views are enigmatic because of his silence. It appears Morris accepted Jesus as God, but he said so little on the subject it is difficult to say for certain. Franklin had great respect for Jesus but had "some doubts" concerning his divinity; Jefferson also respected the teachings and example of Jesus but did not believe he was divine.

- The founding fathers were students of the Bible. They quoted it authoritatively and made frequent allusions to Scripture in their writings and speeches. All of them except Thomas Jefferson indicated that they considered Scripture to be revelation from God. John Adams believed Scripture to be God's revelation, but he suspected that certain passages of Scripture were not part of the original text. Jefferson preceded both Albert Schweitzer's "quest for the historical Jesus" and Rudolf Bultmann's "demythologization," by preparing a compilation of Bible verses in which some passages appeared to have held an orthodox view of Scripture as God's authoritative revelation to man. They respected the Scriptures and studied the Bible extensively. John Jay and Charles Cotesworth Pinckney were leaders in the American Bible Society.

- All of the founding fathers except Jefferson concurred with the Bible that man is basically sinful and self-centered; they did recognize that man is capable of certain civic virtue (Rom. 2:14–15). Jefferson had more faith in the goodness of man than the other founding fathers did, but he recognized that man has a sinful side; he did not share the beliefs of the French philosophies in human perfectibility. Franklin did not adhere to the Calvinist view of total depravity, but he had a lower view of human nature than Jefferson.

In this respect and others, Jefferson (and to a lesser extent Franklin) stand out from the other founding fathers. The worldview of the others was strongly Christian even if several questioned certain Christian doctrines. The other 11 were spiritual descendents of John Calvin; only Jefferson, and to some extent Franklin, were children of the Enlightenment. And yet, modern thinkers are likely to cite Jefferson above all the others as representing the spirit of that age.

- All 13 of the founding fathers had great respect for organized religion, particularly for Christianity. Several were not church members, but, including Jefferson and Franklin, they attended church and contributed to churches. Some contributed to several different denominations. Most believed in Christian unity and rose above the narrow denominationalism of that time.

Thomas Jefferson disagreed with the Calvinist leaders of New England but respected Christianity in general. Ben Franklin held bitter feelings toward his Calvinist upbringing early in life, but he reversed these feelings later in life and wanted his grandson brought up Presbyterian.

Most of these founding fathers sincerely believed the tenets of orthodox Christianity. The few who had reservations about certain doctrines recognized the positive influence the Christian religion had on society. They all agreed that, in Washington's words, "national morality (cannot) prevail in exclusion of religious principle." They realized that the only way a free society can exist is among a highly religious and moral people.

The founding fathers who did not choose to be Christians expressed gratitude for Christianity's influence within their nation. If the founding fathers were to see the hostile contempt with which modern thinkers treat Christianity, I believe they would consider it strange, offensive, and self-destructive.

Endnotes

Taken from *Christianity and the Constitution: The Faith of Our Founding Fathers* by John Eidsmoe (Grand Rapids, MI: Baker Book House, 1987), used by permission, www.bakerbooks.com.

1. Thomas Jefferson to John Adams, August 30, 1787, reprinted in H.A. Washington, editor, *The Works of Thomas Jefferson* (New York: Townsend, 1884), 2:260.
2. Thomas Jefferson to M. Dumas, September 10, 1787, Ibid., 2:264.
3. Benjamin Franklin, quoted by James Madison in *Notes on Debates in the Federal Convention of 1787* (Athens, OH: Ohio University Press, 1966, 1985), p. 209. Benjamin Franklin probably never became a Christian in the orthodox sense of the word, but as his autobiography reveals, he had come a long way from the deism of his teenage years. He clearly believed in a prayer-answering God.

"Beware lest anyone cheat you through philosophy and empty deceit, according to the tradition of men, according to the basic principles of the world, and not according to Christ."

— *Colossians 2:8*

CHAPTER ELEVEN

Pavlov's Child

Samuel Blumenfeld

"A state government education system is a socialist system. . . . It made sense to a lot of people who bought the idea that man was morally perfectible and that all you needed was a good education."

SAMUEL BLUMENFELD

Dr. Samuel L. Blumenfeld has spent the last 30 years writing about American education and seeking answers to such questions as: Why is America experiencing a decline in literacy? Why are so many American children afflicted with learning disabilities? Why are the schools dead-set against intensive phonics and memorization of arithmetic facts? His best-selling exposé, *N.E.A.: Trojan Horse in American Education*, has become a classic in critical educational literature. His other books include *Is Public Education Necessary?*, *How to Tutor*, and *Alpha-Phonics* — used by thousands of parents and homeschoolers to teach their children the three Rs in the traditional manner. His articles have appeared in many publications, and he has lectured and held seminars in all 50 states and Canada, England, Australia, and New Zealand. He has tutored and taught in both private and public schools. The following article by Dr. Blumenfeld was taken from *The New American* magazine.

PAVLOV'S DOGS AND AMERICAN EDUCATION

For the past century, behavioral psychology and revolutionary socialism have combined to wreak educational and social havoc.

You might ask, what have Pavlov's dogs got to do with educating American children? More than you think.

Ivan Petrovich Pavlov, the Russian experimental psychologist, was born in 1849 in the town of Rayazan. His father was a priest, and he was raised in the Russian Orthodox tradition. He was attracted to the study of science, and in 1870 entered St. Petersburg University. In 1875, he got his degree in natural sciences. He then went on to study medicine, after which he entered the Veterinary Institute where he stayed for ten years doing research on digestion.

After a visit to Germany, where he studied at the laboratories of Rudolf Heidenhain in Breslau and Karl Ludwig in Leipzig, he returned to Russia and decided to focus his attention on the study of glandular secretions — saliva and gastric juices. He selected the dog as his experimental animal and devised surgical techniques that made it possible to establish "permanent fistulas (tubes)" in connection with the principal organs of digestion (salivary glands, stomach, liver, pancreas, parts of the intestine).

His experiments were difficult to carry out while keeping the dogs not only alive but healthy. It took the sacrifice of 30 dogs before he could get the surgical procedure right. How did Pavlov get his dogs? He relates: "At that time dogs were collected with the help of street thieves, who used to steal those with collars as well as those without. No doubt we shared the onus of the sin with the thieves."[1]

In 1895, Pavlov was appointed to a chair in physiology at the Military Medical Academy in St. Petersburg, and in 1904 was awarded the Nobel Prize. Pavlov had discovered that in every case, glandular secretion was determined by one or more reflex actions.

Actually, Pavlov recognized that there are two types of reflexes: unconditioned and conditioned. An unconditioned reflex is an innate response to stimuli that occurs naturally, without any learning involved. For example, when you are driving a car and enter a dark tunnel in daylight, your eyes automatically adjust to the change in light. However, a conditioned reflex is a learned response, as when you see a red light, you automatically put your foot on the brake. You have acquired an automatic response to stimuli — a conditioned or learned reflex, a habit.

Rejecting his religious upbringing in favor of the materialist worldview, Pavlov came to believe that science had to free itself from religious dogma concerning the soul. The soul had no place in science, he concluded, and the mind was simply the monitor and transmitter of signal-stimuli from the external world on the one hand, and the organism's responses on the other. Pavlov disliked any talk of "freedom of choice." To him, such talk was an offense against scientific rigor.

Although the Communists took control of Russia in 1917, Pavlov was able to continue his work unhindered in what became the State Institute of Experimental Psychology supported by government funding. Since Pavlov was both a Darwinist and a behaviorist, there was no ideological conflict between him and the new Marxist-Leninist government, which denied God and viewed man as nothing more than an animal whose behavior could be shaped by the state.

In 1920, Pavlov and his colleagues embarked on a long-term experimental investigation. The aim of the experiments was to learn how to artificially create human disorganization for the purpose of controlling and reorienting human behavior. In *The Nature of Human Conflicts* (1932), influential Soviet psychologist Dr. A.R. Luria gives us a full account of the experiments and what they revealed. "The chief problems of the author," Luria wrote in his preface, "were an objective and materialistic description of the mechanisms lying at the basis of the disorganization of human behavior and an experimental approach to the laws of its regulation."[2]

FROM THE FILM: "A state-controlled teachers college, can be 'an engine to sway the public sentiment, the public morals, and the public religion, more powerful than any other in the possession of government.'"

Why would these Soviet psychologists spend so much time and effort trying to find out how to deliberately drive people crazy? The answer is simple. The Soviet Union believed itself to be the leader in a world revolution to convert everyone to communism, which required the conquest of all its capitalist enemies. And this was to be done not by military invasion but by psychological warfare under the guise of objective science. Pavlov wrote in 1935:

> The power of our knowledge over the nervous system will, of course, appear to much greater advantage if we learn

not only to injure the nervous system but also to restore it at will. It will then have been proved that we have mastered the processes and are controlling them. . . . In many cases we are not only causing disease, but are eliminating it with great exactitude, one might say, to order.[3]

PAVLOV TO POWER

Luria described quite explicitly the key to creating behavioral disorganization. "Pavlov" he noted, "obtained very definite affective 'breaks,' an acute disorganization of behavior, each time that the conditioned reflexes collided, when the animal was unable to react to two mutually exclusive tendencies, or was incapable of adequately responding to any imperative problem."[4]

In short, the methodology Luria describes is exactly the way our schools teach children to read. The child is taught to look at printed text as a string of little pictures, whole configurations, memorized in

FROM THE FILM: "If teachers were being trained by the government, then they would do the government's will, which is what we have today in America."

sight-vocabulary exercises. As a result he develops a whole-word conditioned reflex. At the same time he is taught something about the letters standing for sounds, a phonetic way of looking at words, which is very difficult to do if you are looking at the words as little pictures. For many children it is simply impossible; they cannot react to two "mutually exclusive tendencies," and thus become reading disabled, or dyslexic. On the other hand, if the child is taught exclusively by the look-say method, he is unlikely to be able to master reading our alphabetic writing system and is very likely to become functionally illiterate.

To understand why this is so, we must have an appreciation for the unique advantages of the alphabetic system of reading and writing. This is how I summarized it for the *New American* in 1997:

Somewhere around 2000 B.C. someone made a remarkable discovery: All of human language is composed of a small number of irreducible speech sounds. And that person decided that instead of using a writing system composed of many thousands of symbols (which linguists call ideographs), none of which looked like the things they represented and took years to learn and were easily forgotten, it would be better to create a set of symbols to represent only the irreducible speech sounds of language. The result was the world's first alphabetic system, which greatly simplified writing and required memorizing a very small number of symbols that stood for sounds. . . .

In learning to read English by intensive, systematic phonics (as opposed to the phony "incidental" phonics which has been added as window dressing to some look-say and whole-language methods), the child first learns to recognize the 26 letters of the alphabet, and then learns the 44 sounds the letters stand for. . . .

This is the way reading in alphabetic languages was taught for thousands of years, and, indeed, this is the only sensible way of teaching it.

Pavlov's laboratory was used by the Soviet State to devise scientific methods of waging psychological warfare in a manner that would enlist behavioral scientists worldwide. Of course, if you were a dedicated Marxist, you considered this scientific activity to be to the ultimate benefit of mankind.

They also experimented on creating another form of behavioral disorganization, which today we recognize as Attention Deficit Disorder. Luria writes:

The experiment is done very easily: we violate the rules of our usual laboratory procedure for the study of the reactive processes; instead of isolating the subject from everything which might distract his attention, we do just the opposite — while performing the experiment we converse with him, give him a book to read, and at intervals interrupt him by the auditory signal requiring the motor response.

Such a functional exclusion of the higher cortical mechanisms from participation of the simple reaction evokes a return to the primitive, diffuse type of reactive processes and a sharp lowering of the "functional barrier."[5]

DYSFUNCTIONAL BY DESIGN

In other words, when a child is prevented from using his intellect where it is needed without distraction, he reverts to a more primitive behavior, which is a symptom of ADD.

Apparently, there were many behavioral psychologists at that time working on the same problems. In his book, Luria draws special attention to the work of Kurt Lewin in Germany. "K. Lewin, in our opinion, has been one of the most prominent psychologists to elucidate this question of the artificial production of affect and of the experimental disorganisation of behavior," Luria writes. "Here the fundamental conception of Lewin is very close to ours."[6]

Such a plaudit from one of Soviet communism's most important theorists of psychological warfare for a top American educator should be worthy of note, if not alarm.

Who is Kurt Lewin? He is the same Kurt Lewin who came to the United States in 1933, founded the Research Center for Group Dynamics at M.I.T., and invented "sensitivity training." He is frequently recognized in the professional literature as the "father of social psychology." Shortly before his death in 1947, Lewin founded the National Training Laboratory at Bethel, Maine, under the sponsorship of the National Education Association. There teachers were, and still are, instructed in the techniques of sensitivity training and how to become effective agents of change.

Lewin's emphasis on collectivist group behavior to replace individualistic behavior was very much in harmony with what socialist John Dewey, the "father of progressive education," had advocated for his new curriculum. Dewey's work at his Laboratory School at the University of Chicago was known by Lenin's wife, who got the Communist government to reform Russian schools according to the Dewey model.

Dewey was greeted with enthusiasm by Soviet officialdom when he visited Stalin's Russia in 1928; and he, in turn, was smitten by the

Bolshevik experiment and became one of its most prominent pro-
moters. In his 1929 book, *Impressions of Soviet Russia*, he rhapsodi-
cally refers to the Communist system as "nobly heroic, evincing a
faith in human nature which is democratic beyond the ambitions of
the democracies of the past."

"The Russian educational situation," Dewey averred, "is enough
to convert one to the idea that only in a society based upon the cooperative principle can the ideals of educational reformers be adequately carried into operation." Dewey acknowledged that Soviet
propaganda was omnipresent and heavy-handed, but that was okay,
since "in Russia the propaganda is in behalf of a burning public
faith." He was particularly appreciative of "the role of the schools in
building up forces and factors whose natural effect is to undermine
the importance and uniqueness of family life" in Soviet Russia.[7]

The Communists returned Dewey's fulsome praise. *The Great
Soviet Encyclopedia* described him as "an outstanding American philosopher, psychologist, sociologist, and pedagogue."[8] Much of his
pedagogical system was adopted by Stalin's regime.

However, the Dewey-Soviet experiment came to an abrupt halt in
August 1932 when the Central Committee of the Communist Party
abandoned the laboratory method and ordered a return to a structured curriculum. The communist leaders wanted the Soviet schools
to produce competent engineers, not semi-literate basket weavers.

DEWEY'S DISMAL SYSTEM

But in America, where capitalism and individualism still reigned,
the progressive educational leadership had no intention of going
back to the structured pro-capitalistic-individualistic curriculum.
And anyone who visits an American elementary school today will
see the continued implementation of the Dewey-Lewin concept of
education. And with that concept have come all of the problems we
now associate with the public schools.

Countless articles have appeared in the major media over the last
three decades critical of American education. The litany of problems
is always spelled out: poor academic performance, high dropout
rates, student violence, low teacher morale, etc. And the solutions
offered are always the same: more tax money for education, smaller
class size, higher teacher pay, new buildings, new curricula, and

more computers and high-tech paraphernalia. Nobody has bothered to read Luria's book.

But because most of the reporters are young and have no idea how education was conducted back in the days before the Progressives took over — when children actually learned to read and there were no school massacres — they are incapable of asking the right questions. We who went to school in those halcyon days and are still around to talk about them are generally ignored.

Those of us who were witnesses to the past and have spent our lives monitoring the decline of American education know what happened. It all started at the turn of the last century when the Progressives took control of the education system and gradually imposed their new collectivist philosophy on the curriculum.

The most destructive thing they did was reform the teaching of reading by throwing out the true and tried phonics method and imposing a whole-word method that would teach children to read our alphabetic English as if it were a pictographic language like Chinese, which would ultimately lead to the general decline of literacy in our country.

Why were these crucial changes made? They were made so that the Progressives could shape future generations of American children to become collectivists instead of individualists. The Progressives were socialists. They were members of the Protestant academic elite who no longer believed in the religion of their fathers. Their new religion was science, which explained the material world; evolution, which explained the origin of living matter; and psychology, which explained human behavior and offered scientific ways to control it. They believed that evil was caused by ignorance, poverty, and social injustice, and that a collectivist society could eliminate all of that.

The guiding light and chief philosopher behind the Progressive Education movement was John Dewey, whose seminal essay, "The Primary-Education Fetich," published in 1898, provided the blueprint for the new educational agenda. In that article he advocated shifting primary education away from concentrating on individual literacy to placing the emphasis on socialization through group activities. "The plea for the predominance of learning to read in early school life because of the great importance attaching to literature seems to me a perversion," he wrote.

And because his view would be considered so radical by parents and teachers, he wrote:

> Change must come gradually. To force it unduly would compromise its final success by favoring a violent reaction. What is needed in the first place is that there should be a full and frank statement of conviction with regard to the matter from physiologists and psychologists and from those school administrators who are conscious of the evils of the present regime.

In other words, deceiving parents would become an important and implicit part of the plan for radical reform. And psychologists, of whom Dewey was one, would play an important role in creating this elaborate deception. "There are already in existence a considerable number of educational 'experiment stations,' which represent the outposts of educational progress," Dewey wrote. "If these schools can be adequately supported for a number of years they will perform a great vicarious service."

FROM THE FILM: "The public schools themselves were a form of socialism. A state government education system is a socialist system. People do not realize that socialism was an ideology in this country as early as the 1820s."

Unfortunately for American education, the experimental schools to which Dewey referred were "adequately supported" by generous grants from the Carnegie and Rockefeller Foundations. Indeed, Dewey himself conducted such an experimental school at the University of Chicago, and the book he wrote about that experiment, *The School and Society*, became the bible of progressive education and the basis of 20th-century school reform.

And so, the major work of reform would not be done by educators, but by psychologists, who found in education a lucrative source of support for their profession. The new behavioral psychology was born in the laboratories of Professor Wilhelm Wundt at the

University of Leipzig. His two American students, G. Stanley Hall (1844–1924) and James McKeen Cattell (1860–1944), came back to America anxious to apply scientific psychology to American education. Hall became a professor of psychology at Johns Hopkins University, where he taught the new psychology to John Dewey. He later founded Clark University. Cattell introduced mental testing in education as part of the new scientific racism called "eugenics."

But it was John B. Watson, the most arrogant behaviorist of them all, who revealed the true contempt that he and his fellow behaviorists had toward their fellow human beings. In his book, *Behaviorism*, published in 1924, he wrote:

> Human beings do not want to class themselves with other animals. They are willing to admit that they are animals but "something else in addition." It is this "something else" that causes the trouble. In this "something else" is bound up everything that is classed as religion, the life hereafter, morals, love of children, parents, country, and the like. The raw fact that you, as a psychologist, if you are to remain scientific, must describe the behavior of man in no other terms than those you would use describing the behavior of the ox you slaughter, drove and still drives many timid souls away from behaviorism.[9]

In other words, behavioral psychology was not for the timid. "The interest of the behaviorist in man's doings," wrote Watson, "is more than the interest of the spectator — he wants to control man's reactions, as physical scientists want to control and manipulate other natural phenomena. It is the business of behavioristic psychology to be able to predict and control human activity."

And so one can see that what Pavlov and his assistants were doing in Moscow was not too different from what Watson and his ilk were teaching their students.

But even as Dewey had cautioned that change must come slowly, it didn't take long before an increasing number of discerning Americans began to realize what was happening. In fact, by 1955 the reading problem had become so bad that Rudolf Flesch was compelled to write his famous book, *Why Johnny Can't Read*. "The teaching of reading — all over the United States, in all the schools, in all the textbooks — is totally wrong," wrote Flesch, "and flies in the face of all logic and common sense."[10]

As for how the educators were able to perpetuate such "error" without effective reaction from conservative teachers, he explained:

> It's a foolproof system all right. Every grade-school teacher in the country has to go to a teachers' college or school of education; every teachers' college gives at least one course on how to teach reading; every course on how to teach reading is based on a textbook; every one of those textbooks is written by one of the high priests of the word method. In the old days it was impossible to keep a good teacher from following her own common sense and practical knowledge; today the phonetic system of teaching reading is kept out of our schools as effectively as if we had a dictatorship with an all-powerful Ministry of Education.

And if you think the situation has improved significantly since 1955, try getting a good intensive phonics program into your local school. As an author of a very effective intensive phonics reading program used successfully by thousands of home-schooling parents, I have tried to get the program adopted by local schools, only to be told thanks, but no thanks.

ABCs OF PSYCHO-CONTROL

There is indeed a Ministry of Education in America, and it is called the National Society for the Study of Education. It was founded in 1901 by John Dewey and colleagues who were interested in psycho-education and the application of science to educational issues. The society publishes an annual two-volume yearbook filled with discussions of educational interests.

FROM THE FILM: "[Robert Owen (1820s)] believed that the cause of all of our problems was religion and that children could be educated in such a way without religion to become anything you wanted."

The NSSE describes itself as "an organization of education scholars, professional educators, and policy makers dedicated to the improvement of education research, policy, and practice." On its board of directors is a former president of the NEA, Mary Hatwood Futrell. The membership list in the 1969 yearbook is 94 pages long, and you've probably never heard of the organization. The subject for their 2008 yearbook was "Why Do We Educate?" It's a question the educators seem to be totally confused about.

But some of them are not confused at all. One of them is Anthony G. Oettinger of Harvard University, professor of information resources policy and a member of the Council on Foreign Relations. He said the following at a conference of communications executives in 1982:

> The present "traditional" concept of literacy has to do with the ability to read and write. But the real question that confronts us today is: How do we help citizens function well in their society? How can they acquire the skills necessary to solve their problems?
>
> Do we, for example, really want to teach people to do a lot of sums or write in "a fine round hand" when they have a five-dollar hand-held calculator or a word processor to work with? Or, do we really have to have everybody literate — writing and reading in the traditional sense — when we have the means through our technology to achieve a new flowering of oral communication?
>
> What is speech recognition and speech synthesis all about if it does not lead to ways of reducing the burden on the individual of the imposed notions of literacy that were a product of nineteenth-century economics and technology? . . .
>
> It is the traditional idea that says certain forms of communication, such as comic books, are "bad." But in the modern context of functionalism they may not be all that bad.[11]

For Oettinger and his fellow elitists, the ideal society is one in which the vast majority of people are minimally educated to a subliterate comic-book level, a collectivized social order of unthinking docile workers who are dependent on an intellectual clerisy (Oettinger and company) for informational sustenance.

I doubt that there are any parents in America who send their children to school to learn to read comic books. If anything, they want their children to be taught to read and write in the traditional manner. They don't consider learning to read as a burden imposed on the individual. Rather, if taught properly, learning to read can be a joyful experience for children eager to explore the wonderful world of the written word.

And what's the solution for parents? If they want to get their children out of Professor Oettinger's clutches, they'll have to home-school them or enroll them in private or parochial schools where literacy is not a burden, but a liberating force for good.

As for the NSSE's question, "Why do we educate?" the answer is quite simple. We educate to pass on to the future generation the knowledge, wisdom, and values of the previous generation. It's a concept we find in Deuteronomy 6. But we can expect that the NSSE will come up with something enormously complicated that will guarantee the perpetuation of the present problems.

Endnotes

Taken from "Pavlov's Dogs and American Education" by Samuel Blumenfeld, *New American* (September 2008), used by permission, www.thenewamerican.com.

1. Ivan Petrovich Pavlov, *Twenty Years of Objective Study of the Higher Nervous Activity of Animals*; sixth edition (Moscow, USSR: State Biological and Medical Publishing House, 1938), p. 690.
2. Alexander Romanovich Luria, *The Nature of Human Conflicts* (New York: Grove Press, 1932), preface.
3. A.G. Ivanov-Smolensky, "Essays on the Patho-Physiology of the Higher Nervous Activity According to I. P. Pavlov and His School" (Moscow, USSR: Foreign Languages Publishing House, 1954), p. 201.
4. Luria, *The Nature of Human Conflicts* p. 12.
5. Ibid., 385.
6. Ibid., 207.
7. John Dewey, *Impressions of Soviet Russia and the Revolutionary World*, (New York: New Republic, 1929).
8. A. M. Prokhorov, editor, *Great Soviet Encyclopedia* (New York: Macmillan, 1973).
9. John B. Watson, *Behaviorism* (New York: W.W. Norton & Co., Inc., 1924).
10. Rudolf Flesch, *Why Johnny Can't Read* (New York: Harper, 1955).
11. *Innisbrook Papers*, February 1982, Proceedings of a meeting of the Northern Telecom Worldwide Corporation, at which Anthony Oettinger spoke.

"Do not remove the ancient landmark which your fathers have set."

— *Proverbs 22:28*

CHAPTER TWELVE

The History of History Textbooks
Geoffrey Botkin

"The Protestants began to compromise and they surrendered their children to a curriculum that was not neutral."

GEOFFREY BOTKIN

Geoffrey Botkin is an international traveler, political consultant, veteran film-maker, husband, and father. He currently serves as a senior consultant to the Western Conservatory of the Arts & Sciences — a public charity working to help Western nations understand and fulfill the responsibilities of family, church, and community reformation, both home and abroad. For the last five years, Mr. Botkin has been probing the connections between national culture, public justice, and personally held theological belief. He has lectured on philosophy and history at Hillsdale College, on political media at the Heritage Foundation, and on theology around the world. He and his wife, Victoria, have seven children who work with them to effect the recovery of functional family culture in the United States and beyond. The following article by Mr. Botkin was taken from the Western Conservatory of the Arts and Sciences.

WHY THE PUBLIC SCHOOL SYSTEM TEACHES REVISIONIST HISTORY

Anyone who attended public schools knows that history is a boring mass of confused, causeless, and meaningless names and dates. History has been made practically irrelevant. That generations of American minds have been laid waste by this idea is not accidental. At the end of the 19th century, a group of committed men determined that history must go. Here is why.

THE STORY OF AMERICAN HISTORY TEXTBOOKS
IN THE 20TH CENTURY

One of the most direct summaries of education in the 20th century was written by American educator Sam Blumenfeld:

> The plain truth is that there has been in this country a deliberate plan to change the nature of American education so that the American people could be easily led into socialism.[1]

While it is beyond the scope of this article to trace it completely, the story of the theft of American history starts at the beginning of the 20th century with a cabal of men that was small but whose objectives were clear and whose unity was strong. In two short decades, 1912–1932, the country was put on a dangerous course by social engineers who were immediately satisfied with the outcomes, especially the mind-slaughter. They were not out to make men better and smarter. They were out to create small men who would accept a new world with another, a modernized, messiah. Their ideas made the horrors of modern statism possible. Complicity of Christians made these ideas widely acceptable. What is important for students of history to know is that these educators had a clear central ambition. They wanted all men to take every thought captive to the demands of the welfare state.[2]

We pick up the story in 1900. Widespread compulsory government schooling had been in place for one generational cycle — kindergarten to kindergarten. John Dewey's Pedagogic Creed of 1897 had just been distributed to teachers, and it was among these that the energetic attackers of history found willing allies:

> Every teacher should realize he is a *social servant* set apart for the maintenance of the *proper* social order and the securing of the right social *growth*. In this way the teacher is always the prophet of the *true God* and the usherer in of the *true kingdom* of heaven [emphasis added].

Harold Rugg was part of Dewey's small circle of social engineers, headquartered at Columbia Teachers College. Rugg stands out as the most effective strategist for the new social order they intended to create through an education cartel. For his purposes, he required a large war chest — the equivalent of multi-millions — which he obtained from large family foundations like Rockefeller[3] and Carnegie. These foundations had become like a fourth branch of government in their power to create and steer American policy.[4]

In later years, the U.S. Congress took the initiative to find out how Rugg's self-appointed educators, backed by these foundations, were so effective at changing the opinions of Americans. U.S. Congressional Reece Committee researcher Norman Dodd discovered that the Carnegie Endowment formulated a policy the success of which would be "entirely in the changing of the teaching of the history of the United States." Dodd's report continues:

> [In 1909] they approached . . . five of the then most prominent historians in this country with the proposition that they alter the manner of the teaching of the subject, and they get turned down flatly; so they realized then they must build their own stable of historians, so to speak. . . .
>
> Ultimately, a group of twenty are so assembled, and that becomes the nuclei of the policies which emanate to the American Historical Association. Subsequently, around 1928, the Carnegie Endowment granted to the American Historical Association $400,000 in order to make a study of what the future of this country will probably turn out to be and should be. They came up with a seven-volume set of books, the last volume being a summary and digest of the other six. In the last volume, the answer is as follows:
>
> ". . . the future in the United States belongs to collectivism administered with characteristic American efficiency."
>
> And that becomes the policy which is finally picked up and manifests itself in the expression of collectivism all along the line, of which the dividing of this country into regions [is part] . . . in order that regional government, in turn, be effective, there must be a new Constitution of the United States.[5]

According to John Taylor Gatto, the records of these foundations reveal seven clear motivations, which line up perfectly with the Columbia Teachers College agenda:

1. There appears a clear intention to mold people through schooling.

2. There is a clear intention to eliminate tradition and scholarship.

3. The net effect of various projects is to create a strong class system verging on caste.

4. There is a clear intention to reduce mass critical intelligence while supporting infinite specialization.

5. There is clear intention to weaken parental influence.

6. There is clear intention to overthrow accepted [theological] custom.

7. There is striking congruency between the cumulative purposes of GEB projects and . . . perfectionism, a secular religion aimed at making the perfection of human nature, not salvation or happiness, the purpose of existence.

The agenda of philanthropy, which had so much to do with the schools [and social order] we got, turns out to contain an intensely political component.[6]

In 1919, Columbia worked with the Soviet government to arrange field trips for American teachers so they could see the glories of Soviet life firsthand and better envision the coming collapse of American capitalism. Lenin had said the goal of the proletariat was to establish heaven on earth, and students at Columbia believed he was succeeding.

FROM THE FILM: "In 1819, both in Prussia and in Boston, the very first compulsory, forced education classrooms opened, forcing the population to send their children there."

Tragically, instead of upholding the biblical theory of history, as more and more church leaders and members were exposed to the new educational curricula in the schools, churches felt the need to conform. That same year, the American Baptist Society published its own book, Samuel Z.

Batten's *The New World Order*, referring to the need for social control and a "world federation."

Edward L. Bernays, author of the book *Crystallizing Public Opinion*, concluded that by 1928 America's worldview was in complete control of the people who had positioned themselves to shape the minds of schoolchildren.

There is much more to this story than can be related in a lightning-fast overview, but Neal Frey, senior textbook analyst at Education Research Analysts, summed it up nicely in 2006: "No textbook used by the public school system has ever presented accurate American history."[7]

The bottom line is that historical revisionism is the hammer in the blueprint for societal transformation toward humanistic utopia. The early 20th century saw self-appointed educational "experts" using a centralized system of forced schooling to eliminate meaningful history as they built the framework for a new social order. They understood that the past must be eliminated in order to reshape society and the future on man's terms.

Historical revisionism has captured American education. But why is it wrong?

Historical Revisionism Is Rebellion Against God

History is the record of God's working in time to accomplish His purposes, in particular the exaltation of His Son as sovereign over all things (1 Cor. 15:24–25) and the creation of a people for Himself (Rom. 8:28–30). Therefore, to pervert history's meaning is to attempt to subvert God's design.

The legacy of modern statism is a move away from the inheritance of Christendom toward the scientific management of a secular society. The model demanded by Marx and his followers is a rebellious model: an anti-Christian elite rules over the minds, consciences, families, and property of all men. This requires maintaining a dictatorship over the past, present, and future of all men.

God's providence, which refers to His work in carrying out His plan for history, must be attacked in order to abstract God from reality and leave humanistic man "free" to operate on his own.

Rebellious men hate the past because it is full of providential meaning, and they hate the future because it is unpredictable and uncontrollable by man. Rebellious men also hate time because it is limited and reminds them of their appointment with death, and they hate eternity because they cannot control it or access it on their terms. But since time is inescapable and since what has happened shapes what is and what will be, rebellious men seek to make God and Christ remote from the present and future by abstracting them from the past.

Historical Revisionism Is Blasphemy

Webster's dictionary of 1828 defines blasphemy as "an injury offered to God, by denying that which is due and belonging to him, or attributing to him that which is not agreeable to his nature." As the Westminster Shorter Catechism states it, the third commandment requires "the holy and reverent use of God's names, titles, attributes, ordinances, Word, and works," and forbids "all profaning and abusing of any thing whereby God maketh himself known."[8]

Historical revision is a pre-eminent abuse of God's works, but as we have seen, it is totally necessary for God's enemies. The stories on which the revisionists must focus their greatest creativity are those in which God's providential grace is most evident.

Historical Revisionism Robs and Emasculates Man in Order to Place Him Under a New God

Rebellious men seek to make all men passive (emasculated) through ignorance of history. Men without purpose become passive, so the rebellious planners aim at making mankind forget that God said to them, "Be fruitful and multiply; fill the earth and subdue it; have dominion . . ." (Gen. 1:28). Psalm 78 confirms what happens to courage when men forget their history:

> The Ephraimites, armed with the bow, turned back on the day of battle. They did not keep God's covenant, but refused to walk according to his law. They forgot his works and the wonders that he had shown them (Ps. 78:9–11; ESV).

As he becomes passive and cowardly, this emasculated man places himself under the domination of a new god for protection and provision — the social planners and their scientific secular sovereign state.

This is why it has been so necessary for the modern statist governments to deny God's history and theology. If God's predestination is ruled out, man's predestination or total planning can then take its place. When God's enemies replace history with sociology, the purpose of history ceases to be understanding; it becomes an instrument of control.

CONCLUSION

Revision of American history is rampant. It is treasonous. And it is no accident. For four generations of Americans, the significance of the past has been eliminated in order to reshape society and the future on man's terms.

What should be a Christian's response? Do not bury your head in the sand. Recognize and face the fact that a battle is being waged.

Your children need to learn how to take original sources — not doctored textbooks — and to analyze them biblically through a grid of good theology and come to their own conclusions about them. Parents can train their children to do this.

Finally, do not despair. God has always had enemies who hate and conspire against Him. The battle has gone on since the Garden of Eden (Gen. 3:15). Psalm 2 gives us the necessary perspective:

> Why do the nations rage and the peoples plot in vain? The kings of the earth set themselves, and the rulers take counsel together, against the LORD and against his Anointed, saying, "Let us burst their bonds apart and cast away their cords from us." He who sits in the heavens laughs; the Lord holds them in derision (Psalm 2:1–4; ESV).

Endnotes

Taken from "Why the Public School System Teaches Revisionist History" by Geoffrey Botkin, *Western Conservatory of the Arts and Sciences* (January 2010), used by permission, www.westernconservatory.com.

1. Samuel Blumenfeld, "The Dumbing Down of America" in *Faith for All of Life*, Chalcedon Foundation (Nov/Dec 2005): p. 20.

2. The antithesis: "We destroy arguments and every lofty opinion raised against the knowledge of God, and take every thought captive to obey Christ" (2 Cor. 10:5, ESV).
3. Gatto comments: "The Rockefeller Foundation has been instrumental through the century just passed (along with a few others) in giving us the schools we have. It imported the German research model into college life, elevated service to business and government as the goal of higher education, not teaching. And Rockefeller-financed University of Chicago and Columbia Teachers College have been among the most energetic actors in the lower school tragedy." — John Taylor Gatto, *The Underground History of American Education* (New York: Oxford Village Press, 2001), p. xxxiv.
4. Gatto comments: "Edward Berman, in *Harvard Education Review*, 49 (1979), puts it more brusquely. Focusing on Rockefeller, Carnegie, and Ford philanthropies, he concludes that the 'public rhetoric of disinterested humanitarianism was little more than a façade' behind which the interests of the political state (not necessarily those of society) 'have been actively furthered.' The rise of foundations to key positions in educational policy formation amounted to what Clarence Karier called 'the development of a fourth branch of government, one that effectively represented the interests of American corporate wealth.' " — Ibid., p. 252.
5. Norman Dodd, *Transcript of Public Hearing — Joint Committee on Regional Government*, September 26, 1978, Edwardsville, Illinois, p. 51–61, republished at sweetliberty.org:http://www.sweetliberty.org/issues/regionalism/dodd.htm.
6. Gatto, *Underground History*, p. 251.
7. Interview with Geoffrey Botkin, February 2005.
8. *Westminster Shorter Catechism*, Question 54.

"*Do not be unequally yoked together with unbelievers. For what fellowship has righteousness with lawlessness? And what communion has light with darkness?*"

— *2 Corinthians 6:14*

CHAPTER THIRTEEN

What Has Athens to Do with Jerusalem?
The Deep Pagan Roots of Modern Educational Methods
Douglas W. Phillips

"G. Stanley Hall, a child development theorist, took Darwin's theory of evolution and applied it to the development of children."

DOUGLAS W. PHILLIPS

Douglas W. Phillips is the founder and director of Vision Forum Ministries, a discipleship and training outreach that emphasizes Christian apologetics, worldview training, multi-generational faithfulness, and creative solutions whereby fathers can play a maximum role in family discipleship. He is a passionate communicator with a heart for home education and the restoration of Christian family and culture to the glory of God. He and his wife, Beall, have eight children — Joshua, Justice, Liberty, Jubilee, Faith Evangeline, Honor, Providence, and Virginia Hope. They live in San Antonio, Texas. The following is comprised of excerpts from Mr. Phillips' article "Education Choices are Not Neutral," as well as his message "The History of the Sunday School Movement."

METHODOLOGY IS NOT NEUTRAL

For thousands of years, men have debated over educational methodology, or "pedagogy," which is defined as the art, science, or process of teaching. All of these debates have centered around questions such as: "What is the true nature of the child?"; "What are the true goals of education?"; "What is the role of the state vs. the parent in training the child?"; and "How are values, ideas, and information best taught to a child?" — just to name a few. The answers to these questions are at the heart of the greatest religious battles of all time.

These questions can only be answered in terms of religiously driven, faith assumptions about God, man, and the state.

From the ancient Greeks to the evolution-driven pedagogical theory of the 19th, 20th, and 21st centuries, religious beliefs have always driven educational models; it is inescapable. The modern government school classroom is a reflection of the religious priorities of men who are at war with the God of the Bible. The government school model is a self-conscious rejection of the biblical model, and an advancement of a humanistic, evolutionary, and statist view of the child. It was built on the philosophies of some of the most virulent God-haters in history, from Plato to Rousseau to Dewey.

Ultimately, there are only two pedagogical models — that which was known to Abraham, Moses, and Solomon, and everything else. The former model can be described as the biblical, or Hebraic, approach to discipleship. This model sees God's Word as pre-eminently authoritative, and it recognizes and utilizes the unique and completely singular nature of the parent-child bond in the education of children from one generation to the next. "Everything else" might be described as the Greek model of education. This model comes in many shapes and sizes, and it too recognizes the strength of the parent-child bond, but it sees this bond as dangerous to the advancement of society. At the end of the day, it grants to the state a jurisdiction reserved to the family as it seeks to diminish the parents' influence on the beliefs of their own children. As an invention of man, this model is based on wrong views of the goal of education and the very nature of the child.

The Rise of Hellenism

The Greeks followed the doctrine of the gymnasium, which would later become a model of training in Europe and even in American school systems. The gymnasium was the antithesis of the Hebrew discipleship training program.

Gymnasium comes from the Greek word *gymnos*, which means "the place to be naked." In this model of education, Greek boys were taken away from their parents and families, brought into schools, and stripped naked. In this system, young boys would come together with their grown male teachers in a state of nudity to practice athletics, philosophy, and warfare.

The Greeks worshiped youth. In fact, the first Olympics which took place in Olympia in 776 B.C., and the Olympic games that followed it in Greece until A.D. 393, were performed in the nude because of their culture's worship of the body. And yet this perverse act of training young boys in the nude is looked back on by many of today's theologians and philosophers as one of the glory moments in all of history.

In Plato's *Republic*, the Greek philosopher explained that the goal of training was to capture the hearts and minds of children from a young age:

> They will begin by sending out into the country all the inhabitants of the city who are more than ten years old and will take possession of their children, who will be unaffected by the habits of their parents. These they will train in their own habits and laws.

To give a full history of Greece would be well beyond the scope of this article. However, to grasp the pervasive influence that Greek thinking has had on pedagogy, it is critical that we understand the background of the founding of the Academy[1] and the implementation of its methods as they have been passed down since.

FROM THE FILM: "If it's true that there is this evolutionary process that transcends every aspect of life, why not view training that way? And thus developed age-segregated, peer-based, grade-based education."

From the fall of Troy in 1200 B.C. through the rule of Alexander the Great around 330 B.C., the worldview of Greece gained increasing influence on Western culture. The fourth century B.C. was the high-water mark of Greek philosophy, spearheaded by the famous triumvirate: Socrates, Plato, and Aristotle, who founded the Academy and refined the Greek methodology of training. Their philosophies would spread throughout the West with the rise of Alexander the Great — a personal disciple of Aristotle — whose stated vision was not just to conquer new lands, but to transmit Greek culture to the territories he subjugated. The Jews were placed under Greek rule in 333 B.C., the Persian Empire fell in 331 B.C., and at his death in 323, Alexander's empire dominated the Middle East, Egypt, and the Eastern Mediterranean.

Even as Alexander's empire was broken apart, Greek culture and philosophy continued to advance, as the Romans adopted the Greek language and embraced Greek culture — what's known as Hellenism — incorporating it into their own efforts of territorial conquest.

The rise of Hellenism has had a profound influence in shaping the educational philosophy of the West, giving us models and standards regarding pedagogy — standards of child training and discipleship that are still pervasive to this very day.

In speaking of the influence of Greek thinking on the West, R.J. Rushdoony noted:

> It is in philosophy, however, that the Hellenic mind exercised its greatest influence on the West. The Greek perspective can be summed up in the expression "Man is the measure." The Biblical answer would be, "God is the measure." These two polar opinions form the antithesis of Western culture, two positions ever at war with one another. Many other influences are present in Western culture, but they are mediated through one or another framework, notably the Hellenic. Even Christianity has been extensively influenced by Hellenic thought, so that much of church history is more Hellenic than Biblical.[2]

This dilemma has been a problem for more than 2,000 years. The modern Church today is still wrestling with the fallout, with millions of Christians embracing Hellenism — exchanging our spiritual heritage for a mess of Hellenistic, Greco-Roman pottage.

What Has Athens to Do with Jerusalem?

The Greek model of training is an age-segregated educational model that takes children from their parents at an early age to be trained alongside their peers. The goal is to minimize parents' influence and train children to embrace the values of the state. The Hebrew model, in direct contrast, places the responsibility of child training on fathers and mothers, calling on them to direct their children's upbringing in a walk-along, talk-along discipleship model that is relationship-driven. In Deuteronomy 6, we read the following:

> Hear, O Israel: The LORD our God is one LORD: And thou shalt love the LORD thy God with all thine heart, and with all thy soul, and with all thy might. And these words, which I command thee this day, shall be in thine heart: and thou shalt teach them diligently unto thy children, and shalt talk of them when thou sittest in thine house, and when thou walkest by the way, and when thou liest down, and when thou risest up (Deut. 6:4–7; KJV).

During Rome's occupation of Palestine, the Jews became increasingly Hellenized. Many forsook the Hebraic model of training and placed their children in Hellenistic schools. Some Christians today appeal to this fact as a defense for placing their children in government schools. They argue that if the Jews at the time of Christ's first coming borrowed from the Hellenism of their day, isn't that proof that it's "biblical"?

Please consider this reasoning carefully. The fact that the Jews embraced Hellenism during "Bible Times" doesn't mean they acted rightly. Their decision to embrace a Hellenistic educational methodology finds no warrant whatsoever in Scripture. The move came as the Jews integrated with Roman practices that came — not from Scripture — but from the pagan philosophy of the Greeks. In adopting a Hellenistic approach to child training, the Jews rejected the Hebrew model that God commanded in the Old Testament.

This compromise contributed to a generational disconnect that existed between parents and children during Christ's earthly ministry, a disconnect that was anticipated by Malachi's prophecy in the last two verses of the Old Testament:

> Behold, I will send you Elijah the prophet before the coming of the great and dreadful day of the LORD: and he shall turn the heart of the fathers to the children, and the heart of the children to their fathers, lest I come and smite the earth with a curse (Mal. 4:5–6; KJV).

Malachi prophesied that John the Baptist would come in the spirit of Elijah, and that he would turn the hearts of fathers to their sons.

Why did the hearts of fathers need to be turned? Because there was a massive generational crisis at the time of the coming of John the Baptist and the Messiah. It was a broken-down father-to-son family relationship crisis, and God sent John the Baptist to lead a revival that would mend this heart disconnect between fathers and sons.

Something was terribly wrong with this generation. And the choice that fathers made to place their children in Greek schools directly contributed to the crisis. It is therefore foolish to elevate this generation's error in embracing a Hellenistic educational model as a good thing when God sent a revival to rescue them from its disastrous results.

Yet less than two centuries later, Christians forgot this lesson, as the redeemed people of God began putting their children in Greco-Roman schools. This led noted church leader Tertullian to pose a famous and important question around the year A.D. 200: "What indeed has Athens to do with Jerusalem? What concord is there between the [Greek] Academy and the Church?"

With compromise on educational choices still lingering, this is a question we should be asking ourselves today.

PEDAGOGY EVOLVES

In considering the origins of our modern concepts of child training, we must also discuss important late-19th-century trends, as evolutionary theory captured academia, and grade-based, age-segregated training programs were resurrected, resulting in the transformation of the classroom.

FROM THE FILM: "Hall was the first president of the American Psychological Association and brought Sigmund Freud to the United States, who was of course a radical evolutionary psychiatrist who stated that religious belief was a neurotic obsession."

Perhaps you have heard of "phylogeny recapitulates ontogeny" or "embryonic recapitulation theory" ideas advanced by Ernst Haeckel. It is important to note that Ernst Haeckel was a bigot of remarkable proportions. As an ardent evolutionist, Haeckel said that white Europeans had no relationship with black men, even going so far as to compare them to gorillas — all based upon his belief in Charles Darwin's theory of evolution (significantly, the full title of Darwin's famous book is: *On the Origin of Species by Means of Natural Selection, or the Preservation of Favoured Races in the Struggle for Life*).

Ernst Haeckel essentially said this: Let's take the model of evolution and look at it in the microcosm of the womb of a mother, embracing the idea that evolution and the development of species is a paradigm for all of life. Even as we evolve from one stage to another — from australopithecine to ramapithecine to Cro-Magnon to Neanderthal to Homo sapiens sapiens; from amphibious creatures to land-based creatures to mammalians — we should look at all things in this same light, including the development of children. And so in a woman's womb, according to Haeckel, there is a recapitulation of the entire evolutionary process, with each embryo starting in the early stages of evolution from a non-human, developing to the form of an aquatic creature, and then somewhere down the line — probably in the third trimester — humanity emerges.

Haeckel created a memorable picture that was in biology textbooks until the 1970s. In his chart, he visualized his viewpoint, making the case that we can look at the fish, the turtle, as well as other animals and humans, and see that they each go through aquatic to gill stages, etc. — they all recapitulate evolution.

But here's the problem: the picture is a fraud; he doctored it. Haeckel put things on his chart that were preposterous fabrications. Yet for more than a hundred years, people viewed his chart as accurate, though now it is rejected. In fact, Stephen J. Gould, a committed evolutionist who was no friend of Christianity, wrote an important book on phylogeny and ontogeny in which he shows that Haeckel's theory is patently false.

This said, in the early 1900s, psychologist and child development theorist G. Stanley Hall posited that if Darwin and Haeckel's assumptions were true, then shouldn't their theories apply to the way we view child development and training? In other words: we don't want Cro Magnons to be with Neanderthals; we want to break children up along their different evolutionary stages and rigidly create an age-segregated program that allows us to educate them within the context of their biological development. It was based on neither merit nor maturity. Its context was taken completely outside of the family and classified children as to how they fit into a scientific model.[3]

John Dewey, a member of the American Humanist Society and a signer of the Humanist Manifesto, also embraced this idea and was a key leader in the modern progressive education movement of the 20th century, advocating age-segregated, family-fragmenting education based on Darwin and Haeckel's bankrupt theories.

Conclusion

As Christians, we must ask ourselves this: What is our standard for determining how to train our children? If all we had was a Bible on a desert island, would we naturally conclude that you should fragment children along age groups and put them in grade-based classrooms with family-fragmenting approaches to discipleship? Would that be the pattern you derive from the Scripture? Would you see foundation for it there? Would there be any pattern or refuge in God's Word that would lead you to mimic this approach?

When God gives us a revelation and we see through our study of Scripture that we're not on target, it's time to take action.

I thank God for a generation that said: "Get your kids out of government schools." I thank God for a generation that said: "Let's start discipling them ourselves."

And I thank God for a generation that has declared: "Let's reform our ways concerning education. Let's learn the lessons of history and answer Tertullian's question the right way: 'What indeed has Athens to do with Jerusalem?' "

Endnotes

Taken from "Education Choices Are Not Neutral," and transcript of "The History of the Sunday School Movement," both by Doug Phillips (September 2011 and October 2006), respectively, used by permission from Vision Forum Ministries, 4719 Blanco Rd., San Antonio, TX 78212, www.visionforumministries.org.

1. Plato's Academy, forerunner to the gymnasium, was founded ca. 387 B.C. and is thought to be the first Hellenic school.
2. Rousas John Rushdoony, *A Christian Survey of World History* (Vallecito, CA: Chalcedon/ Ross House Books, 1974, 2008), 2008 edition, p. 39.
3. For more about G. Stanley Hall's influence on modern schooling methods, see "The Invention of Adolescence" by Christian historian and journalist Otto Scott, reprinted in its entirety in Appendix B.

"*The kings of the earth set themselves, and the rulers take counsel together, against the LORD and against His Anointed, saying, 'Let us break Their bonds in pieces and cast away Their cords from us.'* "

— *Psalm 2:2–3*

CHAPTER FOURTEEN

The Co-Opting of Big Education by Big Business

John Taylor Gatto

"Back in colonial days in America if you proposed an idea like that they'd burn you at the stake, you mad person."

JOHN TAYLOR GATTO

John Taylor Gatto was born near Pittsburgh, Pennsylvania, and attended public and private boarding schools throughout his youth. He did undergraduate work at Cornell, University of Pittsburgh, and Columbia, and graduate work at Cornell, Yeshiva, Hunter College, and the University of California. After college, Mr. Gatto held a variety of jobs before becoming a schoolteacher for 30 years, a career he climaxed as New York State Teacher of the Year. In 1992, he was named Secretary of Education in the Libertarian Party Shadow Cabinet, and in 1997, he was given the Alexis de Tocqueville Award for his contributions to the cause of liberty. His books include *Dumbing Us Down: The Hidden Curriculum of Compulsory Schooling* (1992), *The Exhausted School* (1993), *A Different Kind of Teacher* (2000), and *Weapons of Mass Instruction* (2010). The following excerpts are taken from Mr. Gatto's book *The Underground History of American Education*.

An Angry Look at Modern Schooling

Today's corporate sponsors want to see their money used in ways to line up with business objectives. . . . This is a young generation of corporate sponsors and they have discovered the advantages of building long-term relationships with educational institutions.[1]

A Change in the Governing Mind

Sometimes the best hiding place is right in the open. It took seven years of reading and reflection for me to finally figure out that mass schooling of the young by force was a creation of the four great coal powers of the 19th century. It was under my nose, of course, but for years I avoided seeing what was there because no one else seemed to notice. Forced schooling arose from the logic that fossil fuel in conjunction with high-speed machinery imposes on flesh and blood.

This simple reality is hidden from view by early philosophical and theological anticipations of mass schooling in various writings about social order and human nature. But you shouldn't be fooled any more than Charles Francis Adams was fooled when he observed in 1880 that what was being cooked up for kids unlucky enough to be snared by the newly proposed institutional school net combined characteristics of the cotton mill and the railroad with those of a state prison.

After the Civil War, utopian speculative analysis regarding isolation of children in custodial compounds where they could be subjected to deliberate molding routines began to be discussed seriously by the northeastern policy elites of business, government, and university life. These discussions were inspired by a growing realization that the productive potential of machinery driven by coal was limitless. Railroad development made possible by coal, startling new inventions like the telegraph, seemed suddenly to make village life and local dreams irrelevant. A new governing mind was emerging in harmony with the new reality.

The principal motivation for this revolution in family and community life seems on the surface to be greed, but appearance concealed philosophical visions approaching religious exaltation in intensity — that effective early indoctrination of children would lead to an orderly scientific society, one controlled by the best people, now freed from the obsolete strait-jacket of democratic traditions and historic American libertarian attitudes.

Forced schooling was the medicine to bring the whole continental population into conformity with these plans so it might be regarded as a "human resource" and managed as a "workforce." No more Ben Franklins or Tom Edisons could be allowed; they set a bad example. One way to manage this transformation was to see to it that individuals were prevented from taking up their working lives until an advanced age when the ardor of youth and its insufferable self-confidence had cooled.

EXTENDING CHILDHOOD

From the beginning, there was purpose behind forced schooling, purpose which had nothing to do with what parents, kids, or communities wanted; but instead was forged out of what a highly centralized corporate economy and system of finance bent on internationalizing itself was thought to need; that, and what a strong, centralized political state needed, too. School was looked upon from the first decade of the 20th century as a branch of industry and a tool of governance. For a considerable time, probably provoked by a climate of official anger and contempt directed against immigrants in the greatest displacement of people known to history, social managers of schooling were remarkably candid about what they were doing. This candor can be heard clearly in a speech Woodrow Wilson made to businessmen before the First World War:

FROM THE FILM: "Confining people in rooms and monitoring every minute of their lives in those rooms couldn't possibly fit into any definition of education that's come from any corner of the world."

> We want one class to have a liberal education. We want another class, a very much larger class of necessity, to forgo the privilege of a liberal education and fit themselves to perform specific difficult manual tasks.[2]

By 1917, the major administrative jobs in American schooling were under control of a group referred to in the press of that day as "the Education Trust." The first meeting of this trust included representatives of Rockefeller, Carnegie, Harvard, Stanford, the University of Chicago, and the National Education Association. The chief end, wrote Benjamin Kidd, the British evolutionist, in 1918, was to "impose on the young the ideal of subordination."[3]

At first, the primary target was the tradition of independent livelihoods in America. Unless Yankee entrepreneurialism could be put to death, at least among the common population, the immense capital investments that mass production industry required for equipment weren't conceivably justifiable. Students were to learn to think of themselves as *employees* competing for the favor of management. Not as Franklin or Edison had once regarded themselves, as self-determined, free agents.

Only by a massive psychological campaign could the menace of *overproduction* in America be contained. That's what important men and academics called it. The ability of Americans to think as independent producers had to be curtailed. Certain writings of Alexander Inglis carry a hint of schooling's role in this ultimately successful project to curb the tendency of little people to compete with big companies. Overproduc-

tion became a controlling metaphor among the managerial classes from 1880 to 1930, and this affected the development of mass schooling profoundly.

I know how difficult it is for most of us who mow our lawns and walk our dogs to comprehend that long-range social engineering even exists, let alone that it began to

FROM THE FILM: "I don't teach the kids that education is bad. I teach them that schooling is bad. We spent a long time studying the great people who had never gone to school, and the great Americans who had never gone to school."

dominate compulsion schooling nearly a century ago. Yet the 1934 edition of Ellwood P. Cubberley's *Public Education in the United States* is explicit about what happened and why. As Cubberley puts it:

> It has come to be desirable that children should not engage in productive labor. On the contrary, all recent thinking . . . [is] opposed to their doing so. Both the interests of organized labor and the interests of the nation have set against child labor. . . .[4]

The statement occurs in a section of *Public Education* called "A New Lengthening of the Period of Dependence," in which Cubberley explains that "the coming of the factory system" has made extended childhood necessary by depriving children of the training and education that farm and village life once gave. With the breakdown of home and village industries, the passing of chores, and the extinction of the apprenticeship system by large-scale production with its extreme division of labor (and all the "all-conquering march of machinery"), an army of workers has arisen, said Cubberley, who know nothing.

Furthermore, modern industry needs such workers. Sentimentality could not be allowed to stand in the way of progress. According to Cubberley, with "much ridicule from the public press," the old book-subject curriculum was set aside, replaced by a change in purpose and "a new psychology of instruction which came to us from abroad." That last mysterious reference to a new psychology is to practices of dumbed-down schooling common to England, Germany, and France, the three major world coal-powers (other than the United States), each of which had already converted its common population into an industrial proletariat long before.

Arthur Calhoun's 1919 *Social History of the Family* notified the nation's academics of what was happening. Calhoun declared that the fondest wish of utopian writers was coming true, the child was passing from its family "into the custody of community experts." He offered a significant forecast, that in time we could expect to see public education "designed to check the mating of the unfit."[5] Three years later, Mayor John F. Hylan of New York said in a public speech that the schools had been seized as an octopus would seize prey, by an "invisible government." He was referring specifically to certain actions of the Rockefeller Foundation and other corporate interests in New York City that preceded the school riots of 1917.

The 1920s were a book period for forced schooling as well as for the stock market. In 1928, a well-regarded volume called *A Sociological Philosophy of Education* claimed, "It is the business of teachers to run not merely schools but the world."[6] A year later, the famous creator of educational psychology, Edward Thorndike of Columbia Teachers College, announced, "Academic subjects are of little value." His colleague at Teachers College, William Kirkpatrick, boasted in *Education and the Social Crisis* that the whole tradition of rearing the young was being made over by experts.

THE GENETICISTS' MANIFESTO

Meanwhile, at the project offices of an important employer of experts, the Rockefeller Foundation, friends were hearing from president

Max Mason that a comprehensive national program was underway to allow, in Mason's words, "the control of human behavior." This dazzling ambition was announced on April 11, 1933. Schooling figured prominently in the design.

Rockefeller had been inspired by the work of Eastern European scientist Hermann Müller to invest heavily in genetics. Müller had used x-rays to override genetic law, including mutations in fruit flies. This seemed to open the door to the scientific control of life itself. Müller preached that planned breeding would bring mankind to paradise faster than God. His proposal received enthusiastic endorsement from the greatest scientists of the day as well as from powerful economic interests.

Müller would win the Nobel Prize, reduce his proposal to a 1,500-word *Geneticists' Manifesto*, and watch with satisfaction as 22 distinguished American and British biologists of the day signed it. The state must prepare to consciously guide human sexual selection, said Müller. School would have to separate worthwhile breeders from those slated for termination. Just a few months before this report, an executive director of the National Education Association announced that his organization expected "to accomplish by education what dictators in Europe are seeking to do by compulsion and force." You can't get much clearer than that.

WWII drove the project underground but hardly retarded its momentum. Following cessation of global hostilities, school became a major domestic battleground for the scientific rationalization of social affairs through compulsory indoctrination. Great private corporate foundations led the way.

PARTICIPATORY DEMOCRACY PUT TO THE SWORD

Thirty-odd years later, between 1967 and 1974, teacher training in the United States was covertly revamped through coordinated efforts of a small number of private foundations, select universities, global corporations, think tanks, and government agencies, all coordinated through the U.S. Office of Education and through key state education departments like those in California, Texas, Michigan, Pennsylvania, and New York. Important milestones of the transformation were: 1) an extensive government exercise in futurology called *Designing Education for the Future*, 2) the *Behavioral Science Teacher Education Project*, and 3) Benjamin Bloom's multi-volume *Taxonomy of Educational Objectives,* an enormous manual of over 1,000 pages that, in time, impacted every school in America. While other documents exist, these three are appropriate touchstones of the whole, serving to make clear the nature of the project underway.

Take them one by one and savor each: *Designing Education,* produced by the Education Department, redefined the term "education" after the Prussian fashion as "a means to achieve important economic and social goals of a national character." State education agencies would henceforth act as on-site federal enforcers, ensuring the compliance of local schools with central directives. Each state education department was assigned the task of becoming "an agent of change" and advised to "lose its independent identity as well as its authority," in order to "form a partnership with the federal government."

The second document, the gigantic *Behavioral Science Teacher Education Project,* outlined teaching reforms to be forced on the country after 1967.[7] The document sets out clearly the intentions of its creators — nothing less than "impersonal manipulation" through schooling of a future America in which "few will be able to maintain control over their opinions," an America in which "each individual receives at birth a multi-purpose identification number" that enables employers and other controllers to keep track of underlings and to expose them to direct or subliminal influence when necessary. Readers learned that "chemical experimentation" on minors would be normal procedure in this post-1967 world, a pointed foreshadowing of the massive Ritalin interventions that accompany the practice of forced schooling at present.

The *Behavioral Science Teacher Education Project* identified the future as one "in which a small elite" will control all important matters, one where participatory democracy will largely disappear. Children are made to see, through school experiences, that their classmates are so cruel and irresponsible, so inadequate to the task of self-discipline, and so ignorant, that they need to be controlled and regulated for society's good. Under such a logical regime, school terror can only be regarded as good advertising. It is sobering to think of mass schooling as a vast demonstration project of human inadequacy, but that is at least one of its functions.

Postmodern schooling, we are told, is to focus on "pleasure cultivation" and on "other attitudes and skills compatible with a nonwork world." Thus, the socialization classroom of the century's beginning — itself a radical departure from schooling for mental and character development — can be seen to have evolved by 1967 into a full-scale laboratory for psychological experimentation.

School conversion was assisted powerfully by a curious phenomenon of the middle to late 1960s, a tremendous rise in school violence and general school chaos that followed a policy declaration (which seems to have occurred nationwide) that the disciplining of children must henceforth mimic the "due process" practice of the court system. Teachers and administrators were suddenly stripped of any effective ability to keep order in schools since the due process apparatus, of necessity a slow, deliberate matter, is completely inadequate to the continual outbreaks of childish mischief all schools experience.

Now, without the time-honored *ad hoc* armory of disciplinary tactics to fall back on, disorder spiraled out of control, passing from the realm of annoyance into more dangerous terrain entirely as word surged through student bodies that teacher hands were tied. And each outrageous event that reached the attention of the local press served as an advertisement for expert prescriptions. Who had ever seen kids behave this way? Time to surrender community involvement to the management of experts; time also for emergency measures like special education and Ritalin. During this entire period, lasting five to seven years, outside agencies like the Ford Foundation exercised the right to supervise whether "children's rights" were being given due attention, fanning the flames hotter even long after trouble had become virtually unmanageable.

The *Behavioral Science Teacher Education Project*, occurring at the peak of this violence, informed teacher-training colleges that under such circumstances, teachers had to be trained as therapists; they must translate prescriptions of social psychology into "practical action" in the classroom. As curriculum had been redefined, so teaching followed suit.

Third of the new gospel texts was Bloom's *Taxonomy*,[8] in his own words, "a tool to classify the ways individuals are to act, think, or feel as the result of some unit of instruction." Using methods of behavioral psychology, children would learn proper thoughts, feelings, and actions, and have their improper attitudes brought from home "remediated."

In all stages of the school experiment, testing was essential to localize the child's mental state on an official rating scale. Bloom's epic spawned important descendant forms: Mastery Learning, Outcomes-Based Education, and School to Work government-business collaborations. Each classified individuals for the convenience of social managers and businesses, each offered data useful in controlling the mind and movements of the young, mapping the next adult

FROM THE FILM: "You're stealing these kids and confining them for 12 years, and the kids have to be put in a rigid class system where the classes are encouraged not to cooperate with one another."

generation. But for what purpose? Why was this being done?

BAD CHARACTER AS A MANAGEMENT TOOL

A large piece of the answer can be found by reading between the lines of an article appearing in the June 1998 issue of *Foreign Affairs*. Written by Mortimer Zuckerman, owner of *U.S. News and World Report* (and other major publications), the essay praises the American economy, characterizing its lead over Europe and Asia as so structurally grounded no nation can possibly catch up for 100 years. American workers and the American managerial system are unique.

You are intrigued, I hope. So was I. Unless you believe in master race biology, our advantage can only have come from training of the American young, in school and out, training that produces attitudes and behavior useful to management. What might these crucial determinants of business success be?

First, says Zuckerman, the American worker is a pushover. That's my translation, not his, but I think it's a fair take on what he means when he says the American is indifferent to everything but a paycheck. He doesn't try to tell the boss his job. By contrast, Europe suffers from a strong "steam age" craft tradition where workers demand a large voice in decision making. Asia is even worse off, because although the worker is silenced there, tradition and government interfere with what business can do.

Next, says Zuckerman, workers in America live in constant panic; they know companies here owe them nothing as fellow human beings. Fear is our secret supercharger; it gives management flexibility no other country has. In 1996, after five years of record profitability, almost half of all Americans in big business feared being laid off. This fear keeps a brake on wages.

Next, in the United States, human beings don't make decisions, abstract formulae do; management by mathematical rules makes the company manager-proof as well as worker-proof.

Finally, our endless consumption completes the charmed circle, consumption driven by nonstop addiction to novelty, a habit that provides American business with the only reliable domestic market in the world. Elsewhere, in hard times business dries up, but not here; here we shop till we drop, mortgaging the future in bad times as well as good.

Can't you feel in your bones Zuckerman is right? I have little doubt the fantastic wealth of American big business is psychologically and procedurally grounded in our form of schooling. The training field for these grotesque human qualities is the classroom. Schools train individuals to respond as a mass. Boys and girls are drilled in being bored, frightened, envious, emotionally needy, generally incomplete. A successful mass production economy requires such a clientele. A small business, small farm economy like that of the Amish requires individual competence, thoughtfulness, compassion, and universal participation; our own requires a managed mass of leveled, spiritless, anxious, familyless, friendless, godless, and obedient people who believe the difference between *Cheers* and *Seinfeld* is a subject worth arguing about. The extreme wealth of American big business is the direct result of school training us in certain attitudes like a craving for novelty. That's what the bells are for. They don't ring so much as to say, "Now for something different."

AN ENCLOSURE MOVEMENT FOR CHILDREN

The secret of American schooling is that it doesn't teach the way children learn, and it isn't supposed to. School was engineered to serve a concealed command economy and an increasingly layered social order; it wasn't made for the benefit of kids and families, as those people would define their own needs. School is the first impression children get of organized society. Like most first impressions it is the lasting one. Life is *dull and stupid*, only Coke provides relief. And other products, too, of course.

The decisive dynamics that make forced schooling poisonous to healthy human development aren't hard to spot. Work in classrooms isn't significant work; it fails to satisfy real needs pressing on the individual; it doesn't answer real questions experience raises in the young mind; it doesn't contribute to solving any problem encountered in actual life. The net effect of making all schoolwork external to individual longings, experiences, questions, and problems is to render the victim listless. This phenomenon has been well understood at least since the time of the British enclosure movement that forced small farmers off their land into factory work. Growth and mastery come only to those who vigorously self-direct. Initiating, creating, doing, reflecting, freely associating, enjoying privacy — these are precisely what the structures of schooling are set up to prevent, on one pretext or another.

As I watched it happen, it took about three years to break most kids, three years confined to environments of emotional neediness with nothing real to do. In such environments, songs, smiles, bright colors, cooperative games, and other tension breakers do the work better than angry words and punishment could. Years ago it struck me as more than a little odd that the Prussian government was the patron of Heinrich Pestalozzi, inventor of multi-cultural fun-and-games psychological elementary schooling, and of Friedrich Froebel, inventor of kindergarten. It struck me as odd that J.P. Morgan's partner was instrumental in bringing Prussian schooling to the prostrate South after the Civil War. But after a while I began to see that behind the philanthropy lurked a rational economic purpose.

The strongest meshes of the school net are invisible. Constant bidding for a stranger's attention creates a chemistry producing the common characteristics of modern schoolchildren: whining, dishonesty, malice, treachery, cruelty. Unceasing competition for official favor in the dramatic fish bowl of a classroom delivers cowardly children, little people sunk in chronic boredom, little people with no apparent purpose for being alive. The full significance of the classroom as a dramatic environment, as *primarily* a dramatic environment, has never been properly acknowledged or examined.

The most destructive dynamic is identical to that which causes caged rats to develop eccentric or even violent mannerisms when they press a bar for sustenance on an aperiodic reinforcement schedule (one where food is delivered at random, but the rat doesn't suspect). Much of the weird behavior school kids display is a function of the aperiodic reinforcement schedule. And the endless confinement and inactivity slowly drives children out of their minds. Trapped children, like trapped rats, need close management. Any rat psychologist will tell you that.

THE DANGAN

In the first decades of the 20th century, a small group of soon-to-be-famous academics, symbolically led by John Dewey and Edward Thorndike of Columbia Teachers College, Ellwood P. Cubberley of Stanford, G. Stanley Hall, and an ambitious handful of others, energized and financed by major corporate and financial allies like Morgan, Astor, Whitney, Carnegie, and Rockefeller, decided to bend government schooling to the service of business and the political state — as it had been done a century before in Prussia.

Cubberley delicately voiced what was happening this way: "The nature of the national need must determine the character of the education provided."[9] National need, of course, depends upon point of view. The NEA in 1930 sharpened our understanding by specifying in a resolution of its Department of Superintendence that

FROM THE FILM: "Is there an idea more radical in the history of the human race than turning your children over to total strangers who you know nothing about and having those strangers work on your child's mind?"

what school served was an "effective use of capital" through which our "unprecedented wealth-producing power has been gained." Pronouncements like this mark the degree to which the organs of schooling had been transplanted into the corporate body of the new economy when you look beyond the rhetoric of Left and Right.

It's important to keep in mind that no harm was meant by any designers or managers of this great project. It was only the law of nature as they perceived it, working progressively as capitalism itself did for the ultimate good of all. The real force behind school effort came from true believers of many persuasions, linked together mainly by their belief that family and church were retrograde institutions standing in the way of progress. Far beyond the myriad practical details and economic considerations there existed a kind of grail-quest, an idea capable of catching the imagination of dreamers and firing the blood of zealots.

The entire academic community here and abroad had been Darwinized and Galtonized by this time, and to this contingent school seemed an instrument for managing evolutionary destiny. In Thorndike's memorable words, conditions for controlled selective breeding had to be set up before the new American industrial proletariat "took things into their own hands." America was a frustrating petri dish in which to cultivate a managerial revolution, however, because of its historic freedom traditions. But thanks to the patronage of important men and institutions, a group of academics were enabled to visit mainland China to launch a modernization project known as the "New Thought Tide." Dewey himself lived in China for two years where pedagogical theories were inculcated in the Young Turk elements, then tested on a bewildered population that had recently been stripped of its ancient form of governance. A similar process was embedded in the new Russian state during the 1920s.

While American public opinion was unaware of this undertaking, some big-city school superintendents were wise to the fact that they were part of a global experiment. Listen to H.B. Wilson, superintendent of the Topeka schools:

> The introduction of the American school into the Orient has broken up forty centuries of conservatism. It has given us a new China, a new Japan, and is working marked progress in Turkey and the Philippines. The schools . . . are in a position to determine the lines of progress.[10]

Thoughts like this don't spring full-blown from the heads of men like Dr. Wilson of Topeka. They have to be planted there.

The Western-inspired and Western-financed Chinese revolution, following hard on the heels of the last desperate attempt by China to prevent the British government market in narcotic drugs there, placed that ancient province in a favorable state of anarchy for laboratory tests of mind-alteration technology. Out of this period rose a Chinese universal tracking procedure called "The Dangan," a continuous lifelong personnel file exposing every student's intimate life history from birth through school and onward. The Dangan constituted the ultimate overthrow of privacy. Today, nobody works in China without a Dangan.

By the mid-1960s preliminary work on an American Dangan was underway as information reservoirs attached to the school institution began to store personal information. A new class of expert like Ralph Tyler of the Carnegie endowments quietly began to urge collection of personal data from students and its unification in computer code to enhance cross-referencing. Surreptitious data gathering was justified by Tyler as "the moral right of institutions."

Occasional Letter Number One

Between 1896 and 1920, a small group of industrialists and financiers, together with their private charitable foundations, subsidized university chairs, university researchers, and school administrators, spent more money on forced schooling than the government itself did. Carnegie and Rockefeller, as late as 1915, were spending more themselves. In this laissez-faire fashion, a system of modern schooling was constructed without public participation. The motives for this are undoubtedly mixed, but it will be useful for you to hear a few excerpts from the first mission statement of Rockefeller's General Education Board as they occur in a document called *Occasional Letter Number One* (1906):

> In our dreams . . . people yield themselves with perfect docility to our molding hands. The present educational conventions [intellectual and character education] fade from our minds, and unhampered by tradition we work our own good will upon a grateful and responsive folk. We shall not try to make these people or any of their children into philosophers or men of learning or men of science. We have not to raise up from among them authors, educators, poets, or men of letters. We shall not search for embryo great artists, painters, musicians, nor lawyers, doctors, preachers, politicians, statesmen, of whom we have ample supply. The task we set before ourselves is very simple . . . we will organize children . . . and teach them to do in a perfect way the things their fathers and mothers are doing in an imperfect way. . . .

This mission statement will reward multiple re-readings.

Change Agents Infiltrate

By 1971, the U.S. Office of Education was deeply committed to accessing private lives and thoughts of children. In that year it granted contracts for seven volumes of "change-agent" studies to the RAND Corporation. Change-agent training was launched with federal funding under the Education Professions Development Act. In time, the fascinating volume *Change Agents Guide to Innovation in Education* appeared, following which grants were awarded to teacher training programs for the development of change agents. Six more RAND manuals were subsequently distributed, enlarging the scope of change agentry.

In 1973, Catherine Barrett, president of the National Education Association, said, "Dramatic changes in the way we raise our children are indicated, particularly in terms of schooling. . . . We will be agents of change." By 1989, a senior director of the Mid-Continent Regional Educational Laboratory told the 50 governors of American states assembled to discuss government schooling that year, "What we're into is total restructuring of society." It doesn't get much plainer than that. There is no record of a single governor objecting.

Two years later Gerald Bracey, a leading professional promoter of government schooling, wrote in his Annual Report to clients: "We must continue to produce an uneducated social class." Overproduction was the bogey of industrialists in 1900; a century later underproduction made possible by dumbed-down schooling had still to keep that disease in check.

Bionomics

The crude power and resources to make 20th-century forced schooling happen as it did came from corporations, powerful families, university people derived from sons of the declining Protestant ministry, and the federal government. All this is easy enough to trace once you know it's there. But the soul of the thing was far more complex, an amalgam of ancient religious doctrine, utopian philosophy, and European/Asiatic strong-state politics mixed together and distilled. The great facade behind which this was happening was a new enlightenment: scientific scholarship in league with German research values brought to America in the last half of the 19th century. Modern German tradition always assigned universities the primary task of directly serving industry and the political state, but that was a radical contradiction of American tradition to serve the individual and the family.

Indiana University provides a sharp insight into the kind of science-fictional consciousness developing outside the mostly irrelevant debate conducted in the press about schooling, a debate proceeding on early 19th-century lines. By 1900, a special discipline existed at Indiana for elite students, bionomics. Invitees were hand-picked by college president David Starr Jordan, who created and taught the course. It dealt with the why and how of producing a new evolutionary ruling class, although that characterization, suggesting as it does kings, dukes, and princes, is somewhat misleading. In the new scientific era dawning, the ruling class were those managers trained in the goals and procedures of new systems. Jordan did so well at bionomics he was soon invited into the major leagues of university existence (an invitation extended personally by rail tycoon Leland Stanford) to become first president of Stanford University, a school inspired by Andrew Carnegie's famous "Gospel of Wealth" essay. Jordan remained president of Stanford for 30 years.

Bionomics acquired its direct link with forced schooling in a fortuitous fashion. When he left Indiana, Jordan eventually reached back to get his star bionomics protégé, Ellwood P. Cubberley, to become dean of teacher education at Stanford. In this heady position, young Cubberley made himself a reigning aristocrat of the new institution. He wrote a history of American schooling that became the standard of the school business for the next 50 years; he assembled a national syndicate which controlled administrative posts from coast to coast. Cubberley was the man to see, the kingmaker in American school life until its pattern was set in stone.

Did the abstract and rather arcane discipline of bionomics have any effect on real life? Well, consider this: the first formal legislation making forced sterilization a legal act on planet earth was passed, not in Germany or Japan, but in the American state of Indiana, a law which became official in the famous 1927 Supreme Court test case *Buck vs. Bell*. Justice Oliver Wendell Holmes wrote the majority opinion allowing 17-year-old Carrie Buck to be sterilized against her will to prevent her "degenerate offspring," in Holmes's words, from being born. Twenty years after the momentous decision, in the trial of German doctors at Nuremberg, Nazi physicians testified that their precedents were American — aimed at combating racial degeneracy. The German name for forced sterilization was "the Indiana Procedure."

To say this bionomical spirit infected public schooling is only to say birds fly.[11] Once you know it's there, the principle jumps out at you from behind every school bush. It suffused public discourse in many areas where it had claimed superior insight. Walter Lippmann, in 1922, demanded "severe restrictions on public debate," in light of the allegedly enormous number of feeble-minded Americans. The old ideal of participatory democracy was insane, according to Lippmann.

The theme of scientifically controlled breeding interacted in a complex way with the old Prussian ideal of a logical society run by experts loyal to the state. It also echoed the idea of British state religion and political society that God Himself had appointed the social classes. What gradually began to emerge from this was a Darwinian caste-based American version of institutional schooling remote-controlled at long distance, administered through a growing army of hired hands, layered into intricate pedagogical hierarchies on the old Roman principle of divide and conquer. Meanwhile, in the larger world, assisted mightily by intense concentration of ownership in the new electronic media, developments moved swiftly also.

In 1928, Edward Bernays, godfather of the new craft of spin control we call "public relations," told the readers of his book *Crystallizing Public Opinion* that "invisible power" was now in control of every aspect of American life. Democracy, said Bernays, was only a front for skillful wire-pulling. The necessary know-how to pull these crucial wires was available for sale to businessmen and policy people. Public imagination was controlled by shaping the minds of schoolchildren.[12]

By 1944, a repudiation of Jefferson's idea that mankind had natural rights was resonating in every corner of academic life. Any professor who expected free money from foundations, corporations, or government agencies had to play the scientific management string on his lute. In 1961, the concept of the political state as the sovereign principle surfaced dramatically in John F. Kennedy's famous inaugural address in which his national audience was lectured, "Ask not what your country can do for you, but what you can do for your country."

Thirty-five years later, Kennedy's lofty Romanized rhetoric and metaphor was replaced by the tough-talking wise guy idiom of *Time*, now instructing its readers in a 1996 cover story that "Democracy is in the worst interest of national goals." As *Time* reporters put it, "The modern world is too complex to allow the man or woman in the street to interfere in its management." Democracy was deemed a system for losers.

To a public desensitized to its rights and possibilities, frozen out of the national debate, to a public whose fate was in the hands of experts, the secret was in the open for those who could read entrails: the original American ideals had been repudiated by their guardians. School was best seen from this new perspective as the critical terminal on a production line to create a utopia resembling EPCOT Center, but with one important bionomical limitation: it wasn't intended for everyone, at least not for very long, this utopia.

Out of Johns Hopkins in 1996 came this chilling news:

> The American economy has grown massively since the mid-1960s, but workers' real spendable wages are no higher than they were 30 years ago.[13]

That from a book called *Fat and Mean*, about the significance of corporate downsizing. During the boom economy of the 1980s and 1990s, purchasing power rose for 20 percent of the population and actually declined 13 percent for the other four-fifths. Indeed, after inflation was factored in, purchasing power of a working couple in 1995 was only 8 percent greater than for a single working man in 1905; this steep decline in common prosperity over 90 years forced both parents from home and deposited kids in the management systems of daycare, extended schooling, and commercial entertainment. Despite the century-long harangue that schooling was the cure for unevenly spread wealth, exactly the reverse occurred — wealth was 250 percent more concentrated at century's end than at its beginning.

I don't mean to be inflammatory, but it's as if government schooling made people dumber, not brighter; made families weaker, not stronger; ruined formal religion with its hard-sell exclusion of God; set the class structure in stone by dividing children into classes and setting them against one another; and has been midwife to an alarming concentration of wealth and power in the hands of a fraction of the national community.

WAKING UP ANGRY

Throughout most of my long school career, I woke up angry in the morning, went through the school day angry, went to sleep angry at night. Anger was the fuel that drove me to spend 30 years trying to master this destructive institution.

Endnotes

Taken from *The Underground History of American Education: An Intimate Investigation into the Problems of Modern Schooling* by John Taylor Gatto (New York: Oxford Village Press, 2001), used by permission, www.johntaylorgatto.com.

1. Suzanne Cornforth of Paschall & Associates, public relations consultants, as quoted in *The New York Times,* July 15, 1998.
2. www.goodreads.com/quotes/show/35754.
3. Benjamin Kidd, *The Science of Power* (New York: G.P. Putnam's Sons, 1918).
4. Ellwood P. Cubberley, *Public Education in the United States* (Boston and New York: Houghton Mifflin, 1934). This is the same Ellwood P. Cubberley who wrote in his Columbia Teachers College Dissertation of 1905 that schools were to be factories "in which raw products, children, are to be shaped and formed into finished products . . . manufactured like nails, and the specifications for manufacturing will come from government and industry."
5. Arthur W. Calhoun, *A Social History of the American Family from Colonial Times to the Present* (New York: Cornell University Library, 2009).
6. Ross L. Finney, *A Sociological Philosophy of Education* (New York: The Macmillan Co., 1928).
7. This document bears the U.S. Office of Education Contract Number OEC-0-9-320424-4042 (B10).
8. A fuller discussion of Bloom and the other documents mentioned here, plus much more, is available in the writings of Beverly Eakman, a Department of Justice employee, particularly her book, *The Cloning of the American Mind* (Lafayette, LA: Huntington House, 1998).
9. Ellwood Patterson Cubberley, *Public Education in the United States,* (Cambridge: The Riverside Press, 1919), p. 355.
10. Harry B. Wilson, *The Motivation of School Work* (Boston and New York: Houghton Mifflin Co., 1916).
11. The following questions were put to schoolchildren in the South Dearborn School District in Aurora, Indiana, in 1994, with which they were asked to Strongly Agree/Agree/Disagree/Strongly Disagree: "I approve the practice of sterilizing the feeble-minded living in state institutions," and "I think it is unacceptable to society to use medical procedures to keep genetically defective humans alive so they can marry and reproduce."
12. Edward Bernays, *Crystallizing Public Opinion* (New York: Boni and Liveright, 1923).
13. David M. Gordon, *Fat and Mean* (New York: Martin Kessler Books, 1996).

"And you will cry out in that day because of your king whom you have chosen for yourselves, and the Lord will not hear you in that day."

— *1 Samuel 8:18*

CHAPTER FIFTEEN

When a Nation Forgets God:
Authoritarianism and Government Schools

Erwin Lutzer

"The child is at home being taught certain absolutes and values, but he goes to school and learns that mom and dad are wrong, there are no absolutes."

ERWIN LUTZER

Dr. Erwin W. Lutzer (B.Th, Winnipeg Bible College; ThM, Dallas Theological Seminary; MA, Loyola University) has been senior pastor of Chicago's Moody Church since 1980. Prior to taking that position, he served as the pastor of Edgewater Baptist Church in Chicago and later became an assistant professor of Bible and theology at the Moody Bible Institute. Dr. Lutzer has authored numerous award-winning books, including *One Minute After You Die*; *Is God on America's Side?*; *Seven Reasons Why You Can Trust The Bible*; *The DaVinci Deception*; *When You've Been Wronged*; *Christ Among Other Gods*; *The Serpent of Paradise*; and *Hitler's Cross*. He is the featured speaker on three radio programs: *The Moody Church Hour*, the popular programs *Songs in the Night* and *Running to Win*. He and his wife, Rebecca, have three married children and seven grandchildren. The following is taken from Dr. Lutzer's book *When a Nation Forgets God*.

PARENTS—NOT THE STATE—ARE RESPONSIBLE FOR A CHILD'S TRAINING

In January 2008, Germany's youth welfare office and police officials surrounded the Gorber family's Uberlingen home in a surprise raid. Mr. Gorber was visiting his wife at a local hospital where she had been admitted because of pregnancy complications with their ninth child. Despite the children's repeated protests, all but the oldest son, age 21, and the daughter, age 20, were taken into custody by authorities. Their crime? They refused to send their children to the local public school but instead chose to homeschool their children.[1]

Andre and Frauke R., a Christian family in Hanburg, suffered a similar fate. They chose to educate their children at home on the grounds that they wanted to be obedient to the Lord and keep their children from the influences of the public school system. In response, state officials promised to "apply the full power of the state until this family yielded to compulsory education laws."[2] Their ordeal began with a "coercion" fine of 850 euros (approx. $1,000). Next, five officers arrested Andre; next, the officers showed up to forcibly escort the children to school. Finally, the family lost custody of the children and they became wards of the state. The family eventually fled to Austria in an RV to join other homeschoolers who have fled Germany so that they could homeschool their children. Although there are some families who are homeschooling in Germany, they do so at their own peril, knowing that they too could at any time have a knock on the door and suffer arrest.[3]

Unfortunately, the German media portrays homeschoolers as "extreme fundamentalists," or as belonging to a cult. No matter that children who are homeschooled usually do better than those in the official educational system in all tests. Compulsory public education is mandated not just in Germany but in some other countries of the European Union.

My purpose is not to trumpet homeschooling as though it is the only option for concerned parents; there are some public schools in America where learning does take place and the wishes of the parents are honored. And, of course, there are private schools that might be an alternative. My point, however, lies in a slightly different direction: the fact is that laws making education in public schools compulsory have historically been found in the most totalitarian of governments where state-sponsored indoctrination was a major goal of the educational system. Although it is still legal to homeschool children in America, we can't assume that freedom will continue.

The Shadow of Hitler

Today's law in Germany that makes homeschooling illegal reminds us of a Nazi-era law instigated by Hitler back in 1938. He declared that public education was compulsory and that children could not be educated at home. The state, not the family or church, had first dibs regarding the child's education. He understood the value of educating a child:

The Youth of today is ever the people of tomorrow. For this reason we have set before ourselves the task of inoculating our youth with the spirit of this community of the people at a very early age, at an age when human beings are still unperverted and therefore unspoiled. This Reich stands, and it is building itself up for the future, upon its youth. And this new Reich will give its youth to no one, but will itself take youth and give to youth its own education and its own upbringing.[4]

If Germany was going to be the country Hitler envisioned it to be, the children would have to belong to the Reich. To parents, Hitler calmly said, "Your child belongs to us already . . . what are you? You will pass on. Your descendants, however, now stand in the new camp. In a short time they will know nothing else but this new community."[5]

FROM THE FILM: "This is not a case of every child making up his own mind. The goal of values clarification has been achieved; the outcome has already been determined by the curriculum."

Hitler believed quite rightly that he who controls the youth controls the future. Parents, he insisted, needed to understand the limits of their responsibility; and if they cooperated, all would be well, if not, the law was on Hitler's side! In effect, what Hitler said was that the parents had the responsibility of raising the child's *body*, but the Reich would educate the child's *soul*.

Private or denominational schools were later closed in Germany due to increased taxes and excessive regulation. Hitler knew that institutions he disliked could be shut down by multiplying laws and by requiring permits for any number of code requirements and procedural regulations. In the end, educational options for parents were squeezed out.

State-Sponsored Indoctrination

The children in Germany were subjected to films that presented the Nazis' view that the Jews were subhuman and that they were an unnecessary burden on society. Darwin's evolutionary notions were also presented in the classroom to extol the virtues of the Aryan race (the Germans) and that the evolutionary idea of survival of the fittest could be hurried along by the extermination of the weak. Since only the fittest survive, it makes good sense that "might makes right." Hitler asked, "Why can't we be as cruel as nature?"

With private schools abolished by 1938, all education was unified under the Nazi ideology. Textbooks were rewritten to reflect the view of racial fitness, the rationale for military expansion, and an emphasis on German history and culture. Those who did not fall in line with the Nazi agenda were reprimanded, expelled, or executed. If teachers wanted to keep their jobs, they had to take an oath of loyalty to Hitler.

Even by 1937, 97 percent of the teachers belonged to the National Socialist Teachers' Union. Each teacher had to use the official courses and textbooks prescribed by the Reich. One teacher's manual taught that German children have an inborn aversion to Jews and that intermarriage with Jews is unnatural because it does not follow the natural biological order. Even Jesus was used to promote the Nazi agenda: In some textbooks He was portrayed as a hero who waged war against the Jews until He was betrayed by them and killed.

FROM THE FILM: "[Values clarification in the schools] undercuts parents, it undercuts church, and most assuredly, it undercuts the absolutes of the Bible."

To my knowledge, the most important source of information regarding Hitler's view of education is found in the book *Nazism: A History in Documents and Eyewitness Accounts* by Jeremy Noakes and Geoffrey Pridham. They present 30 pages of documents detailing how

Nazism attempted to capture the heart of the youth. Hitler could not have been clearer:

> German youth must no longer . . . be confronted with the choice of whether they wish to grow up in a spirit of materialism or idealism, of racism or internationalism, of religious or godlessness, but *they must be consciously shaped according to principles which are recognized as correct . . . according to the principles of the ideology of National Socialism* [italics added].[6]

The purpose of school was not independent thought, but rather to transform the attitude and values of children to conform to what the state wanted. The child, like putty in one's hand, was to be shaped into a true German citizen, meaning, of course, a citizen that surrendered himself/herself to the larger goals of the state.

Hitler's educational philosophy was patterned after that of the Soviet revolutionaries. His goal was to build an army of young radicals who would pay lip service to the past but forge a new path that would ensure that German ideals were passed on from generation to generation. Censorship was practiced:

> The teaching . . . aimed to encourage a "consciousness of being German." . . . In the selection of teaching materials teachers should eschew those works which "contradict German feelings or paralyze energies necessary for self-assertion" and only those modern works would be selected which "have an affinity with the spirit of the new Germany."[7]

Truth was now defined as that which promoted the Nazi state; the goals of a revived Germany were to take precedence over individual thought and research. For example, "Munich professors [were warned]: 'From now on it is not up to you to decide whether or not something is true, but whether it is in the interest of the National Socialist Revolution.'"[8] Truth was whatever the Nazis preferred it to be.

Not Facts but Attitudes

Whether history or sociology, Hitler demanded a shift take place in the educational philosophy of the schools, a shift that would no longer be concerned about whether a matter was true or false, but whether it was useful to achieve the ends of the Reich. The values children had derived from their parents needed to be replaced by the new values taught in the classroom. Children had to be indoctrinated and understand that groupthink was more important than the individual. Through psychological pressure, any student who did not agree with the educational agenda stood out as an embarrassment. This, of course, ensured compliance with the unified philosophy of national socialism, which had freed itself from all absolutes and serious religious considerations.

The educational system became more focused on setting *affective*, not *cognitive* goals (outcomes): "The more enthusiastic they get, the easier are the exams and the sooner they will get a position, a job. . . . The new generation has never had much use for education and reading. Now nothing is demanded of them; on the contrary, knowledge is publicly condemned,"[9] wrote Noakes and Pridham. Young people were instructed to encourage their parents to become good Nazis.

In Germany there was an emphasis on teaching right attitudes using the cult of "experience." Unlike knowledge that involves the intellect, experiences that involved feeling provided "access to the deep truths of Nazism which were essentially based on [ideological unity]. Such an 'experience, . . . was regarded as essential to character-building."[10] What the child ate was the parents' responsibility; what he believed and felt was the responsibility of the Reich.

In Germany, as in America today, authority figures would have to be discredited through the experience of what we call "values clarification." Many teachers exploited the child's natural desire to be independent from parents and from the Church. "It appealed to the desire of youth to be independent of the adult world and exploited the conflict of generations and the typical tendency for young people to challenge authority figures, whether parents or teachers."[11] Parents who tried to contradict what their children were being taught were punished.

Of course, students' values had to be confused before they could be "clarified." Even in math classes, the ideology of the Reich was promoted. Children were asked questions such as these: "If the construction of a lunatic asylum costs 6 million Reichsmarks, how many houses at 15,000 Reichsmarks each could have been built for that amount?"[12] The goal, of course, was to get students to shed their natural inclination to sympathize with the needs of lunatics (read anyone who didn't agree with the Reich) and to see such issues through pragmatic, economic eyes.

Hitler understood that young people are very conscious of what their peers believe — how they dress and talk:

> The slogan "youth must be led by youth" . . . was ritually echoed and to some extent followed in practice. But the spirit in which it was applied was very different. These young leaders were not representing an autonomous youth culture but were functionaries of an official bureaucracy regimented by rules and regulations and following set patterns of training.[13]

Even as they were being indoctrinated, young people were given the "freedom" to form their own clubs and peer groups, just as long as they promoted rebellion against parents and church, and as long as they advanced the larger, grander cause of national socialism. Group peer pressure was used to silence, if not change, the mind of any student who still believed in the values of home and church.

Teachers were expected to develop an optimistic atmosphere of victory, of confidence, and of the certainty of Germany's success. "All other values were subsumed under this rubric. Through arts, crafts, and multicultural experiences the children were indoctrinated."[14] The point, of course, was to condition students to compliance. "It was preferred that people should not have a will of their own and should totally subordinate themselves,"[15] write Pridham and Noakes.

All of us know there is no such thing as a completely unbiased historian. Even choosing a curriculum — deciding what should be included and what should be left out — in all such decisions human bias is brought into the educational process. What makes Nazi Germany unique is the way in which facts were deliberately distorted to promote an agenda. Lies were taught: lies about Jews, lies about Germany's history, and lies about Hitler's intentions.

Hitler knew, as all of us do, that feelings can be more powerful than reason. And, unless feelings are changed, the mind will revert to its former patterns of thought. Centuries ago in the garden of Eden, Satan in effect said to Eve, "Feel, don't think!" Thinking can change feelings; but *feelings can also change thinking*. The point, of course, is that a person should not pay attention to facts but give credence to how he or she feels.

There was a great deal of emphasis on the relevance of courses to Germany's present historical and sociological situation:

> The course of history must not appear to our young people as a chronicle which strings events together indiscriminately, but, as in a play, only the important events, those which have a major impact on life, should be portrayed.[16]

Thus, a false world was created by carefully selecting the curriculum and eliminating anything that did not promote the politically correct ideology. This philosophy was carried over into all disciplines. The only criterion for curriculum was whether the students understood the Reich's worldview. "New courses were introduced in such fields as racial studies, eugenics, and defense studies and there was a new emphasis on pre-history. . . . Law and political science courses were adapted to fit in with the changes introduced by the regime."[17]

Education was life-related, experience-centered, and adopted with group pressure. You either conformed as a teacher or student or faced the consequences.

American Values Clarified

Unfortunately, our schools are all too often indoctrination chambers where children come to be scrubbed of their trust of parents, their church, and their sexual identity, and are force-fed a diet of secularism and immorality. Many years ago, Dr. Chester Pierce of Harvard University, addressing 2,000 teachers in Denver, made a chilling assessment of the teachers' responsibility. Of course, his extreme comments are not shared by all teachers — indeed there are some public schools that are still committed to education and not indoctrination — but it is indicative of a trend in our schools that cannot be ignored.

> Every child in America who enters school at the age of five is mentally ill, because he comes to school with allegiance toward our elected officials, toward our founding fathers, toward our institutions, toward the preservation of this form of government. . . . Patriotism, nationalism, sovereignty, all that proves that children are sick because the truly well individual is one who has rejected all of those things and is what I would call the true international child of the future.[18]

How are these changes brought about?

Values clarification was invented by Dr. Sidney Simon in order to change the beliefs, convictions, and moral values of a child. It is based on the notion that there are no absolutes — no right or wrong. Such transformation is to come into the life of a child by affirming the following: (1) personal values should be left up to each student, not dictated by parents or the Church,

FROM THE FILM: "Hitler was very clear: the soul, he says, belongs to the Riech, it belongs to the German empire. And in Nazi schools, there was indoctrination. "

and (2) questions are to be used that solicit open-ended answers to teach the child that there are no absolutes. Examples of such questions include: Would you favor a law that would limit the size of families to two children? Do you think parents should teach their children to masturbate? Do you think sex education should include techniques for lovemaking, and contraception? Would you like to have different parents? How often do you have sex?[19]

The child's values are as good as anyone else's and no one can tell him any different.

Now that the child has been stripped of his previous values, three more steps follow: (3) the teacher is to tell the child that he must make up his own mind as to what values he will accept (at this point the child is subject to psychological manipulation), and then (4) the child must publicly declare his "conversion" to the new values systems. He is told he must stand before his peers and tell them what his new values are. Then (5) the child is to regularly act on these values. In the end, the child firmly believes that no one — neither his parents nor his church nor the Bible — has the right to tell him what is right and what is wrong. Because all values are preferences, they are not subject to argument or to be judged by any other authority. The child's values are as good as anyone else's and no one can tell him any different.[20]

The students are then force-fed the idea that if they still have conflicts in their mind, they must realize it is possible to hold two points of view, no matter how contradictory they may appear. With this accomplished, the child is now defenseless against an onslaught of humanistic beliefs: evolution; socialism; the normalcy of homosexuality, abortion, euthanasia, etc. Then the student is told that consensus on these issues is reached through group discussion. The child does not know that the values that will be adopted by the group are predetermined by the curriculum. This is a field-tested methodology that has been used successfully in Communist countries; now it operates in many of our nation's classrooms.[21]

THE SEXUALIZATION OF CHILDREN

On May 22, 2009, a headline read, "Gay Curriculum Riles Elementary School Parents." It reports that parents say they are being bullied by school administrators into accepting a new curriculum that includes compulsory lessons about the lesbian, gay, bisexual, and transgender community that will be taught to children as young as five years old.

These parents, in the district of Alameda, a suburb of San Francisco, also say that they will not be allowed to keep their children out of such classes. Attorneys for the school board agree that if the curriculum is adopted, the parents will have no legal right to remove their children from the classes. Obviously, the First Amendment rights of parents are ignored; and even though most parents oppose the plan — their opinions have no effect.[22]

Why this desire to sexualize children? Tammy Bruce, who is a past president of the Los Angeles Chapter of the National Organization for Women, was a firsthand witness of attempts by "progressive" political groups to undermine our millennia-old code of morals and values. Now she exposes the liberal social agenda and says that these groups have the intention of reordering society as we know it. They are intent on *bending society to mirror their warped view of the world*.

I shall quote one of her passages at length. It deserves a careful read:

> The radicals in control of the gay establishment want children in their world of moral decay, lack of self-restraint, and moral relativism. Why? How better to truly belong to the majority (when you're really on the fringe) than by taking possession of the next generation? By targeting children, you can start indoctrinating the next generation with the

false construct that gay people deserve special treatment and special laws. How else can the gay establishment actually get society to believe, borrowing from George Orwell, that gay people are indeed more equal than others? Of course, the only way to get that idea accepted is to condition people into nihilism that forbids morality and judgment.[23]

Tammy Bruce believes the reason these ideas are widely accepted is that "sexualizing children," as she calls it, guarantees control of the culture for future generations. She writes, "It also promises sex-addicted future customers on which the porn industry relies. By destroying those lives, they strike the final blow to family, faith, tradition, decency, and judgment."[24]

Yes, it is to the advantage of the radical left to have a sex-addicted culture! Parents often have no idea that these techniques are being used on their children. They do not know that sex education classes are often little more than "how to" classes — how to have sex without guilt and without a baby. They do not realize that teachers in North Carolina, for example, were told what values they should instill in their children. The seven-point list:

- There is no right or wrong, only conditioned responses.

- The collective good is more important than the individual.

- Consensus is more important than principle.

- Flexibility is more important than accomplishment.

- Nothing is permanent, except change.

- All ethics are situational; there are no moral absolutes.

- There are no perpetrators, only victims.[25]

Again, I must emphasize that all public schools do not subscribe to these agendas, but parents must investigate what their children are being taught. If not, our children are mentally confiscated by an intentional humanistic point of view.

Politically Correct Textbooks

Last week, before writing this chapter, I watched a special on television dedicated to the $10 billion-dollar textbook industry here in America. I was not surprised but deeply grieved at what I learned. Some of the textbooks in American history do not mention the Pilgrims in order that all groups might have "equal opportunity." America is presented in a negative light as an oppressive, capitalistic country, without an equally critical assessment of other countries and cultures. One history textbook mentions the terrorist attacks of 9/11, but nowhere does it indicate that the terrorists were Muslims. Thanks to Muslim committee members, Islam was presented as a historical fact, but Christianity and Judaism were couched in the language of doubt along these lines, "It is said that Moses received the ten commandments; and it was believed that Jesus was the Messiah," etc.

And yes, I should mention that the language police were at work — yes, they do exist! The TV special reported that the word *snowman* is replaced by *snow person* in one textbook. No pictures were allowed of a woman in the kitchen for that too is a kind of stereotype that must be avoided.[26]

In college your child can expect that history just might be taught as a weapon to be used to promote certain agendas. Many in the politically correct (PC) movement believe that the purpose of history is to redress past wrongs. American history is deemed as racist, sexist, and classist and therefore must be considered primarily as the history of oppression. The crimes of Europeans are emphasized. The positive contributions of European society (some think there are none) must be swept aside.

FROM THE FILM: "So what you are really doing is having them affirm together those values that they have now accepted. And what are the values? Relativism, humanism."

When the University of Pennsylvania announced mandatory "racism seminars" for the students, one student expressed her concerns by saying that she had

"A deep regard for the individual and my desire to protect the freedoms of all members of society." A university administrator sent her a note back with the word "individual" circled and the comment, "This is a RED FLAG phrase today, which is considered by many to be RACIST. Arguments that champion the individual over the group ultimately privilege "individuals" who belong to the largest or dominant group."[27]

"In PC land, the middle ground disappears," educator Les Parrot explains. "Either you are pro-gay rights or you are homophobic. Either you are fighting for feminist causes or you are a chauvinist."[28] In the PC world no one can be opposed to abortion on the grounds that it is the killing of human beings. One can only be opposed because one is sexist, opposed to women's rights, and on the side of oppression. Homosexuality cannot be opposed on the grounds that it is condemned in the Bible or violates natural law. Those who oppose it do so because they are homophobic, morally oppressive, and hate-mongers. God cannot be called Father because one adheres to the Bible; those who refer to God as male are sexist.

The most important assumption of the PC movement is that there is no objective truth — either in history or morality. Truth is changing, and the truth of the moment arises out of the particular social/ethnic context. Like the Marxists, PC advocates see history as primarily a record of class struggle and oppression. The basic axiom is that the poor are poor because the rich are rich. The rich are oppressors and the poor are the victims. The capitalism of the wealthy nations is the cause of all the poverty in other countries.

Now we can better understand why the PC movement believes that history can be rewritten to accommodate the wishes of oppressed minorities. History cannot be considered in any sense an objective study of the past along with a sincere attempt to interpret its causes and effects; rather, history is a weapon to be used for whatever purposes seem appropriate for those who are oppressed. It can be molded into whatever shape best suits the liberal agenda.

WHAT ARE YOUR CHILDREN BEING TAUGHT?

Here is a random list of what is happening in some of our schools:

- Some schools use textbooks that favor Islam and that denigrate Christianity.[29]

- In some colleges, administrators or professors would not allow students to give pro-American speeches on campus after the 9/11 attacks of 2001, telling the students that America was the aggressor.[30] On these campuses the American flag was spoken of as "divisive" and not to be honored.

- Marxist ideology often dominates college classrooms. David Horowitz said, "There are more Marxists on the faculties of American colleges than in the entire former communist bloc."[31]

- A California teacher has been forbidden to show his students the Declaration of Independence because it refers to God. In fact, according to one judge, the Constitution itself was deemed unconstitutional.[32]

- In many schools the family is redefined as a "unit of two or more persons, related either by birth or by choice, who may or may not live together, who try to meet each other's needs and share common goals and interests. . . ."

A FINAL PLEA

In closing, I can only plead with you as a parent to take charge of your child's education. For some, this will mean homeschooling; for others a private school; and for those in the public school, it will mean working closely with teachers, school boards, and administrators to monitor what is happening in your child's life. There are no easy answers, but our children are our most important possession.

God places the responsibility for the children's training on the parents, particularly the father, and the passing of the faith to subsequent generations:

> And these words which I command you today shall be in your heart. You shall teach them diligently to your children, and shall talk of them when you sit in your house, when you walk by the way, when you lie down, and when you rise up. (Deut. 6:6–7)

God has not only entrusted the body of your child to your care, but also his/her soul. We cannot let our public educators take over the hearts of those who are most vulnerable and precious to us. If ever parents must be courageous, it is now.

Endnotes

Taken from *When a Nation Forgets God: 7 Lessons We Must Learn from Nazi Germany* by Erwin Lutzer (Chicago, IL: Moody Publishers, 2010), used by permission, www.moodypublishers.com.

1. Michael P. Donnelly, "Germany — It's Time for Some Change," *HSLDA — The Home School Court Report,* vol. 25, no. 1 (Jan./Feb. 2009): p. 8.
2. Dana Hanley, "Courage and Conviction — The Struggle for Home Schooling Freedom in Germany," www.homeschoolenrichment.com, March/April 2007, p. 36.
3. Ibid., p. 39.
4. Quoted in Duane Lester, "The Threats to Homeschooling: From Hitler to the NEA," August 11, 2008, http://www.allamericanblogger.com/3415/the-threats-to-homeschooling-from-hitler-to-the-nea/.
5. Ibid.
6. Jeremy Noakes and Geoffrey Pridham, editors, *Nazism: A History in Documents and Eyewitness Accounts, 1919–1945,* Vol. 1 (New York: Schocken, 1983), p. 432.
7. Ibid., p. 437.
8. Ibid., p. 446.
9. Ibid., p. 427.
10. Ibid., p. 441.
11. Ibid., p. 429.
12. Ibid., p. 439.
13. Ibid., p. 422.
14. Ibid., p. 423.
15. Ibid., p. 428.
16. Ibid.
17. Ibid., p. 446.
18. Quoted in William M. Bowen, *Globalism: America's Demise* (Lafayette LA: Huntington House, 1984), p. 19–20.
19. Marlin Maddoux, *Public Education Against America* (New Kensington, PA: Whitaker House, 2006), p. 84.
20. Ibid., p. 80–88.
21. Ibid., p. 134.
22. "Fox News Reporting: Do You Know What Textbooks Your Children Are Reading?" September 4, 2009, www.foxnews.com/story/0,2993,545900,00.html
23. Tammy Bruce, *The Death of Right and Wrong* (Roseville, CA: Prima Publishing 2003), p. 88.
24. Ibid., p. 195.
25. Maddoux, *Public Education,* p. 414–442.
26. http://www.foxnews.com/story/0,2933,545900,00.html.
27. Dinesh D'Souza, *Illiberal Education* (New York: Free Press, 1991), p. 9–10.
28. Tim Stafford, "Campus Christians and the New Thought Police" *Christianity Today* (February 10, 1992): p. 17.
29. Maddoux, *Public Education,* p. 29.
30. Ibid., p. 65.
31. Ibid., p. 65.
32. Ibid., p. 69.

"A blind man cannot guide a blind man, can he? Will they not both fall into a pit? A pupil is not above his teacher; but everyone, after he has been fully trained, will be like his teacher."

— Luke 6:39–40; NASB

CHAPTER SIXTEEN

Where Are We Headed?
Present-Day UK: A Snapshot of Our Future

Ken Ham

"In secular education they begin with 'Man determines truth.' Therefore, that's the foundation of their entire way of thinking in every way of life."

KEN HAM

Ken Ham is the president/CEO and founder of Answers in Genesis-U.S. and the highly acclaimed high-tech Creation Museum near the Cincinnati Airport — which attracted over 700,000 visitors in its first two and a half years of operation. Mr. Ham is one of the most in-demand Christian speakers in North America. He has authored numerous books on the Book of Genesis, the accuracy and authority of the Bible, dinosaurs, and the destructive fruits of evolutionary thinking, including his co-authored book on the "races" and racism, *One Race, One Blood*, and the best-seller *The Lie: Evolution*. He hosts the daily international radio program "Answers . . . with Ken Ham," heard on more than 800 stations in America, and is one of the editors and contributing authors for AIG's *Answers* magazine (a biblical worldview publication with over 70,000 subscribers worldwide). The following edited excerpts are taken from Ken Ham's co-authored book *Already Gone*.

ALREADY GONE

*T*he large wooden doors shut behind me with a creak and a heavy thud. Outside, the incessant river of life continues to flow as millions of people jam the sidewalks and rush toward red double-decker busses. Beneath the streets, the London Underground moves the masses by the hundreds of thousands — like blood pulsing through the arteries of this vibrant, thriving society.

But inside, I can hear each of my careful footsteps echoing in the dim quiet. I inhale deeply, taking in the aroma of ancient stones and old books. I see rows and rows of ornate pews — seating for more than 3,000 — yet I *am ushered into the small foyer area where around 30 chairs are set up and where I join a handful of elderly people with their heads bowed. Humbly and faithfully, those beside me say their prayers and listen to a brief message by a man who speaks of hope — but whose tired eyes seem to feel none of it.*

It is Sunday. For hundreds of years the faithful have been walking through the heavy wooden doors on this day, at this time, to gather together and share in the timeless rituals of worship, prayer, and proclamation that made this country the bastion of Christendom for centuries. But this morning I realize that I'm part of a funeral. But it is not the funeral of an individual; it is the funeral of an institution. Within months, the older generation will likely disband and the doors of this church will be shut and locked. The candles will never again be lit. The resounding anthem of the great hymns of our spiritual forefathers will never again echo in its passages.

***

Since 1969, over 1,500 churches in England have heard that final thud as their doors were shut after their final service after hundreds of years of active life.[1]

Most of the great churches still stand — great buildings that just 60 years ago were the hub of vital and vibrant activity. Before World War II (and certainly during those turbulent years), churches such as the one I visited that day were the center of community and spiritual life. But now, the community's life, such as it is, takes place outside of those buildings. Inside, many of them have become musty, dusty, and dark. The Victorian Society of the UK summarizes the situation in a publication entitled *Redundant Churches: Who Cares?*

> Invariably, it seems, churches become redundant. The country changes around them and for one reason or another they find themselves bereft of the worshipers needed to keep them going. Many, if not most, of the buildings seem eventually to find new uses, but it is not easy to generalize about how often these uses preserve their architectural and historic interest.[2]

It's not a small concern. Not far from the famous Westminster Abbey in London I found a sign that read: "Advisory Board for Redundant Churches."

"Redundancy." The dictionary defines that word as "exceeding what is necessary or natural . . . needlessly repetitive." That is a disturbing term to describe a former place of worship, don't you think? Who cares about "redundant churches"? It seems not many these days. There are not many left to really care — except for those who see them for their "architectural" and "historical" value. Now emptied of their intended function, many also see the real estate value of these "needlessly repetitive" buildings. A special government agency oversees the distribution and preservation of these buildings. What does that sound like in formal language?

> The Redundant Churches Fund has as its object the preservation, in the interests of the nation and the Church of England, of churches and parts of churches of historic and archaeological interest or architectural quality, together with their contents, which are vested in the Fund by Part III of the Pastoral Measure 1983 (1983 No.1).[3]

In other words, if what's left has some value physically, it is sold or it is preserved. The rest are abandoned or bulldozed. What has become of the buildings worth keeping? Other former places of worship have been turned into museums, clothing shops, music stores, liquor stores, nightclubs, and tattoo and piercing studios. One is even now used as a Sikh temple, and some have been converted into mosques.

FROM THE FILM: "If the textbooks don't start with the Bible as foundational to their thinking, then they are secular in philosophy. If they don't start from the Scripture, then they start with man's opinions."

Hundreds of these churches have ended up in the hands of private owners who convert them into offices or renovate them for use as personal homes or cottages.

It would be something of a relief if these former churches simply represented a shift from traditional worship toward more contemporary worship facilities, but that's not the case. The decline of the Church has followed the plummeting spirituality of a nation that has lost its roots — its foundation. England, the country that was once a cornerstone of western Christianity, is now, by and large, a wasteland of lost souls where the word "God" has many different definitions, with so few these days who would even think of "God" as the Creator God of the Bible.

According to a recent English church census:

- Regular churchgoers (of all denominations) amount to 6.3 percent of the total population.

- The proportion of churches per individuals is now one church to 1,340 people; the size of the average Sunday congregation, however, is 84.

- Between 1998 and 2005, there was an overall decline in regular church attendance of 15 percent — and the trend continues.

- 40 percent of regular churchgoers attend evangelical churches, but even these groups are seeing their numbers decline.[4]

All in all, only 2.5 percent of the population is attending Bible-based churches.

One United Kingdom news source in 2003 stated:

> Holy Week has begun with an expert prediction that the Christian church in this country will be dead and buried within 40 years. It will vanish from the mainstream of British life, with only 0.5 percent of the population attending the Sunday services of any denomination, according to the country's leading church analyst. . . . Only 7.5 percent of the population went to church on Sundays and that, in the past 10 years— billed by the church as the "Decade of Evangelism" — church attendance dropped by an "alarming" 22 percent.[5]

THE SHORT ROAD TO IRRELEVANCE

Westminster Abbey will probably survive, at least for a while. While other churches in England are being converted and bulldozed by the dozens, this stunning and sprawling abbey will continue to stand tall. It was first built to house a group of Benedictine monks in A.D. 1065. For the last 900-plus years it has been attacked, renovated, desecrated, and consecrated over and over, earning it a permanent place in history. Century after century, architects and craftsmen have been adding to its grandeur. When I walk through the corridors beneath the breathtaking expanses of Gothic and Romanesque architecture, I get an entirely different feel than I did in the nearby church where only a few gray-haired parishioners sat in the dusty front rows. Westminster Abbey is alive with people and activity. Yes, it will survive — but not necessarily for the right reasons.

Westminster is part monastery. Its religious life revolves around a daily pattern of worship, prayer, song, and the Eucharist. Until the 19th century, Westminster was the third seat of learning in England, surpassed only by Oxford and Cambridge. It was here that the first third of the King James Old Testament and the last half of the New Testament were translated. But the thousands of people who come to visit every day rarely stop to pray, worship, or contemplate the Scriptures, because the Abbey is also part museum. The architecture, artwork, and icons are timeless and priceless; the architecture is unsurpassed. The abbey is also part mausoleum. The throngs of camera-clad, backpack-toting tourists that flock here come to see the graves of leaders in the fields of religion, literature, and science. It is a pilgrimage of sorts — people coming from around the globe to pay homage before the graves of the likes of Geoffrey Chaucer, David Livingstone, Charles Dickens, Sir Isaac Newton, and Charles Darwin.

Charles Darwin? The founder of modern evolutionary theory? Buried in the floor of Westminster Abbey? It's hard to believe, but I have stood there and looked at the grave myself. Isn't this the man who popularized the philosophy of evolution taking place over millions of years? What is he doing in here? He not only abandoned his church, but he strategically introduced ideas that were contrary to God's Word. Isn't it strange that the man credited with founding modern evolutionary theory should be buried in the same place that the King James Version of the Bible was translated?

No, that's more than strange; it's symbolic — a powerful example of the short road that the Church has followed into irrelevance. A man who popularized a philosophy that hit at the very foundation of the Church (the Word of God) is honored by the Church and buried in the foundation of the Church. It is symbolic indeed.

THE SHORT ROAD[6]

The root of the word "relevance" comes from the word "relate." In order for something to be relevant, it has to connect (or relate) to something that is real and important. The problem we are studying, of course, is that 60 percent of the students who grow up in the Church have lost that connection. They fall into two groups: Group 1 believes that the Bible is irrelevant; Group 2 believes that the Church is irrelevant (unless it's a holiday or it's time to take the kids).

What happened? How did we get here? I believe it all started when the Church gave us "millions of reasons" to doubt the Bible. The Book of Genesis gives us a clear account of the creation of the universe, of the world, and of everything that lives, including humanity. A simple, literal interpretation of these passages makes it clear that this creation took place in six days, with God resting on the seventh, just a few thousand years ago. This history, as it is written concerning the creation of the universe and life, including the first two humans, Adam and Eve, and their fall into sin with the consequence of death — is foundational to all biblical doctrines. This is the foundational history for the gospel.

In the late 18th century and in the early 19th century, however, the idea that the earth is millions and billions of years old (rather than about 6,000) began to emerge in the scientific community of Europe. It wasn't a new idea, actually. Throughout human history, numerous cultures from different points of the globe have considered the universe to be old

FROM THE FILM: "We ought not to get the idea that, 'Ah, in this biology book there is a chapter on evolution, so we'll talk about creation there. That solves that, now we can read the rest of the book and that's okay.' Not at all."

or even eternal. Dr. Terry Mortensen's excellent book, *The Great Turning Point*,[7] chronicles what happened next. At that time, many church leaders in England led their churches to adopt the millions of years and add them into the Scriptures. Some did this by reinterpreting the days of creation as long periods of time; others adopted ideas such as the "gap theory," attempting to fit millions of years into a supposed gap between the first two verses of Genesis. The shift was not arbitrary; it was calculated — particularly by deists who were looking for a so-called scientific justification for rejecting the Flood of Noah's day as an explanation for the fossil-bearing sediments, and for rejecting biblical authority in total, as advocates of this millions-of-years age for the earth. They saw this as devastating to the Bible's account of creation and the Flood and its connection to fossil layers.

Darwin, based on his own writings, was never a believer, and of course readily accepted the millions-of-years ideas. This actually paved the way for Darwin to present his ideas on biological evolution. After all, one needs an incomprehensible amount of time to postulate the idea that small changes observed in animals will somehow add up to the needed big changes for Darwinian evolution — for reptiles to change into birds, for ape-like creatures to change into human beings, etc. Not only did the old-earth idea contradict what the Bible says, but because it is ultimately an attack on biblical authority, it paved the way for the conclusion that the Bible cannot be trusted, and our existence is the result of natural processes.

As the Church compromised on the issue of millions of years, subsequent generations were put on a slippery slide of unbelief. The millions-of-years idea not only undermined the creation account, but it began to undermine the historical account of the Genesis Flood as well. Soon the idea of a local flood rather than a global flood was popularized.

In 1859, Darwin published his major influential work, *On the Origin of Species,* and 12 years later *The Descent of Man,* popularizing the idea of the evolution of animals and the evolution of ape-like creatures into humans. Much of the Church in England (and then across the United Kingdom and Europe) began to also adopt Darwin's ideas, reinterpreting the Genesis account of creation and proposing views such as "theistic evolution" (that God used evolution to bring the different life forms into being).

Such views also spread to America, where various church leaders also adopted such positions to add millions of years and evolutionary ideas to the Bible's account of origins, thus reinterpreting the days of creation, the creation account of Adam and Eve, and so on. Even many theologically conservative churches adopted the gap theory—seeing this as a way of rejecting evolution but allowing for millions of years.

Many other conservative churches, which did not know how to handle the millions of years and evolutionary teaching, basically sidestepped the issues. They would (as they do today) teach Genesis as true, not dealing with the teachings of the secular world that contradicted the account (such as millions of years, evolution, etc.) —

but teaching the account of creation, the Flood, the Tower of Babel, and so on as a wonderful story. They may claim it to be true — but, nonetheless, it is just taught to the students as a story.

The Church began to make a disconnection at this point. It was the beginning of the road to irrelevance: the Church gave up the *earthly* things (e.g., the biological, anthropological, astronomical, geological history as recorded in Genesis 1:11) and focused on *heavenly* things (spiritual matters, relationships, the gospel). When it came to science, the Church gave in to human notions. It was now acceptable to use man's ideas to reinterpret the Bible, rather than to use the Bible to judge man's ideas. At times, the Church has tried to introduce hybrid theories that accommodate both secular science's interpretations and biblical accounts. The day-age theory and the gap theory are two examples. Unfortunately, they hold true to neither scientific evidence nor the Bible!

The real consequence of such compromise can be seen in this quote from Ron Numbers, a modern scholar who stated the following in answer to a question for the media:

> For creationists, history is based on the Bible and the belief that God created the world 6,000–10,000 [years] ago. . . . We humans were perfect because we were created in the image of God. And then there was the fall. Death appears and the whole account [in the Bible] becomes one of deterioration and degeneration. So we then have Jesus in the New Testament, who promises redemption. Evolution completely flips that. With evolution, you don't start out with anything perfect, you start with primitive little wiggly things, which evolve into apes and, finally, humans. There's no perfect state from which to fall. This makes the whole plan of salvation silly because there never was a fall. What you have then is a theory of progress from single-celled animals to humans and a very, very different take on history, and not just human history.[8]

In the past, the most highly recognized and progressive scientists in the field were also highly trained theologians (including Pascal, Newton, and Galileo). They helped maintain the connection between the Bible and science, between the laboratory and the sanctuary. We still have progressive scientists who are strong believers, but when someone comes to church today, they expect to hear about theology (the study of God). Do they expect to hear about biology, geology, and anthropology? The answer is no, of course. This is a major problem. Certainly the Church would not see itself as a research institution teaching people how to use microscopes or develop new electronics and so on. But this is where people have been confused. Observational science, which builds our technology, is very different from historical or origins science, which

FROM THE FILM: "When they threw God and the Bible, prayer, creation out of the public schools, claiming, 'We've thrown religion out, now we're neutral,' they actually threw Christianity out and replaced it with an anti-God religion."

is concerned with the origin of what we observe in the present. It was the historical or origins science that the Church gave up to the world — and thus disconnected the Bible from the real world.

In America today, where do you go to learn about the geological, biological, anthropological, or astronomical history of the universe? School. That's where our kids learn what they perceive is the real stuff, the *relevant* stuff. In Sunday school they learn "Bible stories." (By the way, if you look at the definition of "story," it means "fairy tale." The Bible has become so irrelevant in our culture today that that's what most people think it is — just a spiritual "fairy tale.") What has taken its place? Charles Darwin's evolutionary ideas and the belief in millions of years for the age of the earth and universe are now, by and large, both *welcomed* and *honored* in the European church. And the Bible? It is seen as irrelevant when it comes to issues in the real world. The great disconnect between the Bible and "real" life has taken place. The Bible, God, and the Church became irrelevant in less than three generations. Generations have gone down this slippery slide of unbelief, until they have now basically rejected the entire Bible and its message of salvation.

As our formerly Christianized nations like England and America have been rejecting biblical authority over recent generations, are we surprised to see a collapse of morality in these countries? Without the absolute standards set down in the Bible, should we be shocked to see youth rioting in the streets of London? In America, we see school violence escalating, and an increase in the acceptance of abortion and "gay" marriage. This moral decline has gone hand in hand with a rejection of the Bible and its moral absolutes.

Indeed, what happened in Europe is happening on this side of the Atlantic today. We are on the same road — the same slippery slide — and we have traveled down it a long, long way. We may not be as far along as they are, but understand this: the exact same trend that took place in Europe is happening today. Our spirituality has become compartmentalized. Yes, we go to church, but only to get our emotional and spiritual needs met. Then we walk out the doors and face a pagan world where we have to live by a whole different set of assumptions. We might say this doesn't matter, but let's be honest: in the back of everyone's mind is the question *"If I can't trust the Bible in the earthly things, why should I trust it in the spiritual things?"* This was the same challenge Jesus Christ, our Creator and Savior, put to Nicodemus in John 3:12.

What really happened to the Church in the United Kingdom and Europe, and America — in fact, across the Western world — was that the Church basically disconnected the Bible from the real world.

Churches today in America are not a place where one talks about geology, dinosaurs, fossils, or the age of the earth — that is left up to the schools and colleges. Effectively, the Church basically hands over the history of the universe to the secular educational institutions and concentrates on the spiritual and moral aspects of Christianity. The Church actually disconnects the Bible from the real world. The children (and everyone else, through Sunday school lessons, youth studies, etc.) in the churches are really taught that in church, one doesn't deal with geology, biology, and so on — that is for school. In church, we talk about Jesus — we deal with doctrines and we study moral and spiritual matters — but anything pertaining to understanding geology, biology, astronomy, anthropology, and so forth is left for school.

Please understand this! Ninety percent of children from church homes attend public/government schools.[9] There, they are mostly taught a biological, anthropological, geological, and astronomical history of the universe that totally contradicts the Bible's account of creation, the Flood, and the Tower of Babel.

In the United Kingdom, empty churches now stand in the cities and the countryside as monuments to the triumph of the new

religion of secular humanism. Hollow shells of buildings shadow-
ing streets filled with hollow souls, the disease was the result of a
predictable spread of ideas that seemed harmless enough to start
with, and then mutated into a plague that killed the soul of an entire
nation in two generations.

Today, few people are aware of the spiritual epidemic that has
wiped out the land of our Christian forefathers. Few people are
aware that the same epidemic has reached our own shores, spreading like an unstoppable virus. When it comes to churches in America, our research shows that many are *Already Gone*.

Yes, the epidemic has spread to our shores. Our current generation of children is leaving the church in droves. We are less than one
generation away from being a nation of hollow, empty churches. It
is more than possible that we will be the few, remnant gray-haired
believers who sit in nearly vacant pews on Sunday.

President Obama summed it up in his autobiography, published
just before his election as president of the United States of America:

> Whatever we once were, we are no longer just a Christian
> nation; we are also a Jewish nation, a Muslim nation, a Bud-
> dhist nation, a Hindu nation, and a nation of nonbelievers.[10]

Endnotes

Taken from *Already Gone: Why Your Kids Will Quit Church and What You Can
Do to Stop It* by Ken Ham and Britt Beemer, with Todd Hillard (Green Forest, AR:
Master Books, 2009), www.newleafpublishinggroup.com.

1. The Victorian Society, No 26, November 2007, http://www.victoriansociety.org.
   uk/publications/redundant-churches-who-cares/.
2. Ibid.
3. http://www.opsi.gov.uk/si/si1994/Uksi_19940962_en_1.htm.
4. 2005 Evangelical Alliance, http://www.eauk.org/resources/info/statistics/2005en
   glishchurchcensus.cfm.
5. Ibid.
6. Most of the ideas in this chapter are covered in much greater detail in my book
   Why Won't They Listen (Green Forest, AR: Master Books, 2002).
7. Terry Mortensen, *The Great Turning Point* (Green Forest, AR: Master Books,
   2004).
8. Gwen Evan, "Reason or Faith? Darwin Expert Reflects," *Wisconsin Week*, Feb. 3,
   2009, www.news.wisc.edu/16176.
9. www.news.com.au/couriermail/story/0,23739,25375117-23272,00.html.
10. Barack Obama, *The Audacity of Hope: Thoughts on Reclaiming the American Dream*
    (New York: Crown Publishers, 2006).

"But Jesus said, 'Let the little children come to Me, and do not forbid them; for of such is the kingdom of heaven.' "

— *Matthew 19:14*

CHAPTER SEVENTEEN

Let My Children Go

E. Ray Moore

"I believe the Lord is not going to bless any of these efforts until we first turn back to our own children."

E. RAY MOORE

E. Ray Moore has served for over 35 years in pastoral ministry. Additionally, he has served as a campaign consultant or staff for several major political campaigns. A South Carolina native, he graduated from the Citadel with a BA in political science and from Grace Theological Seminary with a MDiv (Masters of Divinity) in 1974 as well as a ThM (Masters in Theology) in 1979. Mr. Moore is married to the former Gail Laurens Pinckney, and together they have four children and seven grandchildren. He currently serves as president of Frontline Ministries, which focuses on prayer, revival, and Christian education. He is the director of the Exodus Mandate Project (www.ExodusMandate.org) and is the co-author of *The Promise of Jonadab: Building a Christian Family Legacy in a Time of Cultural Decline* with his wife, Gail. The following is taken from Mr. Moore's book *Let My Children Go.*

PUBLIC SCHOOLS IN CRISIS

A terrible crisis has developed in the schools to which most Americans entrust their children. On April 20, 1999, two teenage boys walked into their high school bearing lethal weapons and calmly began shooting their fellow students. Once they had shot and killed 15 people, including a teacher, and wounded several others, they turned their guns on themselves.

The killings at Columbine High School in Littleton, Colorado, shocked the conscience of the nation. There were detailed investigations into the lives of the two shooters, Eric Harris and Dylan Klebold, and the so-called Trenchcoat Mafia to which they belonged, a loose group of chronic misfits at Columbine.

An examination of their personal websites uncovered a preoccupation with Nazi and occult themes and with mass murder. The two youths had entertained fantasies that went much further than what actually happened. They wanted to blow up their school with everyone in it. Then they wanted — of all things! — to go to the Denver Airport, hijack a plane, and fly it into the World Trade Center! In this, the last of their death wishes, they provided stunning prescience of the evil that would come to America's shores two and a half years later.

The Columbine killings had a clear and very ominous, religious dimension. Several of the survivors contended that Harris and Klebold had been *singling out* students known to be Christians.

Rachel Scott was one example, very likely singled out ahead of time. Christian students were shot down in cold blood for their beliefs. Up until that day, Columbine had seemed to be a model public school.

A String of Shootings in Public Schools

But Columbine was only the most dramatic of a string of shootings in public schools that occurred during the 1990s, a period during which the government and the mass media were assuring Americans that the economy was doing well and that the country was on the right course.

Previous shootings had occurred in Bethel, Alaska; Pearl, Mississippi; West Paducah, Kentucky; Jonesboro, Arkansas; Edinboro, Pennsylvania; Fayetteville, Tennessee; and Springfield, Oregon. Many were killed, many were wounded.

The public schools to which today's parents send their children are clearly not the type of places they attended themselves. When the baby boomers were in high school, discipline problems existed, and students sometimes got caught with marijuana in their lockers. But the idea of a pair of students harboring such intense hatred that they would gun down their fellow classmates would never have occurred to anyone.

However, these shootings are extreme cases of a more general phenomenon: today's public schools have grown increasingly violent. Many, especially in large, urban areas, have metal detectors on all their entrances.

Gangs have proliferated, with rival groups both having armed themselves with guns as well as knives and being ready to fight each other on a moment's notice. Many public schools in the inner cities have banned gang insignia in an effort to stem the warfare.

INTELLECTUAL DETERIORATION

There is plenty of less frightening testimony that a terrible crisis has developed in public schools. Abundant evidence assembled from test scores and elsewhere assures us that today's public school graduates do not have the mastery of basic subjects that earlier generations had.

Students are leaving public high schools in record numbers without having acquired basic writing skills, reading comprehension, or mathematical ability. They know little or nothing of this country's founding or its history. They cannot place major historical figures or events in the right century. They cannot walk up to wall maps and point out significant foreign countries. This intellectual deterioration has spread into public colleges and universities that have admitted more and more unprepared students into college-level work. Public universities have had to expand remedial programs that did not even exist 50 years ago. Many colleges have become degree mills, where many students graduate still lacking the basic knowledge needed for intelligent participation in representative government, much less the skills for today's work place.

A FLAWED PHILOSOPHY

Tragically, many of these impaired students have adopted a flawed philosophy: they believe themselves entitled to good grades in school and then to a well-paying job. They have little or no interest in matters of learning. And perhaps saddest of all, if they grow up attending church with their parents, they very often stop church attendance during their college years.

As they enter adulthood, they proceed as if a connection to anything transcending their daily lives is irrelevant. Their transcendent aim is obtaining that high-tech job and taking their place in the global economy, something that doesn't always happen if they haven't developed the necessary skills.

During the 1990s, much of the country seemed to have fallen under a kind of collective hypnosis. President Bill Clinton engaged in

FROM THE FILM: "Christians realize that we're losing our civilization, so they're out there trying to get people elected to office when they have neglected their own sons and daughters sitting in their homes and in their churches."

an extramarital affair with a woman not much older than his daughter, lied under oath to cover it up, and was credibly accused of a number of other sexual indiscretions involving women (one of them a sexual assault).

The majority response seemed to be that Bill Clinton was *personally flawed but politically effective.* Many people remained convinced that all was well because the economy seemed to be doing well. With their 401k accounts surging, the majority wanted no presidential change.

SEPTEMBER 11, 2001

Of course, on September 11, 2001, we received the worst possible wake-up call when terrorists who had received their training in this country reduced the twin towers of the World Trade Center and a portion of the Pentagon to rubble, killing over 3,000 people. It was the worst carnage on U.S. soil since the Battle of Antietam.

Our nation's response to the crisis has been to call for unity and begin what could prove to be a very difficult and very long war against an international terrorist network that is extremely hostile to American values.

As the country has entered this crisis, however, have we thought about where we stand as a nation? We have seen an explosion of signs reading "God Bless America." But has God blessed America? Does America deserve His blessings? What has moved us from the Columbine killings to the more recent crisis?

Deterioration of Christian Values

Secular humanists in America have adopted a piecemeal approach to advancing their cause, removing God from the public scene a little at a time. The consequences of our ceasing to be a Christian nation have been devastating, as they have led directly to *nihilism*, the idea that neither the universe nor our own personal lives have any moral absolutes. This leads to events like the Columbine killings, as well as to a generation of lost young people who fill the emptiness in their lives and hearts with drugs, meaningless and dangerous promiscuous sexual encounters, and mindless televised entertainment, much of it graphically violent.

Humanism can also lead to the idea that the government, or the state, can save us if only citizens give it sufficient power, and that a meaningful life can be secured by conforming to its dictates. Government has become, in the eyes of many secular humanists, a kind of secular god.

Occasionally, humanists have offered entirely forthright statements of what they want to do, and where they want to do it. Consider the following statement from one of the leading humanist publications in the country:

> I am convinced that the battle for humankind's future [the mind] must be waged [and won] in the public school classrooms by teachers who correctly perceive their role as the proselytizers of a new faith: a religion of humanity that recognizes and respects the spark of what theologians call divinity in every human being. These teachers must embody the same selfless dedication as the most rabid fundamentalist preachers, for they will be ministers of another sort, utilizing a classroom instead of a pulpit to convey humanist values in whatever subject they teach, regardless of the education level: preschool day care or large state university.
>
> The classroom must and will become an arena of conflict between the old and the new — the rotting corpse of Christianity, together with all its adjacent evils and misery, and the new faith of humanism, resplendent in its promise of a world in which the never-realized Christian ideal of "love thy neighbor" will finally be achieved. . . .

It will undoubtedly be a long, arduous, painful struggle replete with much sorrow and many tears, but humanism will emerge triumphant. It must if the family of humanity is to survive.[1]

Here, secular humanism is openly acknowledged as a faith — a "religion of humanity," not a science — and promoting a secular humanist invasion and takeover of public schools. Public schools, the author tells us, are to become battlegrounds between Christianity and humanism.

It is clear to nearly everyone, regardless of their worldview, that public schools are deteriorating. We have seen endless efforts to "reform" the public schools — ranging from large-scale government social engineering programs like Goals 2000 to smaller ones such as tax-funded vouchers and charter schools.

We have seen efforts to "rediscover" morality through character education, a movement many Christians are supporting. While some of these efforts are better than others, all are merely detours on the way to failure. In contrast, my assertion is much bolder than to advocate more "reform." Frankly, my plan is the only one that has a chance of sustainable success, and it will result in a marvelous resurgence of Christian values and worldview that will benefit our culture dramatically.

CHRISTIANS ARE NOT POWERLESS: THE CASE FOR A NEW PARADIGM IN CHRISTIAN EDUCATION

The concern expressed by many about the loss of Christian principles in our public schools is commendable. But the Christian community as a whole, especially many pastors, is unsure about what to do.

Because of a string of Supreme Court decisions dating back to the 1940s, it seems clear that a curtain has dropped on any expression of the essence of Christianity — the birth, life, crucifixion and Resurrection of Jesus Christ our Lord and Savior — in the public schools.[2]

Starting with *Everson v. Board of Education* in 1947, the first case to dismiss the Bible from American public schools, the Supreme Court has stripped Christian principles and expression of them from the public school system.

Over a dozen cases have been handed down, including the Santa Fe decision that restricts student prayers at athletic events. While many Christians question the interpretation of the Constitution behind these rulings, they must acknowledge their reality and accept the fact that the public schools and society at large accept them as valid. Such rulings are now so embedded in Supreme Court jurisprudence as to be practically irreversible, at least in the near future. They have become the worldview and law of the land.

What is most important to realize is that the Christian community is not powerless in the face of these rulings. It is one thing to protest, but protests are unlikely to achieve any helpful result. It is one thing to advocate reform in the public schools, but so far, all reforms have failed.

FORMULATING A PLAN OF ACTION

What is needed is a plan that can be translated into action on the part of Christian educators, Christian parents, and their pastors.

The time has come for Christian parents to abandon the state-sponsored public school system in favor of homeschooling and participation in the development of networks of private, Christian schools, many of them based out of churches. This alone can resurrect the God-centered worldview and place it at the center of the education of our children.

In other words, we want to inaugurate a new way for thinking about education in American society, and precipitate a paradigm shift in the thinking of Christians about how they educate their children. This concept of a paradigm is important to understand. The term gained currency following Thomas S. Kuhn's use of it in one of the most important books of the past half-century, *The Structure of Scientific Revolutions*.[3] Paradigms are not worldviews; it is more accurate to say that paradigms presuppose worldviews. Paradigms have more to do with concrete problem-solving strategies, actual achievements, and plans for action.

The current paradigm for thinking about education in American society, even among the majority of Christians, simply takes for granted the idea that "free" public schools are necessary, and that even if the public schools have some problems those problems can be fixed with the right reforms. There is no room in this paradigm for the possibility that the public schools simply cannot be fixed and ought to be abandoned. Yet this is exactly what I endorse.

Our current situation and adherence to biblical principles both call for something much more radical than advocating reform. In the paradigm for Christian education, public schools — state-sponsored schools — cannot be reformed and should be abandoned in favor of homeschools and private Christian schools where a God-centered worldview animates the entire curriculum. According to Scripture, God actually commands us to do this.

ACCESS TO THE MINDS OF THE YOUNG

Educating the next generation is of crucial importance. The secular humanists realized very early in our country's history the importance of gaining control of the schools in order to gain access to the minds of the young. The creation of the state-sponsored school was central to this effort.[4]

It will be important for Christians to realize that state-sponsored schools were never a component of this country's original heritage, as defined by the Founding Fathers. The U.S. Constitution never mentions education, and it never authorized the government to set up and run schools. The state-sponsored school system and the acceptance of it by Christian parents is a kind of hypnosis produced by the modern paradigm of education that takes public schools for granted. The time has come to reject this paradigm, reject the secular humanist worldview behind it, and take back our children.

OUR MISSION AS CHRISTIAN EDUCATORS

It is important to stress, then, that we are not trying to reform the public schools. Nor are we trying, in any sense, to "take them over." Our mission as Christian educators must be nothing less than complete independence from the state-sponsored educational system. We believe that carrying forth this mission could be an important strategy in reversing our present moral and cultural decline and restoring the moral foundation of this nation.

This is, of course, an ambitious order. It must be approached prayerfully, with God's Word, the Bible, firmly before us. Most Christians, like most Americans generally, are accustomed to public schools and just consider them part of the landscape of American life. This is because of the dominant paradigm, which considers state-sponsored education necessary.

Many Christians compartmentalize their faith; that is, they don't allow Scripture to address certain areas. Still, scriptural law is written to be obeyed. One area Christians have historically and tragically compartmentalized has been the education of their children, despite specific biblical instructions in Deuteronomy, Matthew's Gospel, and elsewhere.

God assigned responsibility for education to the family, with assistance from the Church. When secular humanism came to be the dominant worldview among the educational intelligentsia of our society and when the necessity of state-sponsored education became the dominant paradigm, even among Christians, the government — federal, state, and local — was able to usurp the responsibility of the family and the Church. The government, however, has no God-ordained role in education any more than it has a constitutional role.

FROM THE FILM: "Trying to fix public education is like trying to teach a pig how to dance. You get dirty and the pig gets mad. "

ABANDONING GOVERNMENT SCHOOLS

I therefore advocate that Christians abandon rather than attempt to reform public schools. I believe the call to Christians to leave public schools in favor of homeschooling and private Christian schooling is based on Scripture; the historical American constitutional model; sound, Bible-based educational philosophy; and also free-market principles. No one will convince Congress with this argument, or even local school boards.

But progress can be made with Christians, helping them to rebuild their worldview and find their way back to biblical and constitutional thinking that calls for them to remove their children from public schools and begin homeschooling or placing them in private Christian schools.

Can we do this? It is a matter of taking the necessary steps and then trusting God.

We have a powerful precedent in Moses. Moses began his career as a man of no special importance until God spoke to him and commanded him to lead the Jewish people out of bondage in Egypt. Instead of fearing the wrath of Pharaoh, he trusted God. He went before Pharaoh and told him, "Let my people go!"

We have our modern Pharaoh: the federal government and the entire system of state-sponsored schooling. Moreover, we are at a crucial juncture in our history because the situation for Christians in public schools is getting progressively worse, and will get worse still.

I believe God is speaking to us today, just as He spoke to Moses.

The only question is, will we follow the path that Moses followed, or will we continue to follow our own paths, compartmentalize our lives, ruin the education of our children, and endanger the next generation?

If we follow the lead of Moses, it means removing our children from Pharaoh's school system and taking them to the Promised Land of private homeschools and Christian schools.

SETTING FORTH A FOUNDATION

My attempt is to set forth the foundation of what I hope will lead to a major paradigm shift in education in American society. Paradigm shifts, as Thomas S. Kuhn explained, are unpredictable.

I cannot claim to address every problem that will come up or answer every question that can be asked.

All of us are fallible, sinful human beings. The most Christians can claim is eternal salvation and a relationship with Jesus Christ. But I believe that removing our children from public schools is what we as Christian citizens and parents are commanded to do.

We know that God has spoken to us through His Word regarding the education of Christian children, and we had better listen!

The state-sponsored school system has become resolutely hostile to Christianity and to this country's founding principles. Pharaoh's school system cannot be reformed, and we should not try.

Rather, the time has come to tell our modern-day Pharaoh, "Let my children go!"

Endnotes

Taken from *Let My Children Go: Why Parents Must Remove Their Children from Public Schools Now* by E. Ray Moore Jr. (Ambassador-Emerald International, 2002), used by permission from Gilead Media, Columbia, SC, www.gileadmedia.com.

1. John Dunphy, "A Religion for a New Age," *The Humanist* 43 (1), Jan.–Feb. 1983, p. 26.
2. This and ensuing paragraphs, excepting the discussion of Thomas S. Kuhn and paradigms, consist of a much-updated version of an article originally published in *The State* (Columbia, SC), E. Ray Moore Jr., "Christians Not Powerless Against the Court," August 29, 2000.
3. Thomas S. Kuhn, *The Structure of Scientific Revolutions* (Chicago, IL: University of Chicago Press, 1962, 1970, 1996).
4. John Taylor Gatto, *The Underground History of American Education* (New York: Oxford Village Press, 2000/2001). About this book Michael Farris, former president of the Home School Legal Defense Association, wrote, "This is the most important education book of my lifetime."

"Like arrows in the hand of a warrior, so are the children of one's youth. Happy is the man who has his quiver full of them; they shall not be ashamed, but shall speak with their enemies in the gate."

— *Psalm 127:4–5*

CHAPTER EIGHTEEN

Jurisdictional Boundaries:
Who Is Responsible for the Education of Your Child?
Voddie Baucham, Jr.

"Ninety percent [of American Christians] make the exact same educational choice and nobody can point to book, chapter, and verse to justify it."

VODDIE BAUCHAM, JR.

Dr. Voddie Baucham, Jr. is a husband, father, pastor, author, and church planter. He currently serves as Pastor of Preaching at Grace Family Baptist Church in Spring, Texas. He has served as an adjunct professor at the College of Biblical Studies in Houston, Texas, and Union University in Jackson, Tennessee. He holds degrees from Houston Baptist University (BA in Christianity/BA in Sociology), Southwestern Baptist Theological Seminary (MDiv), Southeastern Baptist Theological Seminary (D.Min.), an honorary degree from Southern California Seminary (DD), and additional post-graduate study at the University of Oxford, England (Regent's Park College). He and his wife, Bridget, have been married since 1989. Their seven children are Jasmine, Trey (Voddie III), Elijah, Asher, Judah, Micah, and Safya. They are committed home educators. The following transcribed excerpts are from Dr. Baucham's message, "Whoever Controls the Schools Controls the World," as seen on the *Children of Caesar* DVD from American Vision.

WHOEVER CONTROLS THE SCHOOLS
CONTROLS THE WORLD

Ninety percent of Christians allow our government to educate their children. Recent studies have shown that a staggering 70 to 88 percent of the children of evangelicals are leaving the Church by the end of their freshman year in college. The correlation is clear: If we continue to send our children to Caesar for their education, we need to stop being surprised when they come home as Romans.

How does he who controls the schools control the world? God tells us exactly how in His Word: "A pupil is not above his teacher; but everyone, after he has been fully trained, will be like his teacher" (Luke 6:40). This passage is the New Testament version of "Train up a child in the way he should go, and when he is old he will not depart from it" (Prov. 22:6; NKJV).

It's simple, it makes sense. Whoever is your teacher is also your discipler. Education and discipleship cannot be separated — whoever is educating our children is also discipling them. Which means that whoever educates the majority of children is discipling the majority of children. And if the pupil is not above his teacher, and if everyone will ultimately be like his teacher, one can clearly see the power of education.

The 90 percent of Christian parents who send their children into the public education system often defend their decision in the same general way. First they go through the regular rigmarole of "our school is different" — it doesn't matter who they are or where they're from, their child's school is "different." They'll admit that almost every other school in the United States is having major problems, but *theirs* is the exception.

They then move onto their next point: "Well, I send them there but we make sure to talk through things when they come home." Really? Let's be honest. When they come home and you ask, "What did you learn in school today?" what is their response? — *"Nothin'."* The fact of the matter is that they don't know what they learned at school. They have no idea what is being shoved down their throat — it's their normal. They have no concept of anything else, so they don't know what to discuss with you.

REDEEMING THE TIME?

From K–12, children spend 14,000 seat hours in school — *14,000 seat hours*! The average Christian family spends less than 30 minutes per week discussing spiritual matters. Parents who think that a few conversations centered around "What did you learn today?" will counter the influence that public schools have on their children need to be honest about how vastly outweighed their discipleship efforts are by the time their child spends under government school curriculum — currently controlled by the government and teachers' unions.

What do the precious 24 hours we have to invest each day look like?

The Average School Day:	
Sleep	8 hours
Eating and bathing	2 hours
Travel (to and from school)	1 hour
School	8 hours
Homework	2 hours
Television and social	2 hours
	23 hours

If you have boys you can shave a little off the bathing part. But if you know anything about our culture, two hours for television is way low. That day is already up to 23 hours without including extracurricular activities and not accounting for the lack of overlap between the schedule of parents and their children to take advantage of that one hour that's left — one hour that is designed to overcome all those other hours where our children are being inundated with secular humanism by Caesar. Who are we kidding? There is not enough time in the day to compete with the schools for the minds of our children.

WHAT DOES SCRIPTURE SAY?

For a long time Christians' attitude on this issue has been: "You do what you feel led to do and I'll do what I feel led to do." Well, excuse me if I don't buy into that mysticism. I do what the Bible commands me to do. Leaving this decision up to our feelings is like saying, "There's a beautiful woman standing over there and she's giving my married friend and me the eye." "Hey, you do what you feel led to do, and I'll do what I feel led to do." No, just as the Bible has spoken on the adultery issue, I believe it has also spoken on the education issue. But for so long we've treated this like some sort of mystical decision where parents just meditate until God zaps us with what we're to do with our children educationally.

Before we examine what Scripture says about training the mind, let me admit something to you: the word "school" doesn't exist in any one of the following passages. But there's a good reason for this — the Bible knows *nothing* of schools:

These words which I command you today shall be in your

heart. You shall teach them diligently to your children, and shall talk of them when you sit in your house, when you walk by the way, when you lie down, and when you rise up (Deut. 6:6–7; NKJV).

That would be all the time. An administrator in a public school system in Amarillo, Texas, challenged me on this issue because she's committed to public schools. She said that as a Christian we have to have them and our kids have to be in them. When I mentioned this passage of Scripture to her she responded, "I always thought that meant nonschool hours." Ma'am, where, pray tell, was Moses sending his kids to school?

- How blessed is the man who does not walk in the counsel of the wicked, nor stand in the path of sinners, nor sit in the seat of scoffers! But his delight is in the law of the LORD, and in His law he meditates day and night. He will be like a tree firmly planted by streams of water, which yields its fruit in its season and its leaf does not wither; and in whatever he does, he prospers. The wicked are not so, but they are like chaff which the wind drives away. Therefore the wicked will not stand in the judgment, nor sinners in the assembly of the righteous. For the LORD knows the way of the righteous, but the way of the wicked will perish (Ps. 1:1–6).

- The fear of the LORD is the beginning of knowledge; fools despise wisdom and instruction (Prov. 1:7).

- And do not be conformed to this world, but be transformed by the renewing of your mind, so that you may prove what the will of God is, that which is good and acceptable and perfect (Rom. 12:2).

- We are destroying speculations and every lofty thing raised up against the knowledge of God, and we are taking every thought captive to the obedience of Christ . . . (2 Cor. 10:5).

Is math a thought? Is science a thought? Is history a thought?

- See to it that no one takes you captive through philosophy and empty deception, according to the tradition of men, according to the elementary principles of the world, rather than according to Christ (Col. 2:8).

- O Timothy, guard what has been entrusted to you, avoiding worldly and empty chatter and the opposing arguments of what is falsely called "knowledge" — which some have professed and thus gone astray from the faith (1 Tim. 6:20–21).

How can we obey these principles about the training of the mind without applying them to the way we educate our children?

SLAVES OR FREE?

When compulsory, government-controlled education was originally proposed in the mid-1800s in America, it was fiercely opposed by Christians. For the first 50 years the Church fought tooth and nail against it because they knew better.

Alexis de Tocqueville noted that as late as the 1830s education in America was everywhere in the hands of the Protestant clergy. By 1900, two-thirds of high school children were still educated at home or by the Church.

Remember, a pupil is not above his teacher, but every student when he is fully trained will be like his teacher. I'm a homeschool dad, we homeschool all our children. My 14-year-old son Trey travels everywhere with me, as I am his teacher and discipler. When our sons reach the age of 13 they go through a rite of passage as they enter into manhood. This is when their mother closes up the books and hands them to me; she is no longer their teacher, I am. This is because there are things that I, as a man, am commanded to teach my children — my sons — that my wife cannot. And so when our sons turn 13 they will travel everywhere with me. Trey is my personal assistant. I am his mentor and his teacher in all of his subjects, particularly in the art of manhood — what it means to live and conduct oneself as a man — the good, the bad, and yes, the ugly.

People are always asking the same questions when they find out we're a homeschool family. And these questions are rooted in the fact that they've been discipled by the system. There are three questions that we always get:

1. Is that legal?

2. Where do you get your curriculum?

3. What about socialization?

Why does everyone ask the exact same three questions? Because everyone has been discipled by the same teacher. First of all, "Is that legal?" Where does this question come from? It comes from sheep who have forgotten that they are free men. We ask that question because we believe children are wards of the state; because we've been discipled by the system that says it owns us. Therefore, the first question that everybody asks is "How can *you* educate your own *children*?" The system wants you to be a slave, but I am a free man! My children are mine, not wards of the state; the government has no jurisdiction over my children. Yet everybody asks this first question. Why? Because the pupil is not above his teacher, but everyone, after he has been fully trained, will be like his teacher. And everyone who's been through our education system has had the idea pounded into their head that the state is the educator — that you have to ask permission from the state to educate your own children. In no uncertain terms, the Ninth Circuit Court of Appeals has actually

FROM THE FILM: "Everybody, no matter where they are from, no matter who they are, [say] their schools are different."

expressed this. In my home state of California, when it comes to sex education, if you send your kids to government schools you have *no rights* when it comes to what they're taught — you are sheep and not free men.

The second question stems from the same concept and comes in many forms. "Where do you get your curriculum?" "Who gives you your curriculum?" "Who *approves* your curriculum?" "Who tests your children regularly to make sure that you're keeping up with your curriculum?" Again, a slave mentality is clearly demonstrated here. What these questions really mean to ask is: How is the state exercising its jurisdiction over the child that you and the state *share*?

The other question, as every homeschool family knows, is the question of all questions: "What about socialization?" Again, it comes from the same mentality as the previous two questions because we are sheep and not living like free men. But what exactly do we mean by socialization? Do I really want a group of 14-year-old boys socializing my son right now? Are you kidding me? Besides, when was the last time you were in a room with 25 people your exact same age? — school. It never happens again once school is over. This means that public schools *falsely* socialize children and give them this "skill" that they never needed to acquire in the first place.

Among all the negative social skills acquired through public education, there is only one positive social skill that a kid can learn in school: standing in line. And if you have enough kids you can teach that one at home.

What about Being Salt and Light?

The context of Matthew 5 has nothing to do with sending our children to government schools. The idea of "salt and light" has to do with being distinct, not with assimilating with the world. A city on a hill cannot be hidden. What's great about a city on a hill? It's distinct and set apart. We homeschool *because* we believe in being "salt and light," distinct and set apart.

In fact, when one continues to read just a few more verses in Matthew 5, after Jesus addresses the treatment of salt and light in His Sermon on the Mount, He talks about not a jot or tittle of the Law passing away and He makes a statement: "Whoever therefore breaks one of the least of these commandments, and teaches men so, shall be called least in the kingdom of heaven" (Matt. 5:19; NKJV). Right there in the very passage, right after people go and say, "We need to be salt and light," Jesus says that if you are teaching people to go astray from keeping the Law, you are the least in the Kingdom.

Some Alarming Facts

- Less than 10 percent of American Christians possess a biblical worldview. (I believe the reason for that is because the overwhelming majority of them have been educated by Caesar — the source of their worldview.)

- Two-thirds of American "born again" Christians assert that there is no such thing as absolute truth — I put "born again" in quotations because if they believe there is no absolute truth then they can't believe they're absolutely saved.

- Only four out of ten said they were absolutely committed to the Christian faith — the other six could be in today and out tomorrow.

- Only 44 percent of churched youth assert that humans are capable of grasping the meaning of truth — which makes me want to ask, "How did you grasp the meaning of the 'truth' that you can't grasp the meaning of truth?"

- Eighty-five percent of churched youth agreed with the statement: "What is right for one person in a given situation might not be right for another person who encounters the same situation." This is what's known as relativism, or situational ethics.

- Sixty-two percent of churched youth agreed with the statement: "Nothing can be known for certain except the things that you experience in your life." And of course that must mean they've experienced everything else in their life in order to know that this is true, because that's the only possible way they could logically make this statement.

People with a Christian Worldview

- 11 times less likely to condone adultery
- 15 times less likely to believe homosexuality is acceptable
- 18 times less likely to condone drunkenness
- 31 times less likely to condone premarital cohabitation
- 100 times less likely to endorse abortion

What are pastors always pounding the pulpit about? This list. Why are we always pounding the pulpit about this list? Because people don't have a Christian worldview. If they had a Christian worldview we'd be pounding the pulpit about something else. But because 90 percent of the people who call themselves Christians don't have a Christian worldview, we have to constantly remind them to act like what they are not.

So what is a worldview? Briefly, a worldview is a set of underlying assumptions that interpret existence. Dr. Ron Nash puts it this way: "A worldview is a conceptual theme by which we consciously or unconsciously place or fit everything we believe and by which we interpret or judge reality."[1] James W. Sire: "Our ground-floor assumptions — ones that are so basic that none more basic can be conceived — those compose our worldview."[2] Charles Colson and Nancy Pearcey: "A worldview is the sum total of our beliefs about the world; the big picture that directs our daily decisions and actions."[3]

If you want to find out about someone's worldview, don't ask them what they believe, just watch how they live — that's where you'll see someone's worldview.

How Are Worldviews Formed?

- Informally
- Uncritically
- Intergenerationally
- Intragenerationally
- Over time — 14,000 seat hours!

In other words, there's no formal class where you sit down and the teacher says, "This is your worldview." When our students are in the government education system, nobody's saying to them, "Here is secular humanism" — instead, it is informally communicated. They're also not thinking through it logically. In fact, they're not even being taught to think. They don't teach logic in our schools anymore because you can't shove trash down the throat of a person to whom you've taught logic.

THE POWER OF EDUCATION

Let's take a brief glimpse at what various men at different times in history understood about the power of education, in their own words:

> Non-Christian education puts the child in a vacuum. The result is that child dies. Christian education alone really nurtures personality, because it alone gives the child air and food. Modern educational philosophy gruesomely insults our God and our Christ. How, then, do you expect to build anything positively Christian or theistic upon a foundation which is the negation of Christianity and theism? No teaching of any sort is possible except in Christian schools.[4]
> — *Cornelius Van Til*

This whole process of education is to be religious, and not only religious, but Christian. And as Christianity is the only true religion, and God, in Christ, the only true God, the only possible means of profitable education is the nurture and admonition of the Lord.[5]　　— *Charles Hodge*

I am as sure as I am about Christ's reign that a comprehensive and centralized system of national education, separate from religion, as is now commonly proposed, will prove the most appalling enginery for the propagation of anti-Christian and atheistic unbelief, and of anti-social nihilistic ethics individual and political, which this sin-rent world has ever seen.[6]　　— *A.A. Hodge*

Dr. David Alan Black, who is professor of New Testament Greek at Southeastern Baptist Theological Seminary and a dear friend of mine, said this:

No academic skepticism, no secularist authors, no blatant materialism can so undermine the spiritual life of the country like the completely secularized training of a child under the authority of the State. Bible-based education is mandatory for Christian parents. If we think we can keep our children in a secular school system and escape the dumb down, amoral, and immoral results of secular humanism in schools, we are sorely mistaken.[7]

But Christians aren't the only ones who understand the power of education.

When an opponent declares, "I will not come over to your side," I calmly say, "Your child belongs to us already. What are you? You will pass on. Your descendants, however, now stand in the new camp. In a short time, they will know nothing else but this new community."[8]
　　— *Adolph Hitler*

Education is thus a most powerful ally of humanism, and every public school is a school of humanism. What can the theistic Sunday school, meeting for an hour once a week and teaching only a fraction of the children, do to stem the tide of a five-day program of humanistic teaching?[9]
　　— *Charles Potter*

Our schools may not teach Johnny to read properly, but the fact that Johnny is in school until he is 16 [now 18] tends to lean toward the elimination of religious superstition.[10]
— *Paul Blanchard*

Public education is the parochial education of scientific humanism.[11]
— *Joe Burnett*

Potter, Blanchard, and Burnett were all signers of the Humanist Manifesto and architects of the modern American educational system.

PROGRESS REPORT

So how are the humanists doing? Nehemiah Institute has been conducting the PEERS test for decades. It tests worldviews and ranks them on a scale from "Socialism" to "Biblical Theism." A score from 70 to 100 is classified as "Biblical Theism" — that's where they would expect Bible scholars and professors to rank. The "Moderate Christian" worldview is between 30 to 69 — that's where they'd expect mature Christians to score; if you're a Christian, you have a Christian worldview. "Secular Humanism" is from 0 to 29, and "Socialism" is any score below 0.

Here are some of the latest PEERS test results: Biblical scholars averaged 87.8, right in the middle of the 70–100 range where you would expect. Humanists averaged -45.0 — again, just where you would expect them to rank. Christian school faculty — these are folks who teach in your average Christian high school — averaged 52.9. This, too, is what you would expect, between the 30–69 range. Homeschool students averaged 48.6, just behind Christian school faculty. Now, Christian students in Christian schools only averaged 27.8. This is below the moderate Christian worldview, seeping into the secular humanist worldview. I believe the problem here is that Christian schools actually brag about the fact that they have certified teachers. Certified by whom? The state; Caesar. Many Christian schools are out there basically saying, "Hey, Caesar approves of our teachers!" This is not true with all Christian schools, but it boggles my mind. The final test group is Christian students in public schools. They averaged 7.9 on the PEERS test — the low end of secular humanism, falling into Marxist socialism.[12]

Since 1988, 90 percent of Christian students who have taken the PEERS test have scored below the "Moderate Christian" worldview level — *90 percent.*

The Way Home

Christian Smith was the chair of the sociology department at the University of North Carolina at Chapel Hill when he conducted a study called the National Study of Youth and Religion — a 4.5 million- dollar research project. Now, 4.5 million-dollar research projects in sociology are virtually unheard of. Dr. Smith is no longer at the University of North Carolina at Chapel Hill; he moved on up after this study and now sits as the director for the Center for the Study of Religion and Society at the University of Notre Dame. Now, Christian Smith is not a radical fundamentalist Christian; he's not advocating other forms of education here, but read what he put forth in his peer research:

> Especially when religion is structurally isolated from the primary schedules and networks that comprise teenagers' lives are teens' religious and spiritual lives most weak. It is by contrast when teens' family, school, friends, and sports lives and religious congregations *somehow* connect, intersect, and overlap that teens exhibit the most committed and integral religious and spiritual lives [emphasis added].[13]

The point that Dr. Smith made but wasn't willing to say was the same thing found by the National Home Education Research Institute (NHERI):

The children most likely to remain in the faith of their parents are those who are educated at home. We are currently losing 70–88 percent of young people by the end of their freshman year in college. But homeschooled students remain in the faith of their fathers all the way through college, according to NHERI, at a rate of 90–95 percent.[14]

I'm a Southern Baptist. The second resolution that my friend Bruce Shortt and I brought before the Southern Baptist Convention encouraged Southern Baptists to remove their children from our government schools. In 2005, we brought another resolution that garnered a lot of attention because we were directly opposing the radical homosexual agenda in our schools. We got a version of that one passed, then we got another one through and we continue to be a thorn in the flesh of the SBC. But in 2005, just before the convention, I received a call to come on Al Mohler's program — he's the president of Southern Seminary and one of the most brilliant men in America today, bar none. I wasn't sure about Dr. Mohler's invitation because most of the Southern Baptist leadership had been blasting us in the press — I mean they were creaming us. They threw us under the bus and backed it up a few times. But while I was on Mohler's program he made this statement:

I believe that now is the time for responsible Southern Baptists to develop an exit strategy from the public schools. This strategy would affirm the basic and ultimate responsibility of Christian parents to take charge of the education of their own children. This strategy would also affirm the responsibility of churches to equip parents, support families, and offer alternatives. At the same time, this strategy must acknowledge that Southern Baptist churches, families, and parents do not yet see the same realities, the same threats, and the same challenges in every context. Sadly, this is almost certainly just a matter of time.[15]

TURNING THE HEARTS . . .

In *The Reformed Pastor*, Richard Baxter wrote in the 1600s: "This is the sanctification of your studies: when they are devoted to God, and when He is the end, the object, and the life of them all."

What is my responsibility as a father? It is to equip and train my children in the discipline and instruction of the Lord. It is to raise, train, hone, aim, and launch the arrows that God has given me. And there are those who seem to think that I should take them when they are undeveloped twigs and launch them into a system that will hone them, and sharpen them, and aim them back at me.

News Flash: I'm raising an army — an army of intercontinental ballistic missiles. And one day the silo is going to open over my home, and when it does there will be missiles launched to impact this world for Christ, missileswho have been trained, armed, and honed in my home, and not by Caesar.

Endnotes

All scripture quotes in this chapter, unless otherwise noted, are taken from the New American Standard Bible (NASB).

Transcript taken from "The Children of Caesar: The State of American Education, Where It Is Headed, and What Your Family Can Do about It — Disc 1: Whoever Controls the Schools Controls the World" by Dr. Voddie Baucham, Jr. (2007), used by permission from The American Vision, P.O. Box 220, Powder Springs, GA 30127, www.americanvision.org.

1. Ron Nash, *Faith and Reason*; (Grand Rapids, Zondervan, 1988) p. 24.

2. James W. Sire, *How to Read Slowly*; (Colorado Springs: WaterBrook, 1978), "Identifying the Author's World View."

3. Charles Colson and Nancy Pearcey, *How Now Shall We Live?* (Wheaton, IL: Tyndale, 2004), p. 14.

4. Louis Berkhof and Cornelius Van Til, *Foundations of Christian Education* (Phillipsburg, NJ: Presbyterian & Reformed, 1990).

5. Charles Hodge, *A Commentary on the Epistle to the Ephesians* (New York: Carter, 1856), p. 360.

6. Archibald Alexander Hodge, *Popular Lectures on Theological Themes* (Philadelphia: Presbyterian Board of Publication, 1887), p. 283.

7. David Alan Black, "Our 'Education' President," *DaveBlackOnline.com*, August 21, 2004, http://daveblackonline.com/our.htm, accessed July 5, 2012.

8. Adolf Hitler, from a speech delivered on November 6, 1933, quoted by William Shirer, *The Rise and Fall of the Third Reich* (New York: Simon & Schuster, 1990), p. 249.

9. Charles Francis Potter and Clara Cook Potter, *Humanism: A New Religion* (New York: Simon & Schuster, 1930).

10. Paul Blanchard, from *The Humanist* magazine, 1983, quoted by Blair Adams and Joel Stein, *Who owns the Children?* (Waco, TX: Truth Forum, 1984).

11. Joe R. Burnett, *The Humanist* magazine, 6 (1961), p. 347.

12. Worldview Assessment & Training: PowerPoint, *Nehemiah Institute*, www.nehemiahinstitute.com/Peers-st.pps, accessed July 5, 2012.

13. Christian Smith with Melinda Lundquist Denton, *Soul Searching* (New York: Oxford, 2005), p. 162.

14. This is Mr. Baucham's summary of past NHERI findings. See www.nheri.org/research.html for more studies on homeschooling statistics.

15. Albert Mohler, "Needed: An Exit Strategy," *AlbertMohler.com*, June 17, 2005, http://www.albertmohler.com/2005/06/17/needed-an-exit-strategy/, accessed July 4, 2012.

"Those from among you shall build the old waste places; you shall raise up the foundations of many generations; and you shall be called the Repairer of the Breach, the Restorer of Streets to Dwell In."

— Isaiah 58:12

CHAPTER NINETEEN

The Second Mayflower

Kevin Swanson

"The social systems that we have grown up with are coming apart at the seams, our entertainment is nihilistic, the political state is socialistic-Marxist. This is called devastation."

KEVIN SWANSON

Homeschooled himself in the 1960s and 70s, Kevin Swanson and his wife, Brenda, are now homeschooling their five children. Mr. Swanson has 35 years of experience in the homeschooling movement and serves as the director of Generations with Vision — a ministry he founded to strengthen homeschool families across the country. For the last four years he has hosted a daily radio program — Generations Radio — the world's largest homeschooling and biblical worldview program that reaches families across the United States and in over 80 countries. He has also served as the executive director of Christian Home Educators of Colorado for the last nine years. Mr. Swanson has authored several popular books for homeschoolers, including *Upgrade: 10 Secrets to the Best Education for Your Child*, *The Family Bible Study Guide Series*, and others. The following excerpts are taken from Mr. Swanson's book *The Second Mayflower*.

THE FUTURE OF A CIVILIZATION

Two histories are found side by side in the annals of the world. Sometimes the histories of the city of God and the city of man weave in and out of each other, but they remain distinct. In short summary, the history of the city of man is only a sequence of empires that rise and fall. From Babel to Rome, and from Spain to America, empires collect their force and inevitably dissipate. Immigrations, imperialist insurgencies, civil wars, internal corruption, and natural disasters dismantle the towers that men build. It is quite an amazing thing to consider that the prophet Daniel retained his position through successive empires from Babylon to Persia. Here is a terrific picture of the city of God sustained from one generation to another. Empires come and go, but the church of Jesus Christ now spans the continents. What is done for the kingdom of God does not perish in time or eternity, even while man's empires rot in the ash heaps of history.

What used to be the most powerful Christian church in Europe during previous centuries has now conceded a loss of the continent to the humanists and Muslims. A certain Catholic provost, Joseph Fessio, who was recently interviewed on an American radio talk show,[1] reviewed the status of Western civilization (apparently summarizing a high-level meeting with the pope and other Roman Catholic academicians). Basically, Fessio said that Western civilization is dying in Europe and is soon to be replaced by the Islamic worldview, and religious freedom, at least for Christians, will no doubt die out as it does in most Islamic states. While admitting failure in Europe, Fessio told the listening audience that there was yet some hope for the future of Western civilization in this country because of some who still have a "will to carry on their civilization and faith." Among those who have a vision for their families and the future are the home educators who have removed their children from the culture. He called America's homeschools "the monasteries of the New Dark Age." He quickly added, "You non-Catholic Christians have a lot more of them than we Catholics do . . . and that is where families are having children."

The modern age of empires is about to end with the fall of each major power center from Spain to France to England and, finally, America. But, as with the fall of Rome, Christians are not particularly pained by the fall of these empires. As the bricks began to tumble off of the city of man in A.D. 430, the great Christian theologian, Augustine, penned the classic *The City of God*, in which he contrasted the two cities and suggested that all that really mattered was the city of God. Throughout the succeeding eight centuries, the Church rapidly expanded into Europe, converting pagans from Ireland to Germany, from Scotland to Gaul.

However, with the advent of the secular humanist university during the 12th century, knowledge was separated from faith and life. Education moved from the God-ordained spheres of family and church to the state, and man began building his empires once more. Almost immediately following the establishment of secular universities, the humanist renaissance formed and the Reformation was barely able to slow the headlong rush toward man-centered thinking and living. But even as humanism emerged victorious from the last 300-year "war of worldviews" and built its cultures, societies, and institutions, it planted the seeds of its own destruction. Failure was inevitable.

FROM THE FILM: "We've got to do something. The schools are failing. The society is ripping our families apart. Our young men and our young women are purposeless. They have no vision in life."

By God's providence, in the midst of the raging floods of man-centered humanism that came to characterize Western thought, the 16th-century reformation formed a small stream of God-centered thinking. It retained something of a distinctively biblical worldview, profoundly influencing nations like Scotland, England, Canada, and Holland. But by God's wisdom and mercy, one nation received more of that little stream than any other nation on earth, and that was America. The first Christians settling this land were far more rooted in the perspectives of John Calvin and John Knox than in the thinking of Thomas Aquinas, Desiderius Erasmus, or even Martin Luther. By the time of the Great Awakening of the 1740s, the leading theologians and preachers of the day — such as Jonathan Edwards, George Whitfield, and Samuel Davies — were still more committed to John Calvin and John Knox than they were to Jacobus Arminius, Menno Simons, or Phillip Melancthon. Study the thinking of the men who founded this nation and you will understand their reformational commitment to a theocentric, biblical worldview. Ideas have consequences, and the ideas of the 16th-century reformers culminated in the founding of the most God-blessed nation on the face of the earth.

Nevertheless, these Reformation ideas were relatively short-lived in their cultural impact. Now it is humanist, man-centered thinking that rules our world.[2] What we have today is a post-Christian Europe and America. Despite the efforts of Catholics and Protestant Christianity, the birth rate in Italy is the lowest in all of Europe, and 37 percent of the children in America are born without fathers (up from 6 percent in 1960). The family is unraveling, the culture has become hopelessly nihilistic, and the state has grown tyrannical almost everywhere. For at least four generations, children have been educated in science and history without so much as a mention of the fear of God as the beginning of knowledge. Although some remnants of Christianity are still extant in the forms, these externals are quickly fading. Taking the obvious example of church attendance, we would find that it is still relatively high in America while it has virtually dissipated in Europe. But even while church attendance remains at 19th-century levels in this country, God is hardly a factor in the thinking, the culture, and the reality of the average person. If you compared the art and literature of the modern world to that of the pre-Reformation world, the contrast is stark. There is far less awareness of a transcendent God in the mind of the 21st-century American and Italian than there was in the mind of the 15th-century Italian — 350 years of naturalism, materialism, existentialism, higher criticism, and evolution have taken their toll on the minds of men and their cultures. Humanism has won.

But, as Francis Schaeffer pointed out, men always build their towers so high they fall down. They have been in the habit of doing that sort of thing since Babel. Humanist man insists upon defining himself even as Michelangelo forms his man cutting himself out of the rock. But there was something Michelangelo, as the optimistic humanist, didn't take the time to consider. How can his self-defining man even begin the work if he doesn't have any hands? How can he define a single truth if there is no starting point for truth? Thus, postmodern man gave up his search for a unifying, absolute truth that has resulted in hopelessness, futility, and a loss of the will to continue building empires. His thinking unravels and the towers come down.

Our country's future hangs in the balance. Tremendous forces tear at her, threatening to rip her to pieces. Among those forces is a heritage, that singularly unique heritage shared by no other country on earth. The specters of John Winthrop, William Bradford, Richard Mather, John Cotton, Thomas Hooker, and Jonathan Edwards still loom large over some parts of this nation's consciousness. It is still carried forward in books like this one, along with hundreds of other books and audio-visual presentations produced over the recent decades that depict the obvious contrast between America's godly heritage and the secular departure from the vision. The vision burns even brighter in the hearts of hundreds of thousands of families who, unlike the dying cultures around them, are committed to passing on a vision to future generations. It is a heritage that must not be forgotten.

What concerns people like us is not so much the survival of our nation as it is the survival of the principles upon which this nation was founded — the principles of righteousness and liberty. Of course we are impressed that this nation became the most prosperous nation on earth, a bastion of freedom to which millions have come seeking refuge from tyrannies elsewhere. Yet this nation has, for the most part, abandoned this heritage in favor of building a centralized form of power in what has become the most powerful government in the world.

When the empires of men fight for survival, two trends appear simultaneously: tyranny and anarchy. From historical patterns one can see that as man builds his towers high, the empires trend toward both centralization and decentralization at the same time, with the final breakdown resulting in decentralization. The immigration problem provides an excellent example of this. Centrists want to loosen border control and perhaps even move toward a North America Union, while the current immigration situation produces increasing disunity in the national culture in the name of trans-cultural equality. Some public schools now insist upon teaching in Spanish and Arabic, disrupting the nationally unified culture, and threatening to produce a situation not unlike Bosnia (with multiple religions and cultures) that eventually tends to either civil war or decentralization.

A commitment to humanism itself produces the same phenomenon. When man becomes his own god, he will endow the state (or the civil government) with god-like power, and centralization is inevitable. But, at the same time, the individual retains a desire to be god. Anarchy develops as the family breaks down and as men live more for themselves with less concern for the future. Thus, anarchy and tyranny grow side by side, feeding off of each other for a time.

The one builds upon the other. Eventually, the system cannot bear their weight, and the lack of character and will to survive takes the empire toward decentralization. This is the Babel principle that has persisted since man built his first tower.

Meanwhile, the Christian who retains a biblical world and life view is not interested in the building of empires, for he is busy building the kingdom of God made up of families, churches, and covenanted communities. In fact, between 1620 and 1800, the American experience was a brief experiment in biblical government. But the sway of humanism succeeded in securing the modern "Babel" project during the following century. By the 1900s there was no looking back. America had become one more attempt at the centralization of power in the building of yet another tower that would "reach into heaven" (Gen. 11:4; NASB).

For a while, America maintained a common cultural denominator that was basically Christian at root. This kept the country unified while allowing significant diversity in cultural backgrounds. However, having jettisoned the Christian faith almost entirely from its educational systems, political institutions, and cultural expressions, there is lit-

FROM THE FILM: "Things are bad, but for us, things are really good because we're not relying on the state to raise our children anymore. We're going to raise our own children. We're going to educate our own children."

tle basis for national unity remaining. Now, with so little respect for any universal standard of morality by which freedom could survive, this nation's future hangs in the balance.

THE FUTURE OF THE NATION

So what is the future of this nation? Here is a question that rattles around in the mind of any person who has any stock in it, as I do and, I trust, my reader does as well. As a beneficiary of a tremendous heritage passed on by the fathers who founded the nation and as one who cares deeply for my own children and grandchildren, I seek God's blessing upon this land. What father in his right mind would be satisfied leaving his child in a country that is about to fail morally, economically, and politically?

Short of direct divine revelation, it is impossible for anybody to know the future of the nation with any certainty. But if one were to look at present trends and extrapolate them into the future, he would find a decline in personal morality, more homosexuality, higher incidences of molestations in public schools, more children born without fathers, more devastation to the family, more big government tyranny, more economic stress on the future (with the savings rates falling steadily and the debt rates rising steadily), and lower birth rates. This has been the direction set by at least 100 years of recent history, and it has only accelerated over the last 40 years. If our course is not diverted into massive reformation, there will be little hope that this nation's great heritage will be salvaged for our children and grandchildren. The Christian faith will languish and we may be subject to an Islamic invasion not unlike that seen in European nations. The era of Western Christianity may indeed be over.

But God is in the heavens and He does whatsoever He wills among the armies of heaven and the inhabitants of the earth. None can stay His hand, or say unto Him, "What are You doing?"[3] God is not done with this nation yet. There is a quiet movement of God that has been steadily spreading across this nation since the 1960s, and this movement I call "The Second Mayflower." History is a river that flows like a complex of a thousand currents and streams. From man's perspective, it is impossible to determine the direction it will head even 20 years hence. But one thing is certain: history's direction has always been changed by small minorities of men and women who are self-consciously and intensely committed to either what is right or what is wrong, and remain so committed for generations (Lev. 26:3; Deut. 32:30).

Thus, this rising movement has the potential to impact history regardless of the direction this nation takes. Nevertheless, before I lay the groundwork for building this Second Mayflower, it is important that we consider the three possible scenarios.

Scenario #1: Repentance and Reformation on a Massive National Scale — A complete reversal of direction will only happen if the remnant begins that reformation. Such a reformation must include a renewed interest in the Bible and a conformance to God's demands on our lives, our churches, families, and communities. Although rare in the history of nations, there are several clear examples of this form of repentance recorded in biblical history (2 Kings 22; Jon. 3:10; Matt. 12:41).

Scenario #2: Tyranny — If we were to extrapolate the present situation into the future, we might realistically expect tyranny. That is not much of an extrapolation since the two predominant worldviews in control of modern civil governments (Humanist and Muslim) both produce tyranny. The limitations on government that come through Christian common law — from the Magna Carta (1215) to our own Constitution and Bill of Rights — are rejected by professed statists. For both Muslims, trained in the Koran, and the Humanists, trained in the worldview of Rousseau, Marx, and Plato, the state must play a central role in their lives. That is, the world and life view of either Muslims or Humanists cannot be realized without a coercive state. For both Muslim and Humanist, salvation comes by the power of the sword or the gun. But for the Christian, salvation simply cannot come by means of state coercion — it can only come by the supernatural work of the Spirit of God through the sharing of the Word of God. The Christian state emerges as a derivative of that work.

Totalitarian states subjugate their citizens, maintaining control through fear while expecting fidelity from the masses. Of course, a nation like ours does not produce the oppressive state overnight. It is far more common for a populace to accept tyranny, just as the proverbial frog in the pot passively takes the graduated temperatures until he is good and cooked. As the state tightens its tyrannical grip on a nation, the citizenry tolerate increased regulations on small businesses, increased taxes on families, more violations of privacy, and assorted onerous measures. It may not be long before certain biblical forms of child discipline are disallowed and pastors are imprisoned for preaching against the sin of sodomy. Should such a scenario unfold, there would be all the more reason for another Mayflower. Only men and women with such a vision as this could prepare a haven for such a time of oppression and persecution.

Scenario #3: Fragmentation and Decentralization — With the inevitable collapse of every modern empire, it is far more likely that we will see great decentralization occurring in the near future. Here again, I am only extrapolating trends that are presently seen everywhere. With the advent of the Internet, communication and media have been radically decentralized. The major television networks are fast losing viewers. The webcast for my Generations radio program now reaches 60 nations, and I broadcast from the basement in my home. How many thousands of other such programs now exist, something that was impossible ten years ago? While the major newspapers are losing subscriptions at a rate of 5–10 percent every six months, smaller centers of community and information sharing are rising everywhere. For the first time in a hundred years, the cultural monopoly of a few wealthy investors in Hollywood is unraveling. Developments in technology have enabled small production companies (even local churches) to produce their own feature-length films that have sold millions of reproductions. The world is changing. Even nations that have drunk deeply of the well-packaged humanist, socialist, and materialist worldview coming out of Hollywood now prefer their own productions. For example, film companies in Lagos, Nigeria, have produced 2,500 local features in the last year or two, and film producers in Bombay are pushing out 1,000 films a year.[4]

Already, economic trends toward decentralization can be seen in some forms of manufacturing. For example, micro-coffee "beaneries" provide variety in coffee that mass production could never provide. Smaller, local farms now produce organic food products with a far shorter shelf life. And those who would prefer unpasteurized milk may avail themselves of local provisions.

This trend toward decentralization is also apparent in education. While the American educrats worked hard to centralize the control and funding of education through the Federal Department of Education, millions of parents separated from the system entirely and established the ultimate in the decentralization of education — homeschooling![5]

But will technology continue to drive decentralization? Hardly any form of technology has supported the modern nation states as gas and oil. What will happen when technology enables the decentralization of energy? Whether it be hydrogen technology research developing a cost-effective way to isolate the hydrogen atom from the water molecule, or advancements in solar or wind energy technology, such discoveries will radically free families and communities from centralized control of energy sources. Such developments will bring about significant changes in our geopolitical systems and will allow increased self-reliance and isolation for the state.

Historically, the major catalyst to decentralization comes by way of corruption within (philosophically and morally) and wars from without. Ironically, the centralizing power that formed the empires becomes the means of their own destruction. For example, weapons of mass destruction were first developed in a world where massive centers of power developed around cities and then empires. But these weapons in the hands of rogue nations, employed against the modern centers of power, will result in decentralization away from those centers.

Whenever great empires, like Rome, fall, men are overwhelmed with grief (Is. 21:9; Jer. 51:8; Rev. 14:8) as their faith in man shatters. Many assume that such tragedies must mark the end of the world, and the years following a collapse are always considered "dark ages." But what can we say about towers that fall and the massive decentralization that follows? The Tower of Babel was not the only tower to have met such a fate. For those of us who are not so interested in building empires, these tyrannies will not be missed. The Christian world is not built upon empires. This is not the supreme purpose for our lives. What we are really after is the kingdom of God, which is built on relationships, peace between brothers, righteousness, and joy in the Holy Spirit (Rom. 14:17). It is built upon godly families, churches, and communities that maintain relationship by covenant. It is built upon the righteous laws of God, without which there can be no guarantee of maximum liberty for the people. Conversely, the city of man is always built on centralized, top-down power, and tends to authoritarian rule.

America may very likely fragment into smaller nation-states defined by various socioeconomic, cultural, and moral lines. Some may embrace the Muslim religion, others may embrace socialism, and yet others may realize the vision of the first Mayflower: a country obedient to God and blessed by God. As the economy continues to languish, some states could choose to separate for economic reasons. Unfortunately, racial and cultural differences continue to inspire hate in some parts of the country. This hatred is particularly encouraged by multicultural education and ethnic awareness programs that do little or nothing to unify the nation. It is also quickly becoming clear that religious pluralism without biblical constraints will always break down into ethnic, religious, and cultural

FROM THE FILM: "We're going to pass an inheritence on to our children. We're going to rebuild our families. . . . We're going to teach our children these values, while the rest of the world is effectively going to hell in a handbasket."

division. The Muslim population in America is growing fast and is now pressuring the public schools to accommodate expressions of their faith as well. Without the choice of a biblical government, multicultural societies like those in France, Germany, Bosnia, and America face either tyranny or fragmentation — or both.

Nobody will be as prepared for such decentralization as those who have spent the last three generations building godly families and churches by cultivating relationships and applying God's law to their own lives!

Whatever the scenario will be — reformation, tyranny, or fragmentation — this great movement of God in the 21st century could not be better timed! For if God is really sovereign and if He blesses nations that bless Him (as He has so singularly blessed this nation), then no social order will ever receive the blessing of God unless the people have covenanted together to obey His laws. The libertarians will never create political and economic freedom apart from a government that bases its judicial laws on the Law of God. It is only God's Law that can effectively restrain the tyrant's pursuit for power while creating a social order in which community interacts peaceably and profitably. The law of the one who is both One and Many can resolve the difficulty of the one and the many in our social structures. As this nation's founding fathers pointed out on numerous occasions, freedom is impossible to sustain without a moral, self-governing people. Peaceful communities are impossible dreams without a virtuous, regenerate people. Certainly secular, multi-cultural programs in our universities will not cut it. We need covenanting Christians who have committed their entire lives to the lordship of Jesus Christ and His revealed Word in the Scriptures.

It is the perfect time for another Mayflower. In many ways, present conditions and circumstances parallel the times surrounding the first Mayflower. Yet, I wonder if there are enough of us to renew the Mayflower Compact of 1620. Have we the dedication and resolve to make a covenant based on the Word of God to form a community that will be blessed by God? Truly, we need hundreds of thousands of people who are willing to commit their lives under the lordship of Jesus Christ. We need tens of thousands of fathers who have a clear vision for the future and are committed to leaving a legacy for their children and grandchildren. We need men and women who are willing to repent of complacency and lethargy, seeking God with their whole hearts, seeking His will, revealed in Scripture, by vigorous study, and who are willing to spend their lives applying His laws to their lives, their family, church, and community government.

Who are these people who make up America's foundations? To understand the nature and character of these people is to understand your history and your heritage. The Puritans and Pilgrims were a people dedicated to the Lord. In the midst of terrible social decay, they raised their children in the fear and teaching of the Lord. In spite of threatened persecution, they worked for doctrinal accuracy and personal obedience to the laws of God. They wrote some of the best treatises on biblical topics that the world had seen to that point. They were courageous, self-disciplined, educated, godly, and never afraid to address any subject from a distinctively biblical perspective. They kept the Sabbath day holy, held family devotions twice a day, insisted upon honesty and uprightness in business, and preached the Bible in the face of kings and princes, risking imprisonment and death. Half of them would die during the first year of their venture into the wilderness.

Do we have the commitment of the Puritans and Pilgrims in our churches today? Do we have what it takes? Are we ready for another Mayflower?

Endnotes

Taken from *The Second Mayflower* by Kevin Swanson (Parker, CO: Generations with Vision, 2008, third edition), used by permission, www.generationswithvision.com.

1. *The Hugh Hewitt Program*, January 5, 2006.
2. Humanism is the doctrine that man defines his own truth and ethics, and ultimately controls his own destiny. (Refer to the *Humanist Manifesto I and II* for a more developed definition.)
3. Daniel 4:35.
4. Isaac Botkin, *Outside Hollywood* (San Antonio, TX: Vision Forum Ministries, 2007), p. 213.
5. This trend toward federal control of education continues in full force. Incredibly, federal funding of education has almost tripled from 2000 to 2006, while funding for higher education quintupled.

"Behold, children are a heritage from the LORD, the fruit of the womb is a reward."

— *Psalm 127:3*

CHAPTER TWENTY

Mind, Body, and Soul:
Three Big Reasons to Homeschool
David and Kim d'Escoto

"By homeschooling, we can really tune in to our children's unique qualities and encourage them to follow their divine appointments..."

DAVID AND KIM D'ESCOTO

David and Kim d'Escoto were once skeptical about homeschooling, never even considering the idea until their firstborn entered first grade. Today, they have six children and have been homeschooling for 14 years. Drawing from his experience as an adult Bible teacher and church ministry leader, and her background in elementary education, the d'Escotos are committed to reaching out to families and spreading the homeschool vision. The d'Escotos' interviews do not appear on the *IndoctriNation* DVD but may be included in a follow-up project on home education. The following excerpts are taken from their book *The Little Book of Big Reasons to Homeschool*.

The Conviction

Homeschooling wasn't something we had always planned on doing. With Kim's bachelor's degree in elementary education and a few years of teaching under her belt prior to motherhood, we didn't even think about schooling our own at home. We believed that children should be educated by professionals, the supposed authorities on education. The homeschool families we met now and then were nice, but we automatically categorized them as being, well, different. Maybe they had bad experiences in public schools and couldn't afford Christian schools, we reasoned. Perhaps they were fear-driven, overly protective parents who refused to let their children out into real the world. Or maybe they were rebels who wanted to make some kind of political statement. Okay, the term *religious zealots* also came to mind. Whatever the case, we figured homeschoolers were a scattered few, treading off the beaten path into the unknown. Eventually they would probably come around and see that schools were where children belonged.

Unlike Paul in his rampage against the early Christians, we weren't out to persecute anyone. However, we did experience a similar, unpredictable about-face in our convictions. Part of the revelation came with the unsettling feeling we faced when the time approached to send our firstborn off to first grade, knowing this full-day arrangement would take her from our nest longer than she had ever been before as a part-time preschooler and kindergartener. Was it already time to delegate to another such a large portion of her training and nurturing? Our apprehension grew stronger as we questioned school board politics, policy changes, and a few ugly scandals. But the biggest factor that drew us to keep our children home wasn't as much the frustration and dissatisfaction with the current school arrangement as it was a sudden awakening and attraction toward the perfect alternative — homeschooling.

The Lord brought Jane, a dear woman of faith and a seasoned homeschool veteran, into Kim's life at just the right time. Through her friendship, words of wisdom, encouragement, and prayers, we began to understand homeschooling in a new way. Meeting her close-knit family and admiring the special relationship they shared sparked a greater desire to investigate this option. A timely visit to our wonderful state homeschool convention preceded lots of reading and research, and we soon became convinced that this was the right path for our family.

Now, we're among the "different" ones. And we love it. In fact, our family has been so blessed by our experience that we are passionate about sharing the homeschool vision. The years have strengthened our conviction that this is the right choice for families who are seeking the blessings of togetherness, richer learning experiences, and a lasting godly legacy.

The Blessings

God is truly moving in our world through the homeschool movement. In a time when we have witnessed the fabric of the family becoming unraveled and the grave results on society, He is turning the hearts and minds of children and parents back toward each other, one family at a time. Many can already testify that there are real blessings to being obedient to God's call, blessings that will carry on into eternity.

Benefits to the Mind

There are many advantages to sharing life and learning with our children at home. First, let's explore the benefits of the mind — the academic side. Naturally, this is a major concern for people considering the path of homeschooling. We all want our children to be literate, to develop their minds, and to use the gifts with which they have been blessed by their Creator. One of the biggest benefits to homeschooling is being able to put aside ineffective "schoolish ways" and take a more successful, individualized approach to learning.

"Meaningful dialogue replaces the need for an overuse of mundane workbooks and worksheets, which teachers too often rely upon as a means of proving that concepts have been learned."

The following passage from the Book of Psalms beautifully illustrates how each of us was created as a unique being:

> For you formed my inward parts; you knitted me together in my mother's womb. I praise you, for I am fearfully and wonderfully made. Wonderful are your works; my soul knows it very well. My frame was not hidden from you, when I was being made in secret, intricately woven in the depths of the earth. Your eyes saw my unformed substance; in your book were written, every one of them, the days that were formed for me, when as yet there was none of them (Ps. 139:13–16).

Our heavenly Father authored a special purpose for each of His children and has given to parents the authority to see that His plan is followed. By homeschooling, we can really tune in to our children's unique qualities, address their individual needs in learning styles, pace, and interests, and encourage them to follow their divine appointments in life.

Learning Styles — At home, parents are able to tailor academics to children's individual learning styles. Ask any number of elementary school teachers and they will probably agree that one of the biggest challenges is meeting the individual needs of 25 or more students simultaneously. Since this is nearly impossible, teachers must gear instruction to the average student. Children above or below this level are expected to conform. By contrast, the personalized instruction of homeschooling creates an optimum learning environment for each child, regardless of level.

Learning styles vary distinctly from person to person. Some children learn best through a hands-on approach. Others lean toward an auditory style. And then there are those who prefer a strong visual learning environment. Add to that the list of multiple intelligences, which also include verbal, logical, musical, interpersonal, and intrapersonal abilities. There are so many ways to assess individual learning strengths. Unfortunately, institutional schooling methods tend to capitalize exclusively on verbal and logical skills, leaving many children out of the loop.

Determining a child's learning preferences takes time as they develop over the years. Can we really expect a classroom teacher to know what's best for our child among a large group in a brief 180-day school year? Parents know their children in an intimate way, far more intimately than a schoolteacher can. The love and appreciation born out of the parent-child relationship fuels the desire to discover our child's unique bent and thus create the optimum learning environment.

"What will children remember most — that they had all the latest toys, the coolest clothes, and the biggest house on the block, or that their parents were there when they needed them most?"

Quality Time — The tutorial style of home teaching results in less wasted time. Because teaching at home is one-on-one, parents can get immediate feedback on a child's progress. Meaningful dialogue replaces the need for an overuse of mundane workbooks and worksheets, which teachers too often rely upon as a means of proving that concepts have been learned. With less pencil pushing required, there is more time for enriching activities. And unlike a classroom environment, less time is wasted on disciplinary challenges, class transitions, waiting in line for help, and the many distractions that are inevitable in a large group setting. Therefore, children are better able to concentrate and engage in complex activities and thought processes. As a result, the typical homeschool day is actually much shorter and more productive than an institutional school day. Many families are done with studies in a fraction of the time that most children are sitting in a classroom or a school bus. Some homeschoolers even schedule a four-day week, setting aside the fifth day for field trips or special activities.'

A Pace of Their Own — Children develop at different rates and should not be forced to conform to the pace and structure of a one-size-fits-all school system. Without the pressure of feeling left behind or the boredom of being unchallenged, children can work in the home at a comfortable pace. When an area is mastered, they can skip ahead to something new. If a concept needs further reinforcement, this can be addressed until the child is ready to move on.

School readiness is an important issue when considering the needs of a child. The unfortunate trend is to require too much too soon of little ones. Despite the government's push to give children a "Head Start," studies show that many children just aren't ready for the rigors of formal schooling until age eight to ten, when they are better able to handle the physical, mental, and social demands. Dr. Raymond and Dorothy Moore, leaders in homeschool and Christian education, point out:

> The sequence for the average child these days often spells disaster for both mental and physical health in a sure sequence: (1) *uncertainty* as the child leaves the family nest early for a less secure environment, (2) *puzzlement* at the new pressures and restrictions of the classroom, (3) *frustration* because unready learning tools — senses, cognition, brain hemispheres, coordination — cannot handle the regimentation of formal lessons and the pressures they bring, (4) *hyperactivity* growing out of nerves and jitter, from frustration,

(5) *failure,* which quite naturally flows from the four experiences above, and (6) *delinquency,* which is failure's twin and apparently for the same reason.[1]

Setting a slow and steady pace in the warmth of the home makes education much less stressful and lays a positive foundation for the child's future.

Delight-Directed Learning — Delight-directed learning means that lessons and schedules are built upon family members' interests. Rather than becoming captives of the state, homeschool families are able to customize schedules and learning goals. Whether your interests include music, art, science, sports, gardening, or traveling, using your family's interests as a springboard is a great way to customize your curriculum. Special-interest projects and field trips can enrich the experience of education at home. Activities like these bring subjects to life and make learning fun and purposeful.

If you look at the lives of famous homeschooled people and their accomplishments, you will find a common thread. They were able to tap into their personal passions at a young age, instead of being confined to a rigorous school day schedule. Just imagine how many masterpieces in art, music, or literature might have been stifled had the potential of these men and women been limited by an institutional education.

Learning in the Context of Life — Instead of 180 days of school per academic year — the average for public and parochial schools — most home educators can honestly say that learning happens 365 days per year. Topics can be discussed at the dinner table or driving in the car. The pastor's sermon in church might tie in with family Bible readings. Vacations can include trips to historic sites or taking in the beauty of God's creation. Great literature is read aloud and discussed together. The entire family develops important life skills by cooking, gardening, and doing household chores and home improvement projects. Even a new baby's arrival is a precious learning experience and a welcome addition to any curricular plans. Many homeschool families also participate together in home-based businesses, ministries, and missionary work. Endeavors such as these offer firsthand preparation for the real world year-round, something that classroom settings just cannot offer.

Benefits to the Body

Physically and socially, children have needs that are best understood and addressed in the loving, nurturing environment of the home. Contrary to a common assumption, children's needs do not diminish as they develop from early childhood into adolescence. The increasing pressures of growing up warrant special parental guidance, attention, and secure family bonds. By following God's original plan, we can bring our children back to the family body to receive the blessings of being nurtured more fully in the home.

Freedom from Confinement — It is an undeniable fact that children need to move. For those who are especially active, this physical need merges with their mental development. These kinesthetic learners simply learn better by wiggling, touching, and doing. For many children, sitting in a desk for a large portion of the day is torture and usually lands them anywhere from the principal's office to the doctor's office, oftentimes joining the ranks of the medicated.

At home the need for physical activity can be addressed in fun, creative ways. Spelling words are recited while bouncing on the trampoline. Math facts are reviewed by rolling giant dice and moving across a life-size game board through the living room and up the stairway. Nature walks take science lessons and marry them with much-needed physical activity. Children learn best by doing, and sometimes that means hopping, skipping, and jumping.

People often ask which room we use for homeschooling, probably picturing straight rows of desks in our living room facing the chalkboard on the wall, and Mrs. Crabtree sitting behind a big desk with stick in hand. The truth is, these parents don't want to sit behind a desk all day any more than their children do. Our school is the whole house, the backyard, the bike trails, the museums, the library, and even the grocery store. We read at the breakfast table, on the backyard swing set, on the sofa, and in bed. If classrooms could only be equipped with such comforts.

Attachment/Detachment — From birth, our babies depend on us for their every need. They do not come with instruction manuals, so we figure out our parental roles as we go. We learn how to comfort them, when to feed them, when they need sleep. As they grow, we understand their cries, their habits, and their unique way of communicating to us. We are there when they learn to walk and speak their first words. We are their teachers from day one, and we love them in a way no one else can.

And then they turn five, or younger in some cases, and we are expected to cut the apron strings and turn them over to the state to continue their education. Some parents do this without batting an eye, accepting it as the norm. For others, it just doesn't feel right. But against strong internal voices, many let go of those little hands that once grasped their own.

The detachment process begins, and almost unknowingly, the gap between child and home widens. Bonds are loosened, and the foundation of trust crumbles. Children who once looked to their parents for leadership now turn to their teachers for knowledge, their peers for wisdom, and their music and televisions for entertainment. When the fabric of the family loses its intended purpose and strength, children are at greater risk of being lost to the world.

This has become the unquestioned norm in our society, and the unfortunate consequence is an epidemic of fragmented families.

Benefits to the Soul

Our children's lives reflect their beliefs, and their beliefs are built upon what they have been taught. The absence of biblical teaching in the home has proven to contribute to the growing problem of biblical illiteracy in the Christian community. Many professing Christians cannot identify more than two or three of the disciples, and 60 percent cannot name even five of the Ten Commandments.[2]

Too many Christians have become complacent in their preschool-level of Bible understanding. While claiming that the gospel is at the core of their beliefs, many are failing to apply its principles to their lives. As a result, the Church has witnessed a severe compromise of standards and behavior, which ultimately nullifies a Christian's testimony. The responsibility of spiritual training belongs to the parents and must be a priority in every home. While the church may provide assistance, Sunday school and youth programs should never be a substitute for the instruction that God has commanded to be carried out first and foremost within the family.

Wise and Foolish Builders — Jesus' Parable of the Wise and Foolish Builders (see Matt. 7:24–27) demonstrates our need to build foundations upon the rock of God's principles. In training up our children, it takes time to build these foundations. "When you lie down, and when you rise," the Bible says (Deut. 6:7). Public schools are built upon the sinking sand of false ideologies and unbiblical agendas — not neutral, but anti-God agendas. It is dangerous to assume that a weekly Sunday school class or youth social event will undo the 40 or more hours that children spend in state institutions where they are influenced by ideas that blatantly contradict God's Word.

Would it be prudent to expect our children's physical health to thrive if they ate candy all week and we threw in a tossed green salad on Sunday morning? Of course it wouldn't. But this is the kind of spiritual diet partaken by many children of born-again Christian families.

A recent Barna Group poll reveals some disturbing information. In a survey of parents across America, research shows that there is a lack of difference in the way born-again Christian parents and their non-believing counterparts are raising their children. In fact, born-again Christian parents partaking in the study were more likely to put an emphasis on seeing that their children received a good education over seeing them become followers of Christ. Among other areas of importance to these parents were helping children feel secure, affirmed, encouraged, happy. Only three out of ten Christian parents even included the salvation of their child in the list. George Barna explains:

> Believers do not train their children to think or act any
> differently. When our kids are exposed to the same influences,
> without much supervision, and are generally not guided to
> interpret their circumstances and opportunities in light of bib-
> lical principles, it's no wonder that they grow up to be just as
> involved in gambling, adultery, divorce, cohabitation, exces-
> sive drinking and other unbiblical behaviors as everyone else.[3]

Make no mistake — our children will be tested. They will have to withstand temptation and weather the storms of life ahead. The time we spend with them now in fervent prayer and preparation will not be in vain. Be sure they truly know, fully understand, and passionately embrace the principles of Christ, the Solid Rock.

Wisdom — Jesus contrasted the two builders as being wise and foolish. Let's talk about wise and what that means in educating our families. The Bible gives us many good passages about wisdom, including its foundation: a fear of the Lord. "The fear of the Lord is the beginning of wisdom; all those who practice it have a good understanding" (Ps. 111:10). Fearing the Lord — respect, honor, reverence, awe, and yes, even healthy fear for His unsurpassed holiness compared to our complete inadequacy, our utter doom without Him — this is the beginning, and foundation, to our goal in training up our children. Every day should be an opportunity for us to say "Come, O children, listen to me; I will teach you the fear of the Lord" (Ps. 34:11).

In the world's eyes, wisdom is measured through academic intelligence or material success. In God's eyes, true wisdom comes from following the principles He has laid out for us in Scripture. These very principles should be the backbone of our teaching. What is worldly wisdom apart from Christ?

Our children may or may not be gifted with the mathematical skill to become engineers, the scientific knowledge to become brain surgeons, or the mastery of language to become best-selling authors. But if they love and fear the Lord, learn to love Jesus as their Lord and Savior, and live to serve Him in whatever area to which they are called, while embracing Scripture as their roadmap throughout life, then we have done our job as imparters of true wisdom.

The Exhortation

It has been said that our checkbooks reveal where our treasure is. It is also fair to say that our daily calendars reflect where our passions and priorities lie. What we sow now, in time, money, and energy, will surely impact that which we and our families will reap later.

Jesus said, "For where your treasure is, there your heart will be also" (Matt. 6:21). The sacrifice of time and material things made by parents who choose the path of home education tells children they are the treasures in their parents' hearts. Oftentimes, this means a second income is sacrificed so that mom can stay home. But families find creative ways to make ends meet, and you cannot put a price on the message that your family's well-being is a priority.

What will children remember most — that they had all the latest toys, the coolest clothes, and the biggest house on the block, or that their parents were there when they needed them most? In the final analysis, the parents who sacrificed the temporal for the eternal will have a greater satisfaction and joy.

To homeschool is to take a step on a narrow path. Jesus encourages us to "Enter by the narrow gate. For the gate is wide and the way is easy that leads to destruction, and those who enter by it are many" (Matt. 7:13). More and more are finding this path, but homeschooling is still considered counter-cultural. Prepare to face skepticism, even criticism, not just by unbelievers, but by fellow Christians as well. Your neighbors may raise their eyebrows, school personnel may question your qualifications, and your mother-in-law may even tell you that you are going to ruin her grandchildren. In time, the blessings and fruit will speak for themselves: happy, well-adjusted (and yes, well-socialized) children who are not only smart but wise; close-knit families; and the joy and peace that come from being obedient to God's Word.

The proof will be in the pudding, as the saying goes. But the bottom line is this — you will be held accountable before your children's Creator. He has entrusted to you the care of His lambs, to nurture their minds, bodies, and souls. This is a task and privilege we must take seriously, for the results will have an everlasting impact. Pray fervently and ask for the heavenly Father's guidance in your decision. With Him on your side, you can move forward with confidence and joy.

Endnotes

Taken from *The Little Book of Big Reasons to Homeschool* by David and Kim d'Escoto (Nashville, TN: B&H Publishing Group, 2007), used by permission, www.bhpublishinggroup.com.

All scripture quotes in this chapter, unless otherwise noted, are taken from the English Standard Version (ESV).

1. Dr. Raymond and Dorothy Moore, "When Education Becomes Abuse: A Different Look at the Mental Health of Children," The Moore Foundation and Academy, www.moorefoundation.com/When%20Education%20Becomes%20Abuse.html (accessed July 29, 2005), http://www.moorefoundation.com/article.php?id=48 (updated url January 13, 2012).
2. Albert Mohler, "The Scandal of Biblical Illiteracy: It's Our Problem," Crosswalk Weblogs, www.goshen.com/faith/1218766.html (accessed July 29, 2005), http://www.christianity.com/blogs/mohler/1270946/print/ (updated url January 13, 2012).
3. George Barna, "The Barna Update: Parents Describe How They Raise Their Children," www.barna.org/FlexPage.aspx?Page=BarnaUpdate&BarnaUpdateID=183 (accessed July 29, 2005), http://www.barna.org/barna-update/article/5-barna-update/184-parents-describe-how-they-raise-their-children?q=parents+describe+raise+children (updated url January 13, 2012).

*". . . Come out from among them
and be separate, says the Lord.
Do not touch what is unclean,
and I will receive you."*

— II Corinthians 6:17

CHAPTER TWENTY-ONE

The Dog Ate My Lesson Plans:
Common Excuses to Keep from Homeschooling

Israel Wayne

"You can't have a student meditating on God's Law both day and night if they're in a government school. It just can't happen."

ISRAEL WAYNE

Israel Wayne is a homeschooled graduate who is leading his generation in defending the Christian faith and developing a biblical worldview. He is a regular columnist for *Home School Digest* and *Brush Arbor Quarterly*, published by Wisdom's Gate (www.WisdomsGate.org), where he currently serves as the marketing director. He is also the site editor for www.ChristianWorldview.net. Learn more about his speaking ministry at www.IsraelWayne.com. The following excerpt is taken from Mr. Wayne's book *Homeschooling from a Biblical Worldview*.

COMMON EXCUSES TO KEEP FROM HOMESCHOOLING

Excuse #1: Homeschooling costs too much money.

When we first started homeschooling, our homeschooling budget was next to zero. My mother called a few curriculum companies who sold to the public schools to find out if they would sell books to her. She figured she would be able to find a good deal on discontinued or outdated books from some of the major curriculum publishers. She was even willing to take their used, damaged books — anything to get started.

The first question they would ask when she called was "Is this a school?"

"Well, no," Mom would answer. "I need the books to teach my children at home."

"Are you a certified teacher?" Again she would admit she wasn't. "Do you have a degree?"

"A degree?" she would echo.

"Yes, like a college degree!"

"Well, no."

"What education do you have?"

"I started the ninth grade . . ." she would begin, until uproarious laughter forced her to pull the phone away from her ear.

"You don't even have a high school diploma, and you want to teach your children yourself?!" More laughter. "That's a good one! Well, I'd like to help you, but we only sell to schools, sorry."

It seemed that no one in the country would sell to an "uneducated" mother who wanted to teach her children at home. But, we were not discouraged. Mom had a plan. We went to every yard sale and K-Mart within a 20-mile radius. She bought used textbooks on every available subject and finally pieced together our first curriculum.

I think the total cost was somewhere around five or six dollars. We had to overlook some of the crayon scribbling and tattered pages, but we finally started our "formal" education. I don't know if we had any two books published by the same company, but we had all of the required subjects represented.

The good news is that parents today have many more options. Nowadays, many parents go to used curriculum swaps to exchange books or to purchase used materials at a discounted price. Several homeschool catalogues offer discounted prices on new material. You also can access the public library for supplementary books, and many parents share resources within a support group.

When possible, try to buy new products. Your children will enjoy using top-quality materials, and it looks better if you have to show your books to skeptical in-laws. Sometimes, because of the finan-cial constraints of a single-income household, you have to learn to be creative, but it can be done. The average expenditure per home-schooled student is $400–500 per year.

For $500 a year you can buy an incredible amount of books, text-books, workbooks, lesson plans, software, educational games, science projects, etc. Most of my friends homeschool their children for less than $100 per child, per year. Let's face it, in America, anyone can do that!

Excuse #2: If I homeschool, my children won't be exposed to a wide scope of ideas, lifestyles, or philosophies.

I had a conversation recently with a secular textbook publisher who was trying to break into the homeschooling market. He told me that most of his books had been readily accepted by Christian parents.

"What do you mean by most of your books?" I asked.

"Well, some homeschoolers didn't like our biology texts because they talk about evolution. Homeschooling parents don't seem to live in the real world. They want their children to know 'creation' and nothing else. What will happen if they attend a mainstream university? They won't know what evolution even espouses. I don't see how parents can call that a real education."

"Do the textbooks simply talk about evolution, or do they promote it as factual?" I sensed an inconsistency in his reasoning.

"I don't see the difference, I mean, modern science has proved evolution as the only explanation for the origin of the species."

"Do you teach creationism as a possible explanation for the origin of life?"

"No."

"Let me get this straight," I pressed. "Are you telling me that your biology textbooks teach evolution . . . and nothing else!?"

A long silence followed, and the man never answered the question. It was evident to me that this man wasn't as open-minded and all-inclusive as he claimed. He was an absolutist, just like those he condemns; it's just that he has differing values.

Homeschoolers may see as much immorality, secular ideology, and sin as your average student who is in a government school; they just don't accept it as normal. They can see the error, and they learn to avoid living a pagan lifestyle. The real issue isn't being too sheltered to see debauchery. It's everywhere in our society. There is no escaping it. The real issue is helping our children to recognize fallacies and live in truth. That approach frightens intolerant liberals.

Excuse #3: I'm not qualified to teach my children.

Qualified by whom? Who do you need authorization from? From an academic standpoint, all you need to do is teach your children how to read and how to learn. If they love learning, they will surpass your greatest academic expectations.

My mother didn't even finish formal studies beyond ninth grade. She has successfully homeschooled six children. I graduated from high school when I was 15 and was studying subjects she never even began. She didn't have to stand by my desk every minute to make sure I understood the material. I know how to read, I could follow instructions, and I was motivated to study. Basically, children who love learning will teach themselves.

John Taylor Gatto, a former New York school teacher who won the teacher of the year award in that state in 1990, says in his book *Dumbing Us Down*, "I dropped the idea that I was an expert, whose job it was to fill the little heads with my expertise, and began to explore how I could remove those obstacles that prevented the inherent genius of children from gathering itself."

FROM THE FILM: "[Do government schools give] godly counsel based in the fear of the Lord? Is it proclaiming Jesus as Lord over all of creation, including math and science and history? No, of course not."

From an academic standpoint, I tend to agree with Mr. Gatto on this point. The danger is inhibiting the learning of the children. You don't need to cram their heads with information; just unlock their learning potential. You do this by reading to the child and developing as many hands-on learning situations as possible. Learning should be interesting and exciting. If a child loves learning, there will be no stopping him. Dr. Brian Ray, of the National Home Education Research Institute, found in his 1997 study that there is less than an 8 percent difference between the scores of children whose parents had graduated college and those who hadn't finished high school.

Test scores showed only a 3 percent difference between parents with teacher certificates and the average parent with no certificate. Imagine then the fact that "uneducated" parents are raising their children who are scoring 35 percentage points above students taught by a certified governmental school teacher. It simply proves that God's ways are always the best.

> The foolishness of God is wiser than men, and the weakness of God is stronger than men (1 Cor. 1:25).

> Wisdom is justified by her children (Matt. 11:19).

From a spiritual standpoint, God has given us a biblical mandate to teach and train our own children. He will never give us a responsibility without giving us the tools to complete the task. We have been commissioned; we must be obedient.

Excuse #4: My children will be deprived of the quality resources available in the public schools.

This belief is absolutely, completely, and totally false. I work as the marketing director for Wisdom's Gate, and talk with educational publishers every day. A homeschooling parent can access anything that is used in a governmental school. You can even order school desks, chalkboards, and American flags if you want. Several school supply catalogs sell directly to consumers and include every conceivable item found in an equipped public school room. Of course, we recognize that parents don't need everything the schools use, but it is all available if someone wanted it. Add to that the thousands of Christian publishers and suppliers who sell to homeschoolers, and we've got 'em beat by a long stretch. I'm amazed at how much is available in the homeschooling market. It's phenomenal! Believe me, anything a parent wants for his or her child is available if the parent just looks for it.

Excuse #5: My children won't receive an adequate education if I teach them at home.

Homeschoolers have consistently exceeded government and private schools in standardized tests. Dr. Ray found that homeschoolers are scoring a composite of 35 percentage points above their governmentally schooled counterparts! Other studies available from the Home School Legal Defense Association show that children with special needs also do significantly better in a home learning environment (Dr. Steven Duvall's research).

Of course, I believe that as we obey God, academic success will be added unto us. Test scores, however, should not be our main motivations. What does it profit us if we have a 4.0 grade average, graduate with our master's degree at 14, and go on to gain worldly success if we lose our own souls? If parents focus on giving their children a biblical worldview, I can assure you, their children will excel in everything they do. It's that natural cause and effect of the blessing of God. When we obey, we are blessed; when we don't, we are cursed.

I've never met a homeschooler who was trained up in the way he should go who couldn't hold his own academically among a secular peer group.

Excuse #6: Homeschooling would take too much time.

I've discovered that many parents are very selfish. They are so concerned with their own comfort and their preferred lifestyle that they ignore the crucial needs of their children. There is no greater priority than for parents to be available for their children. Our life is made up of x amount of time. We spend our precious time on what is most important to us.

Will a wife believe a husband's claim to "love his wife above all else" when he spends every spare minute on the golf course? Of course not. When we say our children are not worthy of our time, we send a clear, unmistakable message to them that other things are more important. Our friends, our activities, our social status, our money — almost anything can become more important than our children's lives.

Grow up! If we are mature enough to have children, we should certainly be able to give them the priority they deserve. It's a responsibility, and although we may still want to act like unfettered teenagers, the time comes to put away childish things.

If we have so many activities in our life that we can't homeschool our children, we need to reassess our lives. Career, church activities, extended family, friends — *nothing* should be taking precedence over our obligation to care for and train our children.

Once we have reorganized we will see that homeschooling doesn't take as much time as we originally thought. Most of our homeschooling friends finish their "school work" by 1 p.m. and spend the rest of the afternoon in family activities. If this isn't realty for your family, that's okay. Everyone is different. I would encourage you, however, to examine the expectations you are placing on yourself and determine if they are self-imposed worldly standards, or if they are God-inspired.

If you find that you are poring over textbooks from 8 a.m. to 4 p.m., you are probably biting off more than you really need to. You should probably scale down the formal part of your school day to incorporate non-traditional, hands-on learning experiences.

Buying a complete curriculum package from a single publisher can be a great tool to keep a parent motivated and organized, but usually it ends up being overwhelming and frustrating to the parent. If it is taking too long and causing friction in the family, look for a way to downscale.

Excuse #7: I can't stand to be around my children. They drive me crazy!

As one of my older relatives used to say, "Are ya braggin' or complainin'?" Having children who are so bad that you can't stand to be around them isn't something to be proud of! If your children are that bad, they most definitely *do* need to be homeschooled! Really, whenever parents make such a statement to me, I can't help but think that homeschooling will help them as parents more than it will help their children.

God wants parents to love their children. The refining fire of being together with the children is exactly what a rebellious parent needs. God will shine His light into the parents' hearts and expose all the character flaws that have inhibited their relationship with their children. Once God has the heart of the parent, He begins on the child.

Excuse #8: I want my children to be "salt and light" in the public school.

Let me ask you a question. Do you have religious cults in your neighborhood? If so, do you send your children to their services every Sunday morning? Shouldn't they be there being "salt and light" to the cult members? I wouldn't advocate that you as parents go, just your children.

Let me ask you another question. Do you have bars and nightclubs nearby? Surely your children should also go to these places to be "salt and light." Perhaps you should have them join a street gang so they can witness to their peers. We can't shelter our children from everything, can we?

You may find my exaggeration abrasive, but I hope you can see the logical fallacy with this argument. Let's face it, it isn't concern for our children or a burden for the lost that causes us to use this excuse. If we cared so much for the souls of these lost children in the government schools, we would be there ourselves. We wouldn't sacrifice our children on a humanistic altar under the supposed desire to "reach the lost." We would lay down our own lives for those lost kids, while still choosing to protect our own children.

In politics they call an excuse like this "smoke and mirrors." In an attempt to cover for our own lack of obedience to what we know is right, we try to conceal our shortcomings in a high and lofty ideal such as, "My children are being salt and light in their school." The fact is, the heart is desperately wicked and deceitful. We will often try to cover our own selfishness, and sometimes we deceive ourselves into believing that our decisions are really in the best interests of the children.

Many parents tell me, "My children have led several of their fellow students to the Lord this year." If this is truly the case, God is blessing in spite of the parents' ignorance, not because of it. I personally knew an alcoholic who would witness to other drunks at AA meetings. The problem was, they wouldn't respect him because he was no different than the rest of the group. How could he show them a better way?

God doesn't want us to throw our children into a spiritual snake pit to be salt and light. The way to reach the unsaved in the government schools is to come out and be separate. I've found that people are drawn to ask questions of homeschoolers because they are different. If children are in a secular school, they are being indoctrinated by humanistic thought and are being exposed to all sorts of immorality. Can we really afford to lose our kids for some vain dream of reaching the lost?

FROM THE FILM: "When your children are in that environment and they are walking the halls and in the locker rooms, they're hearing about all the music and the movies of the world, and the sensuality and the sin of the world. That's the way of sinners."

When I was in sixth grade my sister and I spent a year in K–8th grade private school. I had always assumed that private Christian schools were more wholesome than government schools, and I thought for sure I would be a sterling example of an exemplary young Christian in this new school.

I soon discovered that out of a class of about 30 students, only about three were really Christians. Yes, many were from Christian families, and all of them attended church, but only about three actually had a visible relationship with the Lord. It wasn't more than a month before the atmosphere and lifestyle of the pagans started wearing off on me.

Quite a few of the older students listened to hard-core metal music, drank heavily, swore constantly, lusted after pornography, experimented with drugs, and lied like seasoned con artists. The amazing thing was watching them memorize Scripture or act religious when their parents were around. That was an education in and of itself! The school only went up to eighth grade, or it probably would have been worse.

All in all, I would say it was better than almost any government school, but it certainly wasn't a "Christian" environment. I found myself wanting to be accepted. I wanted to fit in. Because I was around my peers more than I was home, the peer group became more important to me than my family. I soon developed an apathy toward learning and a disdain of authority.

Thankfully (in one sense), my grades plummeted. I was so social, I completely lost interest in academics. My report cards sent warning signals to my mother, who began to realize that something was wrong. Relationally, it really took about two years before our family healed from the wounds of that endeavor. A rift had been caused between us by the keeping of bad company.

I wasn't ready to handle it. I was too impressionable and couldn't stand in the face of ridicule and opposition. So I backed down and took the coward's approach of fitting in. I should never have been placed in that position. When children grow up and become adults, then they can stand against forceful opposition. I've never seen a teenager who could fly in the face of total opposition for more than a few months without being negatively impacted.

That doesn't mean they will become exactly like their peers. My sister wasn't influenced as much as I was, but the young person will still be corrupted to some degree. "Bad company corrupts good morals" (1 Cor. 15:33; NASB). It's true and there is no getting around it.

Excuse #9: We live in a good school district, and most of the teachers are Christians.

If I can believe what I hear from most parents, I think every parent must live in a good school district. I have heard opinion polls from parents on how they view our modern educational establishments. The vast majority say that our schools are in desperate trouble. When asked about their local school district, however, almost every parent says, "We have a great school system here!"

Funny, isn't it, how the problems always seem to be "out there somewhere." We can point out the faults of everyone and everything around us, but we can't see error in things that touch us. I've always liked Linus' philosophy in the *Peanuts* cartoon. He fallaciously says, "I love mankind, it's people I can't stand!"

We like to view our educational system in a similar way. In general, parents feel like our nation's school systems are bad, but when it comes to the school where our children attend, we get out the rose-colored glasses. We don't want to see any faults.

Let's face the truth. Nearly every school, everywhere, is being influenced by secularism — even Christian schools. Where do most Christian school teachers get their teaching degrees? From secular colleges, of course. Do we think they can somehow avoid being influenced by their teachers? Let's not fool ourselves. Schools have problems.

Even if your children are in the best school in the country, which is doubtful, a corporate learning environment still falls short of God's best for your children. Your children will miss the individual tutelage and interaction with you, as their parent, and will be forced to settle for second best. The best school in the world is still a step down from following God's order for your child's education.

The reason we should homeschool our children is not as a reaction to a failing school system, or because of our dislike of institutionalized learning, or especially in retaliation for a falling out with the teachers or administrators in a certain school. We should home educate simply out of obedience to a biblical principle. God designed parents as the best teachers for their children. Why? Who knows? But since He did, it makes sense that we should align ourselves with His natural laws of learning.

Don't homeschool for negative reasons. Do it out of simple obedience to God.

Excuse #10: I went to a public school, and it didn't affect me.

Pioneer homeschooler Karl Reed often says, "When I was a baby my mother tripped over a record player, but it didn't affect me, affect me, affect me!"

The point is, how can we possibly spend over 16,800 hours sitting in the counsel of the ungodly and claim it has no impact on us? We develop our worldview from what goes into our minds at an early age. Someone who has been raised in a secular school has probably been influenced much more than he realizes.

Something that is important to understand is that schools today are radically different than they were 20 years ago. They are much more liberal and godless than they were even in the sixties or seventies. Yes, there has always been peer pressure, and there have always been negative influences, but never has the world been so anti-Christian as it is today.

God's grace is a marvelous thing! Jesus has a way of taking negative things in our past and causing them to work together for good. Parents who survived school campuses need to thank God for keeping them pure, and use God's grace to bring their children up in a more Christ-like manner than they were raised.

Most parents made many mistakes when they were teens, and they most likely suffered the consequences of those choices. That is why they do their best to steer their children away from the mistakes they made. Children can avoid certain pitfalls, if their parents won't lie to themselves and say, "It didn't affect me!"

Excuse #11: I want my children to be involved in sports and extracurricular activities.

If sports or social events have kept you from teaching your children at home, I would

> "Blessed is the man who walks not in the counsel of the ungodly, nor stands in the path of sinners, nor sits in the seat of the scornful."
>
> PSALM 1:1

FROM THE FILM: "Children in these schools develop an attitude of resentment toward authority, towards parents, towards teachers, and that is something we're told to avoid."

encourage you to ask yourself a few questions. Am I being pressured by my child to involve them in activities that are opposed to my conscience? In other words, do you personally want your child involved in sports, gymnastics, band practices, or whatever? If not, perhaps you should evaluate if you are the parent, or if the child is.

If you want your child to participate in school events, ask yourself another question. *Why* do I want my child involved in these things? One lady told me she felt God wanted her son to play professional football, so she quit homeschooling him and sent him to a government school. She said he wouldn't have a chance of going pro unless he had played on a high school team.

I don't know whether it was God's will or not. As far as I know, he hasn't been signed yet, but at least his family had a goal. Most parents know God hasn't called their children to be professional athletes; they simply feel that the social interaction would be good for them. I would question the necessity of such extracurricular activities, but if a parent feels they are essential, most of these programs are available through local or state support groups.

There is even a national homeschooling basketball tournament! My point is, if you simply feel a need to have them involved in social activities, you can do that without sending them to the government schools.

If your child wants to play sports, you should evaluate the call of God on the child's life, and pray for direction. Does God really want to use your child in the sports arena? Help your child to realistically evaluate their skills and potential.

When I was ten I was convinced I would be a professional baseball player. After a year of little league I realized that baseball wasn't my gift. I simply wasn't good enough. Unfortunately, some parents won't encourage their children to honestly face their ability (or lack of ability).

I can just imagine how much time I might have wasted going to school, thinking I was going to be a big leaguer when, in fact, God had totally different plans for my life.

Excuse #12: My children won't be able to attend college if they don't go to a public high school.

As the marketing director for *Home School Digest*, I talk to colleges on a regular basis who are actively recruiting homeschooled students. Home scholars are generally self-motivated, and colleges like the attitude of excellence these young adults bring on campus. Home-educated students usually score higher on their college entrance exams and very rarely have the social difficulties in college that traditionally schooled students do.

Colleges are welcoming them with open arms. Many of my home-schooled friends have gone on to college. One studied quantum physics at the University of Maryland, another majored in political economics at Hillsdale College, and a third studied communications at Liberty University. None of my friends had any trouble getting admission to the school of their choice, and most of them actually received scholarships.

Some schools offer scholarship programs exclusively for home educators. Oral Roberts University in Tulsa, Pensacola Christian College in Florida, Bryan College in Tennessee (15 percent of their students have been home educated), and Bob Jones University are just a few of the more than 200 colleges that have accepted home-schooled students.

Excuse #13: The dog ate my lesson plans.

We can drudge up an inordinate amount of "reasons" why we can't homeschool, but really it all boils down to a heart problem. Let's face it — we don't want to do anything that might make us uncomfortable. Biblical homeschooling works, and God honors obedience. We can overcome any obstacle if we are in God's will. Nothing will be able to prevail against us if we are clothed in His strength and following His voice.

Our family has been homeschooling for over 20 years, and I'll admit, it hasn't always been easy. We have all had to face ourselves and recognize our shortcomings. We have, at times, needed to change our habits and beliefs. But through it all, I've learned that it's better to walk through the valley of the shadow of death with Jesus than to walk in "comfort" in our own wisdom. When it gets darkest, we simply close our eyes and grip tighter the unchanging hand that leads us.

Jesus will never leave us or forsake us. That's a promise! We've got His Word on it! It's better to be back against the Red Sea, with Pharaoh's army breathing down our neck—knowing that God is with us — than to be in the finest chariots devised by men, apart from Him. We'll win every time if we are in His will.

I am convinced that everything, even terrible things, will work together for our good, if we love God and are called according to His purposes. Parents, you can successfully teach your children at home — we did, and we had all the odds against us.

My parents divorced when I was six, my mother's second marriage was marked by abuse and ended with us being abandoned, and my mother was faced with raising six kids as a single parent. I was dyslexic, had ADHD, and struggled with a brain that worked faster than my motor skills.

We struggled financially, my mother had numerous health battles, we faced court hearings, social services, and "friends" who constantly told us we were crazy for trying to home educate. God has been faithful to lead us through.

I've learned that "God resists the proud, but gives grace to the humble" (1 Pet. 5:5). If we humble ourselves before Him, and lay our lives at His feet, He will lift us up. He will pick us up out of our miry pit and set our feet on a rock. There is no way we can lose if we are on God's side. "Be strong in the Lord and in the power of His might. Put on the whole armor of God, that you may be able to stand against the wiles of the devil" (Eph. 6:10–11).

Pray for God's guidance in your family. Always be ready to go through the refining fire that God brings into your lives. The process is sometimes just as important to God as the end result. He wants us to learn to love Him on the way to perfection. Homeschooling isn't a guarantee that your family will be successful, but trusting in the Lord is. If we trust Him, and lean not on our own understanding, He will direct our paths (Prov. 3:5–6). God bless you and your family!

Taken from *Homeschooling from a Biblical Worldview* by Israel Wayne (Covert, MI: Wisdom's Gate, 2000), used by permission, www.WisdomsGate.com.

"Fathers, do not provoke your children to anger, but bring them up in the discipline and instruction of the Lord."

— *Ephesians 6:4; NASB*

CHAPTER TWENTY-TWO

Evangelism in the Home
Scott Brown

"The heart of Christian education begins with the heart of God — and the heart of God is communicated in the Word of God."

SCOTT BROWN

Scott T. Brown is the director of the National Center for Family Integrated Churches and an elder at Hope Baptist Church in Wake Forest, North Carolina. He graduated from California State University in Fullerton with a degree in history and received a master of divinity from Talbot School of Theology. He gives most of his time to local pastoral ministry, conferences on fatherhood, church reformation, and strengthening the family. He has been married to Deborah for 29 years, and they have four children and nine grandchildren. The following challenge to fathers to be active, spiritual leaders in the home is taken from an article by Mr. Brown, from the National Center for Family Integrated Churches.

THE GREATEST UNTAPPED EVANGELISTIC OPPORTUNITY BEFORE THE MODERN CHURCH

I believe that we are involved in the greatest evangelistic opportunity before the Church today: the salvation of millions of children under the evangelistic and discipleship ministry of fathers and mothers in the home. This is not the only mission field, to be sure, but it is perhaps the most neglected mission field before the Church in our time.

The Bible calls fathers to preach the gospel to their children every day, "when you sit in your house, when you walk by the way, when you lie down, and when you rise up" (Deut. 6:7). A father is to pass on the knowledge of God to the next generation. He is commanded to expose his children day by day to the greatness of God, the perfections of His ways, and the great stories that explain His nature and character. This kind of instruction gives children a true understanding of the gospel.

Consider the Evangelistic Impact of Faithful Fathers

Think of the evangelistic impact that we as fathers would have in our generation if we would only heed this command. Consider the example of the faithful father: Daily, he praises God to his children with hundreds of words and practical principles. Day after day, he cries out to them, explaining the stories that glorify the kindnesses of God, His wrath toward sinners, and His vanquishing power over all things. In so doing, he reflects the heart of the heavenly Father who cries out, "Today, if you will hear His voice, do not harden your hearts as in the rebellion" (Hebrews 3:7–8).

In turn, his children observe their father as he personally delights in the Word and places himself under its wonderful teaching. They behold how good and mighty God is and how foolish it is to turn away from Him. They see how their daddy is comforted and confronted by it and is changed before their eyes.

Under this kind of loving and happy ministry, children hear the whole counsel of God from Genesis to Revelation. They see the flow of history from God's perspective. They hear of the great doctrines of the faith that have sustained humble people from one generation to the next. They observe the mighty hand of God working against all human odds. They see the beginning and the end of history and where they themselves stand in its stream. They know who wins the battle. They know that nothing can stand against the will of our Sovereign Lord.

Contrast the Results: Big-Tent Discipleship Falls Short

How different this is compared to sending your children to an evangelistic crusade or a concert in the hope that they might be saved.

The story is all too common: a young person goes to a Christian concert and walks down the aisle or makes a profession of faith absent a real conversion. They go forward because they have an emotional response or a guilty conscience or perhaps because a friend went down — but not because they really understand the gospel. This is why so few who "make decisions" at evangelistic meetings ever continue in a normal Christian life. Without the background understanding of sin and repentance or the specifics of the life they are turning toward, they are like the seeds that fell on the shallow soil that sprouted up and died away because they had no root in themselves.

FROM THE FILM: "It's always mystified me why parents think that it's lawful to send our children into the public education system, which is dedicated to teaching paganism."

Sadly, our churches are filled with young people who have "walked an aisle," but who have never really understood the full breadth of the gospel message. For them, the gospel has been trivialized and reduced to simply "accepting Christ." In contrast to this, the daily diet of a father's gospel teaching gives a detailed understanding of the gospel. It provides both the context and content that is necessary to become a true follower of Christ.

REBELLION AGAINST GOD'S CLEAR COMMANDS TO FATHERS

God's requirements for child evangelism are clear: fathers are commanded to diligently teach their children and care for their souls day by day. The sad reality of father's lives in modern churches is that they are satisfied with Sunday schools and evangelistic crusades (which are never mentioned or commanded in Scripture), but they reject God's direct and undeniable commands to personally teach their children daily. This is outright rebellion against the Lord.

Unfortunately, many fathers continue on in their rebellion because they feel good about their efforts, especially when they compare their parenting practices to their pastor and Christian brothers. Fathers often feel great about their involvement in their children's lives because, rather than defining faithful fathering by what Scripture prescribes, they define exemplary fatherhood as going to the kid's recitals and games and getting them into a good Sunday school or youth group.

In order to rescue this lost generation of children in Christian homes from hell, we must first help fathers understand what God has commanded and exhort them to embrace their

FROM THE FILM: "If people found out that I was going to start sending my children to a Muslim school, they would have a conniption fit. I would probably get fired. But they have no problem sending their children to pagan schools."

responsibilities before the Lord. We must speak clearly of what God has mandated so that fathers do not miss the opportunity to touch the hearts of their sons and daughters with the message of the gospel.

WAKE UP! WE ARE LOSING THE NEXT GENERATION

Because fathers have failed to do their duty in discipling their children, we are losing the next generation to the world. Observations from a number of studies illustrate this trend. Consider the following:

> Researcher George Barna maintains that if current trends in the belief systems and practices of the younger generation continue, in ten years, church attendance will be half the size it is today.[1]

> Dawson MacAlister, national youth ministry specialist, remarked that 90 percent of youth active in high school church programs drop out of church by the time they are sophomores in college.[2]

> Data from the Southern Baptist Convention indicates that we are currently losing 70–88 percent of our youth after their freshman year in college.[3] In a report to the Southern Baptist Convention Executive Committee, T.C. Pinkney observed that 70 percent of teenagers involved in church youth groups stop attending church within two years of their high school graduation.[4] The Southern Baptist Council on Family

Life reported an even more staggering statistic — that 88 percent of the children in evangelical homes leave church at the age of 18.[5]

Those Who Understand the Gospel by Age Group

While church attendance is one barometer for generational continuity for the gospel in the church, another study points to a more fundamental problem. Thom Rainer, Professor at Southern Baptist Theological Seminary School of Evangelism, launched a survey that he hoped would tell him if people understood the gospel. In response to his survey questions, the following percentages of people answered in a way that would indicate they were born again:[6]

- Born before 1946 — 65 percent
- Born between 1946 and 1964 — 35 percent
- Born between 1965 and 1976 — 15 percent
- Born between 1976 and 1994 — 4 percent

Consider the Enormous Leverage of Fathers for Evangelism

Of all the studies recently published, the most telling related to the fathers' role in discipleship is this: According to a report published by the *Baptist Press*,[7] if a child is the first person in the household to become a Christian, there is a 3.5 percent probability everyone in the household will follow. If the mother is first, there is a 17 percent chance everyone else in the household will submit to Christ. Here's the clincher: If the father professes Christ first, there is a 93 percent probability that everyone else in the house will heed the gospel call.

Pray for an Uprising of Men

God's Word declares and studies affirm what this generation needs — an uprising of men committed to discipling their children.

While the church in the 21st century is losing the next generation of children to worldliness, we at the NCFIC are encouraging fathers to return to the biblical role as the head of the household and to preach the gospel and make disciples of their children. We are also encouraging church leaders to have the courage to cancel the programs that steal the father's creation-order role and put their energy into fulfilling the clear commands of God.

The great Messianic prophesy of Psalm 22 shows how God brings the glory of salvation from one generation to the next through those who take seriously the charge to teach their children:

A posterity shall serve Him. It will be recounted of the Lord to the next generation, they will come and declare His righteousness to a people who will be born, that He has done this (Ps. 22:30–31).

Please pray that we as fathers would not miss the greatest untapped evangelistic opportunity before the Church today. Let it be said of this generation of fathers that we did our part to fulfill the Great Commission.

May we preach the fullness of the gospel to our households and give our children a thousand reasons to believe.

Endnotes

Taken from the article "The Greatest Untapped Evangelistic Opportunity Before the Modern Church" by Scott Brown, from the National Center for Integrated Churches (2006), used by permission, www.ncfic.org."

1. George Barna, *Revolution* (Carol Stream, IL: Tyndale House Publishers, 2005), p. 48–49.
2. Reggie McNeal, *The Present Future* (San Francisco, CA: Jossey-Bass, 2003), p. 4.
3. T.C. Pinkney, remarks to the Southern Baptist Convention Executive Committee, Nashville, Tennessee, September 18, 2001.
4. Ibid.
5. Southern Baptist Council on Family Life report to Annual Meeting of the Southern Baptist Convention, 2002.
6. McNeal, *The Present Future*, p. 4.
7. Polly House, "Want Your Church to Grow? Then Bring in Men," 2005 Southern Baptist Convention, *Baptist Press*, www.bpnews.net.

*"I have no greater joy than
to hear that my children
walk in truth."*

— *3 John 1:4*

CHAPTER TWENTY-THREE

The Goal of Education

R.C. Sproul, Jr.

"Freedom, in the end, isn't about having guns, money, or houses — it's about raising our children to serve the Lord Jesus."

R.C. SPROUL, JR.

R.C. Sproul, Jr. is a graduate of Reformed Theological Seminary and Grove City College. He received his doctorate of ministry in 2001. He was the founding pastor of Saint Peter Presbyterian Church, and is founder, chairman, and teacher of Highlands Ministries where he serves as editor of *Every Thought Captive* magazine. He has written or edited 13 books, including *Biblical Economics*, *Almighty Over All*, *Tearing Down Strongholds*, *Eternity in our Hearts*, *Bound for Glory*, and *Believing God*. He is the father of Darby, Campbell, Shannon, Delaney, Erin Claire, Maili, Reilly, and Donovan. The following is taken from the first chapter of Mr. Sproul's book *When You Rise Up*.

THE GOAL OF EDUCATION

War has become the dominant motif of our age. It seems that everywhere we turn there is this battle, that conflict, the other struggle. We are in the midst of a culture war, as left and right clash to define the broader culture. The federal government has declared war on terrorism, an elusive and difficult-to-define enemy. We are in the midst of an ongoing war on drugs, and before that, though Jesus told us the poor would always be with us, the federal government declared war on poverty. Even in the evangelical church, we have the worship wars — churches and denominations heatedly arguing over something indeed worthy of an argument — how to worship God.

Wars are never fought in a posture of indifference. Apathy is not something that inspires soldiers, not something you get a ration of on the front line. Wars are not often waged with cool detachment. When the warfare is more rhetorical than martial, however, we especially need clear thinking. There is one ongoing battle in the culture where cooler heads rarely prevail, and for a good reason. We fight the culture war, the war on terrorism, the war on drugs, the war on poverty, the worship wars in large part for the sake of our children. We want them to live in a safe world, a clean world, a world wherein they can worship God aright. But no battle touches more immediately upon our children than the education wars. Here, perhaps more than in any other battles, our hearts are on the line and our passions run deep. So coming to the education issue with clear minds is particularly important.

The education battles are myriad: battles between this federal education bill and that one, battles between this method of teaching in government-run schools and that method. We have Principle Approach Christian schools, classical Christian schools, and Christian schools that are so far behind the times that all they are is Christian schools — which shall we choose? Within the homeschool movement there are similar internal battles. Parents used to the textbooks they had as children want curriculum A, while others want curriculum C to ensure that their children have well-trained minds. And we haven't even gotten to the wars between the three groups: the government-school people hating the homeschoolers and the Christian schoolers, who of course return the favor, and the Christian schoolers and government schoolers allying themselves against those fools who won't do school.

There are at least three major battlefields in this one great war, three theaters in which the fighting goes on. We fight over who is called to do the teaching. Is the education of children a function of the state, the church, or the family? We fight over what should be taught, the content of our curriculum. Should we be reading the Bible only, the Bible plus Homer, or should we be watching television and reading *Heather Has Two Mommies*? Finally, there is the method battle. Whole language or phonics? Classical or Montessori? School-in-a-box or Charlotte Mason? These are all important questions. But before we can even try to agree on the answers, we need to see if there is anything prior we can agree on. There are three prior questions that we usually skip right over, which helps explain why we have such disagreement.

The first question is, "Is education important and valuable?" Here we have universal agreement. At the century's turn, as a nation we were spending $754 billion a year on education, including both voluntary expenditures and tax money.[1] That's more than three-quarters of a trillion dollars. To make sure you grasp the enormity of that number, let's see it in its fullness: $754,000,000,000. That number ought to suffice to answer our first question. Everybody agrees that education is important.

FROM THE FILM: "All of reality exists so that God's name would be known. And the government school says that you cannot name His name."

The second question is, "By what standard?" The source for our answers as to how Johnny should be educated is not John Dewey or Horace Mann. Nor is it the National Education Association or the U.S. Department of Education (even when there is a Republican in the White House). Neither do we draw our standard from John Calvin or R.L. Dabney or Dorothy Sayers. As Christians, we already know the answer to the question. However much God might have gifted any education theorists through the ages, He made none of them inerrant or smarter than Himself. At least those combatants in the education wars who claim the name of Christ can all agree that whatever the Bible says, that is what we must believe.

The third question relates to the first two. "Just what exactly is the goal of education?" When Alice was walking through Wonderland, she found herself at a crossroads. She was confused over which way she should go. Startled by the Cheshire Cat up in a nearby tree, Alice asked the Cat which way she should go. "That depends a good deal on where you want to get to," said the Cat. Alice replied, "I don't much care where." The Cat saucily answered,

"Then it doesn't matter which way you go." How can you judge the failure or success of the $754 billion, unless you have some goal?

I once spoke at a conference on welfare reform. I was asked to address the group twice. In my first lecture, "The Abysmal Failure of the Welfare State," I argued that welfare has done nothing to help those in need — in fact, it has harmed the very people it purported to help, creating a dependency on the state. In my second lecture, "The Astounding Success of the Welfare State," I argued that creating a dependency on the state was the true goal of those politicians who pushed welfare programs. Success or failure depends upon the goal.

So what are we spending that $754 billion for? If you asked the average man on the street, he would probably tell you that the purpose of education is to prepare children to get good jobs when they are grown. Some might add that education exists to help children learn to get along with each other. We bus children halfway across town because the end goal is an appreciation for diversity. We skew our admissions standards for the same reasons.

FROM THE FILM: "They are forbidden by law to publicly and clearly state that Jesus Christ is Lord."

What if instead of asking the man on the street you were to quiz the religious right? Why do they want to "take back our schools"? For essentially the same reasons. That is, the religious right want children to have good jobs and to embrace their moral vision. To put it another way, we have education wars because the Republicans want to raise little Republicans and the Democrats want to raise little Democrats. Meanwhile, both claim to be simply neutral. Yet both are inadvertently bumping into a hard reality: All education is inherently religious. Robert Louis Dabney rightly argued:

> True education is, in one sense, a spiritual process. It is the nurture of the soul. Education is the nurture of a spirit that is rational and moral, in which conscience is the regulative and

imperative faculty. The proper purpose of conscience, even in this world, is moral.

But God is the only Lord of the conscience; this soul is His miniature likeness. His will is the source of our obliga-tions. Likeness to Him is its perfection, and religion is the science of the soul's relations to God. Let these statements be placed together, and the theological and educational pro-cesses appear so related that they cannot be separated.

It is for this reason that the common sense of mankind has always invoked the guidance of the minister of religion in the education of youth. . . . Every line of true knowledge must find its completeness as it converges on God, just as every beam of daylight leads the eye to the sun.[2]

Puritan poet John Milton understood well not only that educa-tion cannot be "neutral," but also what its purpose is: "The end of learning is to repair the ruin of our first parents by regaining to know God aright, and out of that knowledge, to love Him, to imitate Him, to be like Him."[3] How might the left howl if those on the religious right actually followed Milton's lead? Understand also that when Milton said "God," he did not mean the generic "to whom it may concern" god of our culture. He meant the God of the Bible. Instead, the religious right is content to fight for cultural conservativism. Not long ago there was a public hullabaloo over an American history textbook approved by the New York State Board of Regents. It seems this text informed the students about the person and work of George Washington Carver, yet managed to cover American history with no mention of George Washington. As bad as that is, I am puzzled that those Christians who are a part of the religious right are more upset about the absence of the father of this country than they are about the absence of the King of the universe, the Lord of all things.

The goal of education, biblically speaking, is the goal of every-thing. The biblical bottom line is easy enough to find. We simply have to look to the beginning, to go back before the ruins even needed to be repaired. It is not enough to go back to the days of Ozzie and Harriet. They are the ones who brought us where we are. Instead we have to go back to the Garden. In the Garden, God commanded Adam and Eve to be fruitful and multiply, to rule over the animals, to dress and keep the Garden. They were to reflect the glory of their maker by "gardenizing" the rest of the creation, to rule under God. This is our goal — raising God-glorifying children, rather than raising responsible citizens who can manage to get along with the world around them. Consider what the Psalmist wrote:

> Give ear, O my people, to my law; incline your ears to the words of my mouth. I will open my mouth in a parable; I will utter dark sayings of old, which we have heard and known, and our fathers have told us. We will not hide them from their children, telling to the generation to come the praises of the LORD, and His strength and His wonderful works that He has done. For He established a testimony in Jacob, and appointed a law in Israel, which He commanded our fathers, that they should make them known to their children; that the generation to come might know them, the children who would be born, that they may arise and declare them to their children, that they may set their hope in God, and not forget the works of God, but keep His commandments; and may not be like their fathers, a stubborn and rebellious generation, a generation that did not set its heart aright, and whose spirit was not faithful to God (Ps. 78:1–8).

What might happen if this were our model for education rather than the model put forth by the state? Too often we who serve Christ keep the world's goal but use a different building. Or we keep the goal but hire a different faculty. Those things matter, but nothing matters more than determining where we are going.

Forget about education for a moment and try this little experiment. Suppose you are reasonably sanctified. And suppose that God appears to you as He did to Solomon before you. God says, "I want to give you a gift. I want to show forth My grace by granting you your heart's desire. But instead of giving the gift to you, I'm going to give it to your children." Think for a moment about what you would ask for. You wouldn't want to be rash, so consider your answer carefully. What do you want for them? What would be your request? Would you not reply, "O gracious Lord, this is my request, that my children would dwell in Your house forever. Make them Yours; redeem their souls; remake them into the image of Your own dear Son." If such is not your wish, shouldn't it be?

We need to think through what we value, and how much. Most mornings I exercise using a videotape that features walking. Aerobic dancing is rather too complicated for my pair of left feet. I walk three miles, and every half mile along the way I am reminded of how far I have gone. I have memorized those places on the tape. I know simply by the sound of the background music when the woman on the tape will tell me I've crossed another marker along the way. However, at the end, just when I should be so pleased to be done, she says something that grates on my soul. She asks her audience, "Should I give you the best news in the world? You've done three miles." It is a good thing to walk three miles, but not the greatest news in the world.

Consider the wisdom of John. Though he was probably not speaking of his biological children, he said, "I have no greater joy than to hear that my children walk in truth" (3 John 4). He is abundantly clear here. He doesn't say, "The best news in the world is I've walked three miles. The great news is I just saved a bundle on my car insurance. And I'm reasonably pleased to report that my children walk in the truth."

But if our great goal is to see our children embrace the gospel, what do we do once that has happened? If our child reports to us, "Daddy, while I was away at camp I threw my pinecone into the fire and invited Jesus into my heart," does Daddy in turn reply, "I can die happy now; that's all I need to know. I'm taking a nap now. Your mom and I are going to get in the RV and you'll never see us again. We're just going to run out the clock. Our work is through here." Our goal for our lives includes not only doing the work He has given us to do, what we call the dominion mandate, not only exercising dominion over our children (that is, raising them in the nurture and admonition of the Lord), but seeing that they are about the business of doing the same. You want to see your children, now abiding in the true vine, bear forth much fruit. You want them to grow in grace, to become more sanctified, to become more and more like Jesus. You want them to be consumed with pursuing first the kingdom of God.

First, we want our children to embrace the work of Christ. Second, we want them to do the work of Christ, to pursue His kingdom. And we haven't even gotten to learning to play nicely with others, or learning the periodic table. By now many of you are thinking, *I thought I was reading a book on education. This sounds more like Sunday school or youth group material. When is this guy going to get to education?"* Or, *If I tell anyone this, they'll be sure to think, "When are we going to stop talking about Sunday school and youth group and start talking about education?* This is simply more evidence of our fundamental confusion over education. Thinking that education is something different from discipling our children is a sure sign that we have been "educated" by the state. Education is discipleship.

Not only do we have a war between those who prefer the state or the church or the family as the focus of education, not only do we have a war over which curriculum to use, but we also disagree about the goal. Even within the homeschooling movement there is a battle between those who are for academic excellence and those who are for moral excellence. What is confusing in this battle is that academic excellence and moral excellence are not necessarily at odds. Both sides recognize this, and before the battle begins, both sides insist with vigor that they are both for academic and moral excellence. Yet there is a real battle. How do we resolve this?

The truth is that both sides are saying, "Both academic and moral excellence, but . . ." And I am no different. We are not in favor of moral excellence because it makes you a more diligent student. Instead we are for academic excellence because we believe such is the fruit of character. To make it even clearer, consider this choice. Would you rather have your child graduate at the top of his class at Harvard, become a Rhodes Scholar, win the Nobel Prize, and serve on the board of the Council for Secular Humanists? Or would you rather have your child be unable to make it through high school, become a garbage man, and be a godly husband and father? I know, everyone wants both. We want our children to be godly geniuses. But if we had to choose, and praise God we don't, there really is no choice.

When God regenerates a heart, that heart bears spiritual fruit. And a vital part of that fruit is a renewed mind, the capacity to look at the world through God's eyes, to see all that we do in light of serving His kingdom. When, for instance, we teach our children physics, what is the end goal? Are we motivated to do so simply because studies show that those who master physics make, over the course of a lifetime, 33 percent more income than those who don't learn physics?

Is it so our children can become structural engineers and make a grand living putting up skyscrapers? Is it so in old age we can brag to the neighbors about our children's work? Or is it instead because in building such buildings our children exercise dominion, turn dirt into shelter, and in doing so serve others?

FROM THE FILM: "You get the salt and light argument from people who have their children in government schools. It's not working. If we send out evangelists and they become unbelievers, we're not following a biblical strategy."

Suppose also that we are focused on issues of the heart, that we are seeking to cultivate the fruit of the Spirit in our children. Even here we can take a wrong turn. What motivates us? The fruit of the Spirit doesn't exist so that our children can become heirs of Dale Carnegie, be hugely popular, or become prom queen or class treasurer. Rather, we teach our children these things so that they might, in obedience to God, live in peace with all men, as much as is possible. In short, as we make all our decisions and work them out, we must think through how our thoughts and actions relate to the commands of God. We need to excise from our thinking the merely normal or conventional. All we do for our children must be about raising them in the nurture and admonition of the Lord.

Satan's pull is strong. We are all in the grip of an ideological and a practical inertia. We are prone to slip back into how we've always done things, unless we remain vigilant. I emphasize the Bible's importance not in but as our curriculum. It is an emphasis I bring every time I speak on the subject of education. And every time I find myself having an internal tug-of-war. On one shoulder I have a devil whispering in my ear. On the other side I have an angel. The question is (and I can't tell you which side is the devil and which side the angel, or there would be no more tug-of-war), "Should I throw them a bone, or should I not throw them a bone?" When I am emphasizing the Bible, the Bible, the Bible, I see the terror rising in their eyes. If homeschooling is a radical departure from that we're used to educationally, how much more frightening is it to throw away the mountain of curriculum we've purchased and sit down with a Bible?

But my fear works in the opposite direction. Why should I have this tension? Why, when I believe it is utterly appropriate to teach math and physics, when I believe that both can help us better understand God, and better obey His command to exercise dominion, would I have a reluctance to concede such? Math teaches us the order of God's universe. It manifests His glory, His beauty. It is likewise a part of being a good steward. When Jesus calls us to "consider the cost," we'd better be able to calculate the costs. But I know the temptation. As soon as I concede that math is perfectly legitimate, we'll fall right back into our old pattern, seeing the Bible as a sourcebook for stuff to sprinkle over the world's curriculum. The world has determined a curriculum, and we feel tremendous pressure to follow it, if only because it is normal. And because we are Christians, we want to do normal in a Christian way. Before we can even begin to consider math, we have to start with the Bible.

How then might we do math in our homeschools, in a way that is consistent with Psalm 78, in a way consistent with John Milton's wisdom on the purpose of education, in a way consistent with the injunction in Deuteronomy 6 to teach our children when they lie down and when they rise up? Is it sufficient to stop and say a prayer or two before getting down to brass tacks? It's perfectly appropriate to pray before we do our math. I'm certainly not against prayer. But how you teach math rightly is by always remembering why you teach math, and more important, by always reminding the children. We must first confess, then profess that two and two make four — not apart from Jesus, and not beside Jesus, but because it is Jesus' two and Jesus' two and Jesus' four. It all belongs to Him. We confess and we profess that He invented math and He rules over it. He is the reason for it. Math is always objective, never neutral. That is, it speaks truth because Jesus is the truth.

Let's look again at the psalm, and note first the beauty of it. This, remember, is not a mere lesson to be taught. Instead it is a song and a prayer of God's people. Asaph begins by encouraging the people to listen:

> Give ear, O my people, to my law; incline your ears to the
> words of my mouth. I will open my mouth in a parable; I

will utter dark sayings of old, which we have heard and
known, and our fathers have told us (Ps. 78:1–3).

Covenant theology wasn't invented at the Reformation. The notion of familial solidarity before God that is so central to the homeschool movement is trumpeted here in this psalm. What Asaph is
saying is as simple as it is beautiful: "I'm going to tell you what my
father told me, and his father told him, and his father told him, and
his father before him told him to tell him." The promise is that he
will tell God's wisdom, God's words, that have been passed down
from one generation to the next. There is nothing new under this sun.
Asaph doesn't draw the people's attention by promising to bring the
latest research, the latest folly from the enemies of God.

Asaph's message not only passes down from one generation to
the next, but is itself the message that must be passed down from
one generation to the next. That is, Asaph isn't just telling multigenerational secrets, but the secret itself is, "Pass it on to the next generation." This is always a critical part of God's covenant. To simply
fulfill the immediate demands of the law is never enough. It wasn't
enough that Abraham should receive the mark of the covenant. Nor
was it sufficient that he should place that mark on Isaac. Rather,
Abraham was commanded to teach Isaac to teach his own sons the
covenants of God. In simplest form, the covenant God has made
with man is simply this: Love, trust, and obey God . . . and teach
your children to do the same. And to take it one step further, we
haven't taught our children to do the same unless or until we have
taught them to teach their children.

Like Asaph, I try to teach my own children this same thing during
family worship (family worship is neither a class in our homeschool
nor set apart from our homeschool, but is rather part of the warp
and woof of our family life, both life and school). When I preach to
the children, having read a portion of the Bible (my sermons during
family worship generally last from 30 to 45 . . . seconds), I remind
them that it is not enough that they should know what the Bible is
teaching. They must teach their own children these same truths. In
like manner, if I fail to teach my children to teach their children, I
have failed to keep covenant.

I'm convinced that failure to understand this multigenerational
call of the Christian family is at the root of our failure to manifest

the kingdom of God, that this is why we seem always to take two steps forward and one step back. We haven't taught enough levels of this. We must with sincerity and zeal teach our children to teach their children to teach their children to teach their children to teach their children . . . to keep going until the King's return. Instead we produce the children of Ephraim, children who do not know who they are or whose they are.

Our vision for homeschool, for the raising of our children in the nurture and admonition of the Lord, is not something we do just because we're supposed to. Rather, it is our very vision for making manifest the kingdom of God. And that vision of the kingdom of God isn't something only for today or off at a great distance. It is, through the Holy Spirit's power, this generation's changing the hearts of the next generation, and then their changing the next generation, and the next and the next. It is generation after generation after generation of building the Kingdom, growing to be more like Christ, to love Him, to imitate Him, to know Him aright.

FROM THE FILM: "To proclaim the lordship of Jesus Christ in the government schools will get you thrown out, whether you are a teacher, an administrator, or a child."

Perhaps even before we ask, "What is education for?" we should ask a prior question, "What are children for?" The Westminster Catechism teaches us that man's chief end is to glorify God and enjoy Him forever. Of course, the Westminster Assembly met long before the advent of political correctness. When they spoke of "man's" end, they weren't suggesting that women were to serve some other goal. "Man," in this context (as in my writings as well), refers not only to males but also to females. But it is broader still. "Man" covers not only the gamut of genders, but the gamut of ages. In short, children's chief end is to glorify God and enjoy Him forever.

This summary of man's end brings together the Bible's varying language on the same theme. That is, we are given several "bottom line" assessments of our calling. God begins with the dominion mandate, to exercise dominion over the creation. And since God doesn't change, that ultimate goal abides. The goal is restated in Ecclesiastes — the sum of the matter is this: to fear God and obey whatsoever He commands (Eccles. 12:13). And then Jesus reiterates the same theme in a slightly different key when He tells us that we ought to seek first the kingdom of God and His righteousness. Our children are made to seek God, as we are. Therefore, if we are to train our children rightly, we must expunge from our own hearts that overarching agenda of the culture around us, the pursuit of personal peace and affluence.

So I am sometimes troubled by how we homeschoolers measure our success. It seems that every few months the headlines tell us of another triumph, that this homeschooler got a perfect score on the SATs or the other won the national spelling bee, or a third the Young Inventors contest. And we present this as evidence that we are doing a good thing in homeschooling. Of course, there is nothing wrong with homeschoolers' achieving, nor is there anything particularly surprising about it. But these are not our successes.

Our headlines, instead, should be about stories such as this. Several years ago I took three of my children to the grocery store: Campbell, then six; Shannon, four; and Delaney, three. Not only do I have a pattern of taking our children with me, but we also have a pattern for how we go through the store. We begin with fruits and vegetables, and then finish at the bakery section. At our local store, the good folks behind the bakery counter give away cookies to little children. This, too, is a part of our pattern. Delaney, with a year's experience of going shopping with Daddy, hadn't quite learned all the habits. So every week she had to ask, "Can we get a cookie, Daddy?" She worries unduly, because her daddy is so cheap that it doesn't matter if we have stopped at the grocery store on the way home from a tour of the candy factory. The cookies are free, so the answer is always yes.

The lady behind the counter gave Campbell his cookie and Delaney hers. I did not get one for Shannon, for though she likes cookies, she isn't yet adept at eating them. (My daughter Shannon is mentally retarded, with the mental ability of an 18-month-old.) I realized at this point that I had forgotten piecrusts for my wife (who is probably socking me in the arm right now for letting you know she doesn't make her own crusts — though she does make our bread, oatmeal, granola, etc.), so I left the children and the buggy to fetch some. As I headed back, I caught my son. He did not know I was watching. As far as he knew, no one was watching him. But I saw him do it. He broke off a piece of his cookie and fed it to his little sister Shannon. He didn't do this because Shannon would praise him. He did it because God has worked in his heart, because his mother is an outstanding homeschooling mom, teaching him well. That is the heart of the matter; that is what we ought to be celebrating.

I'm not arguing that it's a bad thing for children to be smart. Rather, I am suggesting that the issue of education is always the heart. Changed hearts is the goal, the function, the very purpose of education. Our goal is not multigenerational personal peace and affluence. Neither are we simply trying to raise clean-cut children. Homeschoolers are adept at doing that. And there certainly may be a parallel between being nice and having the gentle and quiet spirit the Bible calls us to. But what we want is the changed heart.

What is your goal? What are you shooting for? Even if you answer "building the kingdom of God," you might still have it wrong. Be careful here. We are not training our children so one day they might build the Kingdom. We must remember, as we continue to grow in grace and become more effective in our calling, to ditch this notion that school is something you do for a time, and then you work. We continue to learn, while we work. And our children continue to work, while they learn. Your children are not simply in training but are even now about the business of building the kingdom of God. What is the kingdom of God? It is that place where the least of these, Jesus' brethren, my daughter Shannon, gets a piece of cookie, because it was given to her.

My hope is that our reformation is not just in our thinking. I pray that we will not conclude, "Well, that was valuable and important, even interesting," then go back to the status quo. If the heart is the heart of the matter, if our children not only are learning to be Kingdom builders, but are also being Kingdom builders now, if we are to train our children to train their children, then this is something we need to remind ourselves of daily. The devil, you understand, is craftier than the beasts of the field. He doesn't simply whisper in our ears, "Betray your children. Raise them in the nurture and admonition of the state." Instead, he distracts us, pulls us off target, makes us forget our calling, piece by piece.

Our calling is to keep our eyes on the prize — not to long to be at ease in Babylon, but to long for the city whose builder and maker is God. We will not get education right until we get life right. Just as so many peasants of the 13th century sacrificed to build the great cathedrals of Europe (which they would not see finished in their own lives), so we must look into the future, seeing the fulfillment of the promise, the consummation of the Kingdom. Praise God that in His grace we get a taste each week, as we enter the worship experience in our weekly rest, of our eternal rest.

May we remember as parents that we are His children and that He is about the business of changing our hearts, of repairing our ruins, of remaking us. And though He has not finished with us, He has placed in our care His children. May He, in His grace, keep our hearts aflame for these children. May He give us minds like steel traps that we would never be distracted, that we would not forsake our calling. May He, the great Steward, make us faithful stewards of children, the most precious gifts, of which is the kingdom of God.

Endnotes

Taken from *When You Rise Up* by R.C. Sproul, Jr. (Phillipsburg, NJ: P&R Publishing Co., 2004), used by permission, www.prpbooks.com.

1. *Mini Digest of American Statistics, 2002* (Washington, DC: U.S. Department of Education, National Center for Education Statistics, 2003), p. 48.
2. R.L. Dabney, author, Douglas Wilson, editor, *On Secular Education* (Moscow, ID: Canon Press, 1996), p. 16–17.
3. John Milton, *Areopagitica and of Education* (Northbrook, IL: AHM Publishing, 1951), p. 59.

Postscript to Teachers and Administrators

Bruce Shortt

[W]hen good people are working in a bad system,
the system wins.

—Marshall Fritz[1]

If you're reading this, you're almost certainly part of the remnant of capable teachers and administrators trying to stick it out in government schools. I went to "public" schools from kindergarten through high school; I have taught teachers during "in-service" days and in enrichment programs; both of my grandmothers taught in public schools — one of them began teaching in a one-room schoolhouse; my mother was a school nurse; I have more than a few uncles, aunts, and cousins who have taught, or who are teaching, in government schools; I have served in a community arts organization with a number of current and retired public school teachers; and a wonderful Christian woman in our church who teaches at one of our local government schools has also taught our oldest son's Sunday school class. In sum, I have more than a passing personal acquaintance with government schools.

You, of course, live with this strange, expensive, and destructive institution daily, and the odds are that you have seen many of its problems. Whether you are a new or experienced teacher or administrator, you probably feel trapped, beleaguered, isolated, frustrated, betrayed, and, perhaps, a bit persecuted.

You also probably feel a bit conflicted. While the right course of action for Christian parents is clear, your position is ambiguous. For some of you there are compelling reasons to stay and soldier on; for others of you it's time to move on. This is a question that each of you must weigh in light of your circumstances. There are a few things, however, that may be useful to bear in mind as you try to sort out from time to time whether your government school has simply reduced you to the role of an enabler for its many pathologies.

GETTING OUT OF DODGE

One of the recurring themes I have run across in my research is the depth of dissatisfaction with the current state of government schools among the most experienced teachers and administrators. Linda Schrock Taylor, a Michigan teacher, writer, and entrepreneur, voices eloquently why, as she puts it, seasoned teachers "are leaving the teaching profession in droves":

> [W]e began teaching when learning was valued, students were motivated, and administration was supportive of excellence in education. We then spent these 30 years observing, with no power to stop, the trashing of traditional teaching methods; the entrenching of inferior fads and materials; the lowering of expectations . . . the "other-world" craziness of administrative leadership. We have watched our schools be vandalized; traditional curriculum be compromised; students speak, dress, and act like the lowest of classes. We work for young bosses who are proud of never earning anything higher than a C in school, but who expect us to applaud their "achievements." . . . We have no choice but to pick up, turn in our keys, and leave.[2]

This critique is borne out by various studies. One of the most recent was produced by Public Agenda, a New York-based non-profit polling organization, by analyzing a decade of research. Not surprisingly, Public Agenda found that even though many teachers may support higher academic standards, they also often feel that students lack the necessary work ethic to meet those standards and that parents and administrators don't give teachers the support they need to enforce them.[3] Also not surprisingly, students and teachers report unruly students and school violence as significant problems.[4] Apart from these concerns, 47 percent of principals reported that talented teachers are most likely to leave because of "politics and bureaucracy."[5]

The day-to-day reality behind these disturbing statistics was vividly described in a 2002 report by the *Palm Beach Post*, which interviewed dozens of Palm Beach County teachers and school district officials.[6] According to the teachers interviewed, student discipline problems in the Palm Beach County schools are worse than ever. Obscene graffiti written on walls; students cursing at teachers, spitting in teachers' coffee, throwing desks at teachers, and threatening to have them beaten up; and general classroom disruptions were among the problems Palm Beach County teachers have been experiencing with increasing frequency. At the same time, teachers also complained that administrators "brush aside [student] behavior problems," partly out of a desire to avoid a "negative impact" for their schools, partly because they are "overwhelmed with other duties," and partly for fear of litigation if they discipline "too harshly."[7] What's a teacher to do? The answer for many teachers in Palm Beach County schools is to leave the profession. And most of those leaving are very likely those who are competent and who, therefore, can find other suitable employment.

More recently, the Associated Press wrote about "disruptive student behavior" in Oklahoma City's F.D. Moon Academy, a magnet school for mass media communications and technology. On one day of 2004 alone, 120 of 147 sixth graders were suspended from school for picking up tables in the cafeteria and slamming them into the floor and mouthing off to faculty.[8] Earlier in the week another 16 students from the same sixth grade class had been suspended for "class disruptions." At a meeting with parents, the principal, Elaine Ford, said that roughly 85 percent of faculty time is taken up with disciplining students. One parent at the meeting told the reporter that "she wasn't surprised by students' behavior because some of the parents in the audience were yelling while school officials talked."[9] These are the sorts of conditions that are driving many long-time teachers and administrators out of government schools.

But it's not just the capable, experienced teachers who are being driven from the profession. Joshua Kaplowitz recounts in the article "My Classroom from Hell" part of his all-too-brief career as a fifth-grade teacher in a government school in Washington, DC[10] Kaplowitz, a recent Yale graduate, discovered rapidly after arriving at Emery Elementary what government schools have become. Not only were Kaplowitz's efforts to maintain classroom order not supported by the administration, the administration actually thwarted them. Honest grading? Kaplowitz was told, in effect, that it was prohibited by law, and he was cited for insubordination when he insisted on giving students the failing grades they had earned. As for trying to protect students from assaults by other students, he soon learned that his colleagues were in a survival mode and bound by what can only be considered inhumane school district rules:

When I asked other teachers to help me stop a fight, they reminded me that DC Public Schools banned teachers from laying hands on a student, even to protect other children. You have to be made of iron to wait passively for the security guard while one enraged child tries to hurt another.[11]

The *coup de gras* for Kaplowitz's brief teaching career came when an emotionally disturbed child falsely alleged that Kaplowitz had injured his head and back by violently shoving him in the chest. While being acquitted on a criminal charge of misdemeanor assault, and having to endure a civil proceeding in which the boy's mother thought she would win the litigation lottery, Kaplowitz learned the teachers' union is flooded yearly with fabricated corporal punishment charges. Needless to say, Joshua Kaplowitz is no longer a government schoolteacher.

Another first-year teacher in the New York City government schools recently wrote anonymously of the sham that passes for education there.[12] Children, he quickly learned, were "often the last thing on teachers' minds." Instead, school politics, collecting free lunch forms, and otherwise figuring out how to survive in a dysfunctional institution were the order of the day. Moreover, despite the vast budget for New York City government schools, he also learned that little of it was reaching the classrooms. Getting books, chalk, and even staples was a struggle, not to mention figuring out how to teach in a building where there were dead rodents in the hallways and the air conditioning often didn't work.

Yet another young teacher, Matthew Clavel, recently wrote of his frustrations as a math teacher required to use a "fuzzy math" curriculum that was dooming his students to a life of mathematical illiteracy.[13] How did administrators respond to complaints from teachers that the "fuzzy math" curriculum was a disaster? According to Clavel: "District officials told us that we should just keep going — *even if not a single child in our rooms understood what we were talking about*" [emphasis added].[14] Clavel, by the way, is also no longer teaching.

In Piper, Kansas, a second-year biology teacher, Christine Pelton, flunked 28 students who had cheated in a class project that accounted for 50 percent of the class grade.[15] Indignant parents lobbied the school board, and, as a result, the school board instructed Pelton to change the weighting and the scores on the project — changes that would have resulted in 27 out of the 28 students passing the course. Rather than change the grades, Pelton resigned. Afterward, Pelton commented on the effect of the school board's irresponsible action on students' thinking: "I'd lost the kids' respect. I heard kids talking about that if they didn't like what I did in the future, they could go to the board of education and they could change that."[16]

Survival of the "Unfittest"

The point here is that there are powerful forces of "adverse selection" at work in government education. Think of it as a system that encourages the "survival of the unfittest." Moreover, capable veteran teachers and administrators are not merely retiring or walking away. Linda Schrock Taylor reports that there are now many in government school administration who are actively seeking to *drive out* teachers who haven't bought into the latest school of education fads.[17]

The 2004 winner of the National Right to Read Foundation's Teacher of the Year Award, veteran teacher Ann Edwards,[18] expressed the same sentiment in her 1999 testimony before the Subcommittee on Early Childhood Education of the U.S. House of Representatives' Committee on Education and the Workforce:

> I have an idea now what it might have felt like for minorities in the South at the beginning of the Civil Rights Movement when one might have to sit at the back of the bus. It is now as though traditional teachers have to go to the back of the school bus. Sitting with them are students, many of whom will be minorities, that will never become proficient readers and will lack other skills necessary to compete in the real world in the 21st century. Many in the education profession today worship at the "shrine of change" and have a "child-centered" as opposed to a "subject-centered" approach to education. Disciplines needed to have a chance at succeeding in life have been abandoned.[19]

In addition to the loss of veteran teachers, many aspiring teachers who would be great educators never make it to the starting line today because they are repulsed by the rank pedagogical and political stupidities served up in the curricula of schools of education. Of the motivated and capable aspiring teachers who actually do make it into the classroom, many are either driven out, like Joshua Kaplowitz, or leave because, like Matthew Clavel, they cannot stand being accomplices in the destruction of their students' futures. Beyond this, consider that more than a million veteran teachers are nearing retirement.

Government schools are being utterly transformed by the loss of this enormous cadre of teachers that, on the whole, tends to share your values and standards.[20] What will it be like to be surrounded increasingly by "teachers" who have been led to believe that academic standards are an impediment to social justice and that the main function of schools should be to reconstruct identities, values, beliefs, and lifestyles? What will it be like to find yourself increasingly among "colleagues" imbued with high "self-esteem," but many of whom would have trouble passing a tenth-grade literacy test?[21] If you are candid, you will have to admit that this process has been going on for years and is intensifying.

The bottom line is that capable, conscientious teachers and administrators are going to be increasingly isolated. The vast bulk of the survivors are going to be those without real job skills or who are so dim that they think that gross mistakes such as "whole language" reading instruction and "fuzzy math" are just fine. For the diminishing remnant, however, government schools will become lonelier places by the year.

The situation for Christian teachers and administrators is even worse. Your faith has been virtually criminalized within government schools. For many of you, even the slightest affirmation of your Christian beliefs at school would lead to discipline or termination if found out. Further, you must cope with a system in which any pretense to upholding real academic standards has long ago disappeared; faddish curricula make effective teaching all but impossible; and much of the school day for the children in your school necessarily involves indoctrination in leftist ideology, immoral values, and New Age and other pagan theologies. Not in your class, perhaps, but it's there in your school, and the problem is metastasizing.

"Accountability" and Mission Impossible

As the failure of government schools has become more apparent, the public rightly has been demanding more accountability; that is, the public increasingly wants schools, administrators, and teachers to feel some economic or other "pain" if their students fail to learn. For many of you, the lack of discipline within your schools makes effective teaching at best a rather remote prospect. What, for example, can a principal like Elaine Ford do?

Moreover, one of the cruelest ironies you face is that you are being held accountable for achieving results while often being denied — in fact, prohibited from using — the tools you know you need to do your job. Consider the upside-down world in which Matthew Clavel found himself as a math teacher. How could he produce results if he used the mandated "fuzzy math" curriculum? And what about those who teach reading? How can you produce reading results when you are forced to use something other than a sound phonics-based curriculum? During a conversation with a principal over teachers being forced to use a poorly conceived and ineffective new reading curriculum, Ann Edwards expressed well the frustration of a skilled teacher:

> I feel like a doctor with patients who are dying and the district . . . is only allowing me to treat patients with one type of medicine. The medicine that I am required to use does not work as well as the proven treatment I (and other experienced teachers) have used successfully for several years. In fact, several patients are dying with the new medicine. The old medicine works; you know it works and I know it works. *As a professional, I am now in a moral and ethical dilemma. You want me to watch my children fail at reading and not teach what I know works best* [emphasis added].[22]

The truth is, being asked to teach and get results under the circumstances in which many of you must work is a lot like being asked to paint the Golden Gate Bridge with a hammer and a bucket of milk.

WHAT IS TO BE DONE?

Some of you have good reasons to stay in your government schools, but most of you, over time, are going to leave. But whether you stay or go, there are some things that you can and must do as *Christian* educators.

First, if you have a child in government school, take him out. Your witness is important — both to your child and to other parents. Second, you must tell your pastors and the parents in your church the truth about what is happening in government schools — the whole truth, "with the bark off." To remain silent is to collaborate in the destruction of our children. Third, you must help your church think through ways of providing alternatives to government schools and help encourage parents with a "government school habit" to rescue their children from Pharaoh's schools. Fourth, you need to dream. What could you and others like you do if you were free to provide the kind of education that you know Christian children should have, but that you are not allowed to provide? God may be ready to open some doors for you. Finally, and most important, pray — pray that Christian parents be given wisdom in educating their children.

Endnotes

Taken from *The Harsh Truth about Public Schools* by Bruce Shortt (Vallecito, CA: Chalcedon Foundation, 2004), used by permission, www.chalcedon.edu.

1. Marshall Fritz, "The Cement Canoe," available at www.sepschool.org.
2. Linda Schrock Taylor, "Twilight Years or Twilight Zone: Seasoned Teachers Leave Public Schools in Droves," www.Lewrockwell.com, January 24, 2003.
3. Jean Johnson and Ann Duffett, with Jackie Vine and Leslie Moye, "Where We Are Now: 12 Things You Need to Know about Public Opinion and Public Schools," Public Agenda 2003, available at www.publicagenda.org.
4. Ibid.
5. Ibid.
6. Shannon Colavecchio and Kimberly Miller, "Palm Beach Teachers: 'We Leave Teaching Because of Kids' Bad Behavior,' " *The Palm Beach Post*, April 14, 2002.
7. Ibid.
8. "School Suspends Most Sixth-Graders for Mass Rowdiness; 'You'd be Shocked,' Principal Says," Associated Press, available online at http://www.sfgate.com/cgi-bin/article.cgi?file=news/archive/2004/03/26/national1146EST0561.DTL.
9. Ibid.
10. Joshua Kaplowitz, "My Classroom from Hell," *The Wall Street Journal*, January 24, 2003.
11. Ibid.
12. Anonymous, "The System's Failing Grades," *New York Press*, vol. 15, issue 16 (2002).
13. Matthew Clavel, "How Not to Teach Math: New York's Chancellor Klein's Plan Doesn't Compute," *City* magazine, March 7, 2003.
14. Ibid.
15. Andrew Trotter, "Plagiarism Controversy Engulfs Kansas School," *Education Week*, April 3, 2002.
16. Ibid.
17. Taylor, "Twilight Years or Twilight Zone: Seasoned Teachers Leave Public Schools in Droves."
18. Ann Edwards has taught for 24 years in grades K–9. Currently, Mrs. Edwards teaches at Litel Elementary School in Chino Hills, California. The National Right to Read Foundation describes its mission as follows: ". . . to return

comprehensive, scientifically based reading instruction and good literature to every elementary school in America." For more information about this organization, visit its website at http://www.nrrf.org/index.html.

19. Written testimony of Ann Edwards before the Subcommittee on Early Childhood, Youth and Families of the Committee on Education and the Workforce of the House of Representatives, One Hundred Sixth Congress, First Session, hearing held in Anaheim, California, July 6, 1999, written testimony dated Thursday, July 22, 1999, Serial No. 106-57.

20. The estimate of teachers that will shortly retire is from the NEA, "Attracting and Keeping Qualified Teachers," available at www.nea.org/teachershortage/. The NEA also estimates that more than two million new teachers will be needed in the next decade.

21. In the 1998 administration of the Massachusetts teacher certification test, 59 percent of the 1,800 recent school of education graduates flunked. The test was described as being at about an 8th to 10th grade level. In 1997, 75 percent of teacher candidates in Suffolk County, New York, flunked an 11th grade level reading comprehension test. In 2001, the *Chicago Sun-Times* gave ten 9th to 11th grade students the same test of "Basic Skills" used to qualify teachers. The students finished in 11 to 23 minutes, all but two passed the math and grammar portions, and half passed the reading comprehension part of the test. There are many, many stories like this, as well as many, many stories about how the education industry has worked to delegitimize testing or to lower standards to the point of making it almost impossible for someone to fail.

22. Written testimony of Ann Edwards before the Subcommittee on Early Childhood, Youth and Families of the Committee on Education and the Workforce of the House of Representatives, One Hundred Sixth Congress, First Session, Hearing held in Anaheim, California, July 6, 1999, written testimony dated Thursday, July 22, 1999, Serial No. 106-57.

The Invention of Adolescence
Otto Scott

A dolescence is now accepted by most Americans as a strange and difficult period marked by wild swings of mood, outbursts of temper, rudeness, rebelliousness, and personality changes — all involuntary.

They would be surprised to learn that this period was unknown, unrecognized, and unseen in every previous civilization, culture, and society throughout the immensely long history of humanity. It is, even today, unknown in large areas of the inhabited world.

I recall marveling at the calm that pervaded families in South America during my last extended stay there in the early 1950s. I did not hear a single rude response by a teenager to anyone. No doubt it was different in the slums, but this was the atmosphere among the middle and upper classes.

In earlier times, this was once true even in the United States, the land now known for difficult children. There was even a time when there were no adolescents. That was, of course, a time beyond the memory of even our oldest inhabitants: a time before the Civil War, during the First American Republic. Our great social changes began after that conflict; after huge waves of immigration came via the new, safer steamboats; during the period when many Americans, anxious for a higher, more complete education, went to Europe — and especially to Germany — to study.

One of these was G. Stanley Hall, who earned a doctorate in psychology under William James at the new Johns Hopkins University in 1878. Hall went to Germany for two years and was swept up in German psychological research and became especially interested in the mental development of children.

After that immersion in what is usually termed "the latest scientific developments," Hall returned to Johns Hopkins as a professor of psychology and pedagogy (wonderfully impressive terms!). Hall taught John Dewey, Lewis Terman (who later pioneered "mental" tests), and Arnold Gesell, later famed as a "child" psychologist.

Hall conducted numerous "studies" of children during the 1880s and 1890s, and in 1904 issued a landmark book cumbersomely titled *Adolescence: Its Psychology and Its Relations to Physiology, Anthropology, Sociology, Sex, Crime, Religion and Education.*

That title alone should have warned the wary, but it was a time when a number of savants were appearing with novel theories about human behavior. Dr. Freud, addicted first to opium and then cocaine, had convinced many of his patients that he could read thoughts of which they were themselves unaware. Lombroso's theory that a criminal was an anthropological type with certain physical characteristics still had a following; so did phrenology: the idea that the contours of the skull indicated mental and spiritual qualities. It was a time, in other words, when — in the name of science — human beings were being redefined by various individuals who claimed to possess supernormal powers of observation and insight.

Dr. Hall was one of these. His theories fit with Spencer's social Darwinism and the fashionable belief in the perfectibility of man through formal, secular education. He thought the embryo in the womb repeated Darwin's evolution of humanity from the sea, and that the stages of childhood repeated the stages of social evolution from pre-savagery to civilization. He left the definition of civilization unstated and seemed to believe that it was a permanent condition achieved in the West in 1905.

Dr. Hall argued that childhood consisted of "three stages, each with a parallel in racial history" and each requiring a certain set of teaching approaches. Infancy and early childhood were equal to pre-stages of culture, and parents/teachers should allow the child to play with blocks and to exercise freely. At 6 or 7, he believed the child experienced various crises leading to the "pre-adolescent" years of 8 to 12, when behavior is comparable to "the world of early pigmies and other so-called savages."[1] At this point (6 or 7) the child was, in Dr. Hall's view, ready for school — and its discipline. But a new period of crisis, he believed, arrived between 13 and 18 —which he termed adolescence.

Hall compared this to ancient and medieval civilizations. He believed it was a crucial period, "because it prepares the youth for the acquisition of knowledge, mores, and skills that will determine the future of the individual and, by extension, that of the human race." He also believed that it was "a stormy period . . . when there is a peculiar proneness to be either very good or very bad."[2]

There does not seem to be any basis for this conclusion. Throughout all the previous centuries of Christianity — and of Judaism before that 12 had been considered the age of maturity. Both confirmation in the Christian religion in pre-Reformation centuries, and the Bar Mitzvah in Judaism (then and now) took place at that age. Thereafter, a young person was expected to behave as a responsible adult and to assume a place in adult society.

Boys in New England whaling towns went to sea and rose to become masters of clipper ships in their early twenties. Girls married at 16 and set about raising a family, managing a home, and behaving as matrons. Their counterparts around the world behaved the same. Life began early; tantrums may have occurred, but they had no general rationale connected to age: everyone was held responsible, and God was not blamed for anyone's misbehavior.

Social life, however, is replete with imitative patterns. People are apt to behave as they are expected to behave — whether well or foolishly.

Hall's ideas fit the fashion: It would not be fair to say that they were deliberately conceived to do so; it would be accurate to say that Hall was a man of his time, more than a man of original insight. He codified ideas about children and youths that were then floating in the air. That was the reason his argument was so easily swallowed by educators and other professionals. True originality has a much harder time.

In any event, Hall's work provided a basis for segregating school children by age. Elementary school children were segregated from secondary schools along the lines of his "observations." Twelve was the age of the break. The new fashion spread even into religion, and the clergy began to aim different lessons at special age groups: the Bible was too much for the young.

The movement mushroomed into special courses for special ages. At certain ages, a child was expected to learn this much — and no more. To learn behind the group was a cause for concern, so, in time, was to learn ahead of the group. Norms came into being; to fit the norm became (as it is now) more important than to sprint ahead —

and to fall behind is a calamity. Never mind that different children grow at different rates at different times and that even individual progress is sometimes fast, sometimes slow. Differences were put in the background, age in the foreground.

At a certain time, therefore, in the lives of contemporary American children, certain behavior patterns are expected — and subtly mandated. Nor is this only true of children. There is now an expected beginning and an end to a working career: one cannot be too young — or too old.

We have, today, an entire hierarchy of social groups based on age: from Day School to Leisure Village. There are assumptions surrounding each age group: from expected tantrums by adolescents to PMS for women of a certain age — and an end to creativity from the old.

There are many variations of this development — from youth gangs to the forced retirement. In fact, we have almost achieved a society nearly completely segregated by age in which the generations have been narrowed from the traditional 30 years to far fewer. Age now separates us more than ever before in any society; persons raised only a few decades apart find one another nearly incomprehensible. Dr. Hall, therefore, can be said to have influenced us as much (and perhaps more) than Darwin or Dr. Freud and, like these more celebrated "thinkers," has brought us at least an equal load of distress, disturbance, and unhappiness.

Endnotes
Taken from "The Invention of Adolescence" by Otto Scott, *Chalcedon Report* magazine (July 1991), used by permission from The Chalcedon Foundation, www.chacedon.edu.

1. Granville Stanley Hall, *Youth*, (New York: Appleton, 1907), chapter 1.
2. Ibid, p. 135.

Resignation Letter
Mike Metarko

Dear Ladies and Gentlemen,

It is with strong conviction that I write this letter as my formal resignation effective Thursday, July 1, 2010, from my position as principal of Hanover Elementary School, where I have devoted the last 5 of my 14 years in the Bethlehem Area School District. Though there is no job at present to which I will be going, God has clearly persuaded me through His Word and through my research into the foundations of our educational system that I must end my career in public education.

For the last 14 years, I have worked diligently to be the "salt and light" spoken of in Matthew 5:13, but I have realized that while I am plugging up pinholes in the dike that holds back the tumultuous waters of public education, the improperly laid foundation has been eroding beneath our feet. God states, "The fear of the Lord is the beginning of knowledge" (Proverbs 1:7). This means that neither God nor moral character can be separated from true education; in fact, the glorification of God and the building of biblical moral character must be the basis of true education. In the words of Benjamin Rush, signer of the Declaration of Independence, "We profess to be republicans [in form of government], and yet we neglect the only means of establishing and perpetuating our republican forms of government, that is, the universal education of our youth in the principles of Christianity by the means of the Bible. For this Divine Book, above all others, favors that equality among mankind, that respect for just laws, and those sober and frugal virtues, which constitute the soul of republicanism."

But what have we done? We have thrown God, Bibles, and prayer out of our schools based upon an inaccurate interpretation of the "separation clause," while openly proselytizing the religion of secular humanism (*Smith v. Board of School Commissioners of Mobile County, Alabama*). We have divorced morality from education and focused only on what special interest groups perceive as the "right" content knowledge. We manage the masses at the expense of the individual.

As with most educators in the system, I have been sincere in my efforts to apply the doctrines of those we call the founding fathers of education, but I have realized that I have been sincerely wrong. My research into the real philosophies and beliefs behind men such as Rousseau, Dewey, Hall, etc., has opened my eyes. I am now aware that not only have I not been working for God, I have been working in complete opposition to Him. I mistakenly thought I was on neutral ground: there is no neutral territory.

That said, let me assure you that my argument is not against those I have worked with for the past 14 years. I have a love for my colleagues and friends; most are wonderful teachers of a curriculum they have been given; most truly love the children and will do anything for them; most sincerely try to improve our children, our city, our nation. But we have all taken our eye off the mark of what the chief end of man is. The nation's statist system of public education is the real issue.

The Bible is overwhelmingly clear in that the primary responsibility in educating a child rests with the parents (Deuteronomy 6; Ephesians 6:4; etc.). We need parents to be parents once again, families to be families once again, fathers to be the father and leader, mothers to be the mother and nurturer. It does not "take a village to raise a child"; it takes a family entrusted with the Word of God. Our children are not to be wards of the State; on the contrary, they are creations of a God of love, justice, and redemption who loves us so much He sent Christ to die for us so that if we believe in Him and profess Him as Lord and Savior, He will grant us eternal life. He does not need us, but we need Him. He has given us the roadmap to life and to education: the Bible. I pray that He may manifest Himself in your life as He has clearly done so in mine.

Respectfully,
Michael J. Metarko

Resignation Letter
Sarah LaVerdiere

October 4, 2010

Dear Principal,

Since February of this year when I began teaching for the Public School System, I have been wrestling with the nagging feeling that I should not be working in public schools. In my short time as a teacher, it has been made abundantly clear to me that the public school system is not merely neutral in terms of its religious leanings, but it actually propagates ideals that are blatantly anti-Christian. As a Christian woman, it's been extremely difficult for me to come to work each day and be restricted by law from teaching the young children in my classroom values that I hold to be eternal truths — biblical, Christian values that have been proven for thousands of years to build character and generate productive members of society. But, instead of teaching these true biblical values, our schools require that we teach the acceptance of homosexuality as a harmless alternative lifestyle, that radical environmentalism is a noble cause, and most damagingly of all is the system of positive behavior support which essentially teaches children that they are naturally good — this is the antithesis of the true gospel which says that we are not good, but naturally sinful, and that we need Jesus Christ as our Savior.

Therefore, after much thought, prayerful consideration, and discussion with my husband, we have concluded that I cannot continue to work for the public school system and simultaneously uphold my higher duty to my Lord in heaven. After all, it is written in Scripture that if we are not with God, we are against Him (Matthew 12:30), and by working for the public school system, I am in deed working against my Lord Jesus Christ. I hereby submit this letter of resignation of my position as a 5th grade teacher.

Sincerely,
Sarah LaVerdiere

Letter to Parents
Sarah LaVerdiere

October 21, 2010

Dear Parent/Guardian,

Effective Tuesday, November 2, I will be resigning my position as your child's fifth grade teacher. After much thought and prayerful consideration, I strongly feel the Lord leading me away from working in public education. The principal is currently conducting interviews to find my replacement, and I will provide that new teacher with detailed information about the class in hopes of facilitating as smooth a transition as possible.

Over the past several months as a school system employee, I've realized that our public school system is not merely neutral with regards to religion, but it actually approaches education in a way that is completely contrary to biblical principles. "The fear of the Lord is the beginning of knowledge" (Proverbs 1:7) yet, sadly, public school educators are forbidden by law from even mentioning Jesus to students, making our efforts to educate your children feeble from the very start. As a Christian woman, it has been difficult for me to instruct my class without acknowledging the name of Christ throughout the curriculum. The true reason to study math and science is to witness and appreciate the orderly nature of God's creation. Just as the true reason to study history is to witness and appreciate the providential hand of God, and the way He has shaped our modern world. The systematic removal of Christ from education is proving to be deadly for our society as seen in the ever-increasing rates of illiteracy and drop-out among high school students.

Nowhere are the negative effects of a godless education system more apparent than in the instruction of moral issues. In the public school system, your child is subjected to a disciplinary structure that gives ultimate consideration to elevating their self-esteem and does very little in the administration of negative consequences for their immoral behavior. While this may sound positive to us, the results of this unbiblical method of discipline are anything but. Instead of producing focused, self-disciplined children, the fruits of this flawed system are children who are overly confident, self-centered, motivated only by rewards, rebellious, and totally unprepared to face adverse consequences for their bad choices as they move into adulthood. How can we teach morality without God when all true morals come from the Bible? And more importantly, how can we convey to children that they need a savior for their sinful nature when every school day they are being taught that they are naturally good people? Perhaps you have already seen the negative effects of this system manifesting itself in your child's behavior at home. Please do not be mistaken, your child's behavior will continue to worsen unless you take drastic measures to correct course.

The Lord said, "He who is not with Me is against Me, and he who does not gather with Me scatters abroad" (Mathew 12:30). If you are a Christian, please consider that your child is being scattered from the Word of God by spending 35 hours a week in an educational system that effectively teaches that we do not need Jesus. There are Christian teachers and administrators at school and in other public schools who believe they are working for Christ and being salt and light to students, but these educators are silenced by law from proclaiming the lordship of Christ, and they know that speaking out would cost them their job. At the same time, teachers who are homosexuals, radical environmentalists, and atheists are given free rein to pervert the mind of your child and are given special protection by the same public school system that is all too eager to attack Christian educators. How can Christians fight against this evil and be true salt and light to children without the ability to even acknowledge Jesus in the classroom?

Christian parents, if you desire that your children grow in the fear, admonition, and love of our Lord, I strongly encourage you to consider making the personal sacrifices necessary to remove your children from the public school system and start teaching them according to the biblical model for child raising: homeschooling. By giving you a child, God entrusted you with a tremendous responsibility to raise that child in a way that honors Him. He tells parents to instruct their children in the home, all throughout the day, as they lie down to bed, and when they rise up in the morning (Deuteronomy 6:7) — this is not accomplished by sending your child to be under the care of a stranger for 1,300 hours each school year. I pray that you will take up this challenge by educating your children in a way that is honoring to our Lord, and that He will bless your family and make your work prosperous as a result of your faithfulness to Him.

If you are not a Christian, it is my prayer that by God's grace and mercy He will one day fill your heart with grief and shame, convicting you of your sins and leading you to a life of repentance. The love and mercy that our heavenly Father shows us is truly amazing. God loves us so much that He sent His only Son, Jesus, to perfectly uphold the law and be gruesomely put to death on a cross to pay the penalty for our sins — Jesus willingly suffered the death we all deserve. Only through faith in Christ are we able to be washed clean of our transgressions and made worthy in the eyes of God to share in everlasting life in the kingdom of heaven.

I openly welcome the opportunity to discuss the content of this letter in more detail with you. Please feel free to e-mail me with any thoughts, questions, or concerns you might have.

Sincerely,
Sarah LaVerdiere

The Impossibility of Neutrality
Rousas John Rushdoony

Editor's Note:

Several of the authors in this book refer to the work of Dr. R.J. Rushdoony. In 1965 Dr. Rushdoony founded the Chalcedon Foundation to support Christian and homeschools as the most important institutions in reversing the influence of secular Humanism. He played a crucial role in the battle to legalize homeschooling throughout the 1970s and 80s as he served as an expert witness in multiple court cases throughout the United States where home and Christian schools were under legal attack by public school districts. His contributions toward reestablishing the rights of Christian parents for the education of their children in all fifty states, along with his thoroughly Christian philosophy of education are why many Christian homeschoolers today would call him the father of the modern Christian homeschooling movement. His notable books on education include *Intellectual Schizophrenia*, and *The Messianic Character of American Education*. The following excerpt is from Dr. Rushdoony's book *The Philosophy of the Christian Curriculum*.

One of the key myths of humanism is the idea of neutrality. It is held that the mind of man can be neutral with regard to facts and ideas, and that the scientific method is the way of neutrality. Man can, we are told, calmly and objectively approach and analyze facts and arrive at the truth.

Such a view presupposes neutrality *in the knower and the known*. With respect to the knower, man, it assumes that man is not a fallen creature, at war with his Maker. Rather, man is held to be a being capable of approaching factuality objectively and impartially, so that the basic judgments about the nature of things depends upon the mind of man.

For us as Christians, this view is false. If man is not fallen and dead in sins and trespasses, then man can save himself. Man's reason can lead him to Christ without the grace of God. Man, however, is fallen in all his being; he is totally at war with God. Fallen man may manifest no hostility to God, but his indifference is equally an act of war, because he has ruled out God from all consideration in all things. He has in effect declared that God is dead for him, and therefore need not even be considered or thought about. (If my children act as though I do not exist, nor am to be thought about, spoken about or referred to, then they, without a word said, are manifesting hatred of me, and are warring against me.) Man is never neutral with respect to God, nor to anything that is of God. There is no neutrality in man.

Similarly, there is no neutrality in facts, in *the known*. The idea that facts are neutral is a product of humanistic and evolutionary thought, which holds that facts "just happened." They are ostensibly products of some cosmic accident and are thus uncommitted and meaningless facts. Hence, man can study them without any religious commitment; they are a neutral realm of being.

For us as Christians, however, all factuality is God-created, and hence the meaning of all things, including man, can only be understood in terms of the triune God and His word. All things come from the hand of God, and we do not grasp the meaning of anything if we deny its Creator. The facts are never neutral, because they are God-created. Those who ask us to be "broad-minded" and approach the world and all factuality with an "open and neutral" mind are really asking us to presuppose a world which is the product of chance, not God. They are asking us to overlook the most critical factor of all, God, the Creator, and to presuppose that facts are a product of chance.

Cornelius Van Til has pointed out that "The war between Christ and Satan is a global war. It is carried on, first, *in* the hearts of men for the hearts of men."[1] This war is a total war. As Van Til so powerfully states it,

> There is not a square inch of ground in heaven or on earth or under the earth in which there is peace between Christ and Satan. And what is all-important for us as ire think of the Christian school is that, according to Christ, every man, woman, and child is every day and everywhere involved in this struggle. No one can stand back, refusing to become involved. He is involved from the day of his birth and even from before his birth. Jesus said: "He that is not

with me is against me, and he that gathereth not with me scattereth abroad." If you say that you are "not involved" you are in fact involved in Satan's side. If you say you are involved in the struggle between Christ and Satan in the area of the family and in the church, but not in the school, you are deceiving yourself. In that case you are not really fully involved in the family and in the church. You cannot expect to train intelligent well-informed soldiers of the cross of Christ unless the Christ is held up before them as the Lord of culture as well as the Lord of religion. It is of the **nature** of the conflict between Christ and Satan to be all-comprehensive.[2]

This total war is one which must be recognized, and education is at present perhaps the central theater of war. Van Til is right: "There are two, and only two, mutually exclusive philosophies of education."[3] These are Christian theistic and humanistic. Attempts to fuse the two are untenable (Matt. 6:24).

This means that the teacher cannot be neutral nor subscribe to humanistic philosophies with respect to his field of study. Either there is a neutral void behind every fact, or the living God. In our teaching, we will always consciously or unconsciously acknowledge one or the other.

In a neutral world, man stands as the sole voice of reason in a universal realm of irrationality. This makes man the high and ultimate judge and authority. The world is then under his interpretation and judgment, so that man stands over reality as its only lord and master.

Humanistic education fosters in its pupils the basic premises of Genesis 3:5. It asks man to be his own god, determining for himself what constitutes good and evil. Modern philosophers of education are often emphatic in declaring that there are no final answers. Hence their hostility to the Bible. To assume final answers means that there is a truth somewhere which stands apart from man and in judgment over man. To deny final answers and to affirm a perpetual guest, and a perpetual revision of all answers, is to affirm that it is not an answer or truth which is ultimate but *man*. As a result, modern humanism is hostile to the idea of answers. It prefers to speak of tentative answers and of paradigms which provide tools for using reality but never affirming any ultimate truth about reality. The ultimacy of man is thereby preserved.

This is the meaning of progressivism and instrumentalism. The Bible tells us that Jesus is the truth (John 1:17). Jesus makes the same statement about Himself: "I am...the truth" (John 14:6). Humanistic education denies that truth is a person or a thing. Experimentalism tells us that truth is what works for man.[4] With respect to truth, Morris holds that, "Taken literally, the statement 'I have found it' is not a scientific statement but more in the nature of a theological one."[5] Knowing is always a process, never a conclusion. *The truth is always contingent and relative to man.*[6] This, of course, is a theological statement, but Morris's god is man. *For us also truth is always contingent and relative, but to God, not man.* The existentialist also makes truth relative to man and his existential choice.

Truth is never abstract, nor is it some vague idea floating in the heavens. Truth is always relative to whatever is ultimate in our faith. If matter is ultimate for us, then truth is relative to matter, if mind, to mind. If man is ultimate, then truth is contingent and relative to man. For us, however, all things having been created by the sovereign and triune God, are relative to Him and to His word. *Because* the Lord is the ultimate and sovereign Creator, He is therefore the *truth* in all its fulness, and all else is true in terms of its relation to Him. The more we understand the relation of the physical world in relation to God and His order and purpose in creation, the more we know the truth about creation. The logic of the humanist position requires him to say that truth is relative and contingent to man and his society because man is the ultimate truth.

St. Paul was aware of this element of humanism in the Greco-Roman world of his day, and hence his indictment of it as "Ever learning, and never able to come to the knowledge of the truth" (II Tim. 3:7). "Ever learning" is rendered by the Berkeley Version as "forever getting information."

Humanistic philosophies of education, and the state schools, are expressions of a religious faith, faith in man. Perkinson is right in speaking of "the Americans' faith in their schools."[7] Ours is another faith, and we must stand in terms of it, consistently and faithfully.

Endnotes:

Taken from *The Philosophy of the Christian Curriculum* by Rousas John Rush-doony (Vallecito, CA: Ross House Books, 1981, 2001 reprint edition), used by permission, www.chalcedon.edu.

1. Cornelius Van Til, *Essays on Christian Education*, (Nutley, New Jersey: Presbyte-rian and Reformed Publishing Co., 1974), p. 26.
2. Ibid., p. 276.
3. Ibid., p.36.
4. Van Cleve, Morris, *Philosophy and the American School* (Boston: Houghton Mifflin, 1961), pp. 155-165.
5. Ibid., p. 159.
6. Mid.. p. 164.
7. Henry J. Perkinson, *The Imperfect Panacea: American Faith in Education*, (New York: Random House, 1968), p. 219.

Spread the Word
Richard A. Jones

Dr. Richard A. Jones received his degree in Dentistry from the University of Michigan in 1959. He was a general dentist and periodontist in the U.S. Army Dental Corps for 20 years to include two years in Vietnam. He retired as a full Colonel in 1979. Later, in 1981, he moved onto the the mission field as a general dentist for Operation Mobilization with whom he served for two and half years on the evangelism and "good books for all" ship, the MV Doulos. Then came a slow but steady awakening to the joys and duties of the homeschool/discipling philosophy which has kept him busy since, working for its advancement. Dr. Jones is on the board of directors of American Vision and is the Michigan state coordinator for Exodus Mandate.

A project as well-done and inspirational as *IndoctriNation*—one attesting to countless hours of dedication by the film's production team—deserves our grateful thanks. After all, what more could they possibly have done to remind us of the stunning failure of U.S. public schools to provide even so much as a mediocre education? What more to expose the God-rejecting educational bureaucracy's spiritual betrayal of tender, vulnerable children? What more to move Christian parents to see the critical need of withdrawing precious children from the socialist indoctrination camps too many Americans still innocently call schools? The film speaks for itself, making it a pleasure to write a heartfelt congratulatory note.

However, whether wise Christians will rise to the challenge and offer up a victorious result to God remains to be seen. In potential, the film appears to have more than sufficient power to shake parents awake and off of the national dime of apathy. But, we'll proclaim success only if and when the crucial message of *IndoctriNation* is converted into action.

Does it have the power to reverse our school-influenced cultural tailspin: our fanatical obsession with school sports, especially Friday night football; our love of material things, money, two cars, and an impressive mortgage; "free" eight to five babysitting at school that's anything but free and the corresponding need for mom to bring home a second income to help pay for it all? Will we respond to the revisionist, anti-Christian teachings fed to American kids? Will we acknowledge that students are only a secondary concern to many educators? We'll know soon.

That's the heart of the challenge *IndoctriNation* has successfully presented. Of course other films and writers have put the problem in front of us repeatedly and they deserve our thanks. But, the difference this time is that *IndoctriNation* can be, ought to be, should be, the philosophical and pro-Bible straw that breaks the back of national resistance to the uplifting message in Deuteronomy 6:7-9—a call for the direct role of parents in raising up critical thinkers and kingdom-advancing Christians.

If any vehicle involved in youth training and discipling can inspire Christians to obey the decree that we fear God and keep His commandments—especially those commands for parents—*IndoctriNation* has that potential, but only if it is widely and sufficiently viewed. So share it, distribute it, speak about it, and place it by the thousands into the hands of pastors and parents everywhere. If we can all find it within ourselves to respond rightly then Christendom wins and we emerge on the far side with a nation intact, eagerly awaiting a God-honoring happy century ahead. If not, history's record of bad alternatives is a long one.

Keep praying, and stay tuned for the ultimate epilogue of success that the architects of *IndoctriNation* worked so hard to attain. Success can come, but the window of opportunity narrows by the day.

INDEX

Plato 34, 194-195, 286

pornography 31, 313

Portugal 10

Positive Behavior Interventions and Supports (PBIS) 86

post-Christian 12, 282

post-graduate 263

postmodern 34, 209, 282

Potter, Charles 272

Potter, Dr. Charles Francis 122

pre-adolescent/preadolescents 56, 355

pre-Reformation 282, 356

Presbyterian 39, 154, 156, 167, 276, 329, 368

preschool 129, 255

prescription 57-58, 62, 64

presuppositions 94, 148-149

Priest, Karl 5, 8, 107, 122

pro-American 235

pro-Bible 370

problem-solving 53, 257

Proceedings 181

proclamation 240

pro-education 146

pro-gay 235

progressivism 131, 367

propaganda 32, 112, 175

Protestant 176, 217, 267, 282

Protester Voices 107, 122

Proverbs 11, 35-36, 40, 66, 80, 182, 358, 361

Prozac 42, 47, 54, 56, 60-61, 63

Prussia 9, 186, 214

Psalms 295

psychiatric 42-43, 47, 52, 55, 57, 59, 61-62, 64

psychiatrist 47, 52, 56, 198

psychiatry 52, 55, 59

psychology 31, 59, 169, 171, 174, 176-178, 207, 210, 354-355

psychopharmacology 61

Puritan 77, 154-155, 158, 163, 333

qualifications 29, 93, 303

quotients 110

race-based 137

racism/racist 14, 31, 178, 227, 234-235, 239

radical 9, 83, 89, 120, 143, 177, 198, 210, 214, 218, 233, 258, 274, 337, 360, 362

Rainer, Thom 325

ramapithecine 199

Ravitch, Diane 132, 140-141

readiness 297

reforms 131, 141, 209, 257

regulations 131, 143, 225, 229, 286

Reich, Jerome, 158

relativism 114, 118, 232, 234, 270

Republican 136, 143-146, 151, 331, 358

researchers 43, 49, 51-53, 55, 216

Reuters 60, 63

Revisionism 187-188

Revisionist 22, 31, 183, 189, 370

Riskind, Jonathan 61

Ritalin 41-43, 45-47, 49-55, 57-64, 209-210

Rockefeller 177, 184, 190, 205, 207-208, 214, 216

Rockefeller Foundation 190, 207

Rockwell, Norman 111

Rohrbough, Brian 5, 8, 19

Rohrbough, Malcolm 158

Romans 85, 93, 196, 263

Rome 197, 279-280, 288

Rosh Hashanah, 26

Rugg, Harold 184

Rush, Benjamin 358

Rushton, Dr. Jerry 51, 60, 63

Safe and Drug-Free Schools 29

Safe School Czar 29

Satel, Sally 61

SATs 341

Savior 3, 20-21, 90, 248, 256, 302, 359-360, 362

Schaeffer, Francis 282

Schizophrenia 38, 364

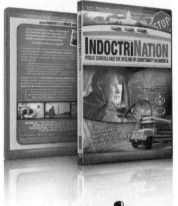